Sex, Power, Control

Sex, Power, Control
Responding to Abuse in the Institutional Church

Fiona Gardner

Foreword by Stephen Parsons

The Lutterworth Press

THE LUTTERWORTH PRESS

P.O. Box 60
Cambridge
CB1 2NT
United Kingdom

www.lutterworth.com
publishing@lutterworth.com

Paperback ISBN: 978 0 7188 9562 4
PDF ISBN: 978 0 7188 4819 4
ePub ISBN: 978 0 7188 4820 0

British Library Cataloguing in Publication Data
A record is available from the British Library

First published by The Lutterworth Press, 2021
Copyright © Fiona Gardner, 2021

All rights reserved. No part of this edition may be reproduced, stored electronically or in any retrieval system, or transmitted in any form or by any means, electronic, mechanical, photocopying, recording, or otherwise, without prior written permission from the Publisher (permissions@lutterworth.com).

*For those who survived
and in memory of those who didn't.*

If you look at it from the outside, it is beautifully decorated. It has lovely stories, it promises so much, it promises everlasting life and redemption; but, if you strip away the veneer, it is a cold machine, it is gunmetal coloured. As with any corporation, its whole reason for being is to maintain itself and to reproduce itself from generation to generation. It's not about love, compassion, or kindness, or sympathy, or any human quality like that. It has inserted itself so firmly in society people don't question it.

Cliff James
from 'Exposed: The Church's Darkest Secret'
aired 14 January 2020.

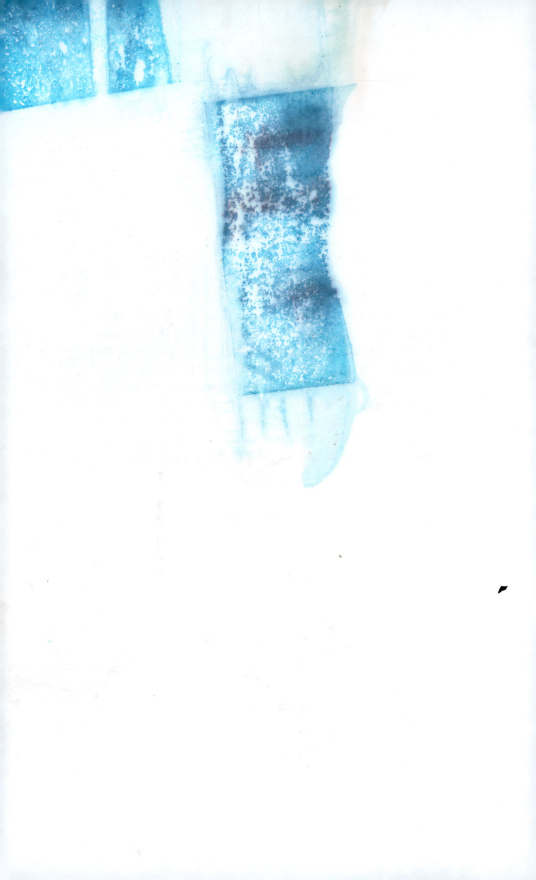

Contents

Glossary	vii
Acknowledgements	ix
Foreword by Stephen Parsons	xi
1. Introduction – Stripping away the Veneer	1
2. Survivor Accounts	14
3. The Mind of the Abuser	30
4. How the Church Has Responded	48
5. Surface Awareness – Policies, Guidelines and Training	65
6. Dynamics of Power and Control in the Institutional Church	83
7. Charismatic Power and Control	100
8. The Influence of the Public School Ethos within the Institutional Church	117
9. Sex and Gender	134
10. Spiritual Abuse, the Spiritual Sickness within the Church and Signs of Hope	151
Afterword	165
Endnotes	167
Bibliography	193
Index	

Glossary

ATL	Allchurches Trust Ltd
CCHH	Churches' Council for Health and Healing
CCPAS	Church's Child Protection Advisory Service, now known as Thirtyone: Eight
CDM	Clergy Discipline Measure
CRB	Criminal Records Bureau check, now replaced by DBS Disclosure and Barring Service
DPP	Director of Public Prosecutions
DSA	Diocesan Safeguarding Adviser, also sometimes called the DSO, Diocesan Safeguarding Officer
EIG	Ecclesiastical Insurance Group
GAFCON	Global Anglican Future Conference
IICSA	Independent Inquiry into Child Sexual Abuse
LGB	Lesbian, Gay, Bisexual (used as shorthand for LGBTQI+, lesbian, gay, bisexual, transgender, queer, intersex and plus – any other identities that might fall under this umbrella)
MACSAS	Minister and Clergy Sexual Abuse Survivors
NOS	Nine O'clock Service
NSP	National Safeguarding Panel
NSSG	National Safeguarding Steering Group
PCR	Past Cases Review; PCR2 is the second Past Cases Review
PCC	Parochial Church Council, executive committee of a Church of England parish consisting of clergy, churchwardens and representatives of the laity
PTO	Permission to Officiate is a concessionary ministry licence usually granted to clergy over the age of 70 that allows them to continue to lead services including administering the sacraments.
SCIE	Social Care Institute of Excellence

Acknowledgements

Early in 2019 I was contacted by Top Hat Productions about my work in the diocese of Bath and Wells between 2004 and 2010. Top Hat had been commissioned by BBC2 to produce a documentary about the Church cover-up involving the late Bishop Peter Ball. After meeting with Esther McWatters who was researching the subject, I agreed to take part, and the documentary 'Exposed: The Church's Darkest Secret' was filmed that year and broadcast in January 2020. I would like to thank Esther, who was at the time series producer, and Ben Steele, who filmed and directed the documentary. It proved a cathartic experience and also led directly to contact from Adrian Brink at The Lutterworth Press, who invited me to write this book. I would like to thank Adrian for the opportunity to do so. I would also like to thank the editorial team at The Lutterworth Press, especially Debora Nicosia for her guidance.

I am very grateful to Stephen Parsons for writing the foreword and for his comments on the material. His website has proved an invaluable resource and also an inspiration.

Many thanks also to Jayne Ozanne, director of the Ozanne Foundation and member of General Synod, for her helpful comments on Chapter 9.

I would like to thank Hugh Gee, psyche-analyst, for his insights about the Church and his support over the years.

A huge thank you to my husband Peter Ellis, both for his loving support when I was working in the diocese of Bath and Wells and in the writing of this book. I also thank him for sharing the research he has undertaken on boarding schools and for his professional editorial skills in commenting on the chapters and compiling the index.

The experiences of survivors provided the impetus for my work in the diocese and their accounts are the foundation of the book. It is right that it is dedicated to them.

Foreword

It is some thirty years ago that I was asked to edit a small magazine for an ecumenical charity called the Churches' Council for Health and Healing (CCHH). This charity had a distinguished history, looking back to an initiative taken by Archbishop William Temple in 1944 to bring the churches of Britain to work together in this area of healing and cooperation with the medical profession. Although the CCHH was hampered by lack of resources and eventually closed in 1999, it possessed one important area of influence. Healing charities had the possibility of being affiliated to our charity. In the event that a group became involved in scandal, the Council had the task of removing it from its association with the central body. So, in the 1990s, I was familiar with the idea that clergy and church leaders could on occasion commit abuse in the context of healing activities. I saw the incidence of sexual abuse while offering divine healing as a blasphemy, but the wider Church generally did not want to contemplate this area of evil. The pastoral, theological and psychological resources were not there to deal with it or adequately respond. My studies for a book I was writing at the time, *Ungodly Fear*, showed me clearly that sexual abuse in the Church was common but I saw it only within a narrow perspective. My main insight was to treat it as a misapplication of the power of a few leaders.

In the perspective of the 1990s, I was unable to see this evil of abuse as being deeply embedded within aspects of the Church's own culture. Patriarchy, deference, sexism and negative attitudes towards sexuality inherited from our Puritan ancestors, all fed into the culture that enabled this abuse. Also, no one at that time was predicting the tsunami of cases that surged during the present century. Alongside the (post-Jimmy Savile) awareness that has entered our churches and society in the past ten years, there has also been a vastly improved understanding of the topic within the academic and professional worlds. The Church itself has, in many ways, lagged behind. While it has started to provide improved training for clergy and church workers to be aware of the issue, it has found it hard to provide adequate care and support for the traumatised cohort of abuse survivors. The Church has also failed to understand how its own teaching and understanding of human sexuality have contributed to the incidence of cases. These failures have impacted negatively on the reputation of the Church. It still remains possible that the damage caused by these institutional failures has been so severe that the trust and respect for the Church held by society at large has been lost for ever.

At one level, this present work by Fiona Gardner is about Christian leaders in the Church of England behaving badly. However, it is much more than that. Three things make this book a product of this decade and not from the period when I was doing my own study. In the first place, Fiona is able to avail herself of three decades of detailed reports about church abuse, much of which can be studied via the internet. The work of the Independent Inquiry into Child Sexual Abuse and other reviews have turned over many stones and revealed dark places for which the Church should feel much shame.

In the second place, Fiona has brought into her writing much theoretical background to help the reader understand at a deeper level the phenomenon of abuse, both from the abuser's perspective and the point of view of the survivor. Her commentary is informed by a deep appreciation of the psychological literature, gleaned from her professional training and practice and her reading. I have especially appreciated her insights in the area of narcissism.

The third aspect of her writing, which is helpful to the reader, is the way she locates sexual abuse in its social setting within the Church. She writes, for example, about the role of the British public school and the way that it is one of the social entities that has in some ways enabled and fostered abuse. The Church, by combining institutional blindness, naïve optimism and malevolence in itself, has unwittingly come to be a major part of the problem.

The issue of how the scourge of sexual abuse can be banished in the future cannot be fully resolved in a book of this size. However, there are here the outlines of suggestions and pointers as to what the Church needs to do. In the first place, the Church has to listen to the experts who bring to bear their insights from other professions and disciplines. Survivors also need to be heard. They continue to suffer years after the original abuse and they demand and expect to encounter a church organisation that understands their experience. So often the survivor is made to feel that he/she is the enemy rather than the one in desperate need of help. Fiona's work points the way towards providing the rounded, holistic approach to the topic that both church leaders and survivors need on their common journey towards wholeness and healing.

Stephen Parsons

Stephen is an Anglican priest, author and blogger. He is the editor of a blog addressing power issues in the Church: http://survivingchurch.org/.

1.
Introduction
Stripping away the Veneer

Why has everyone involved been so inept, had no sense of urgency, given their rhetoric on safeguarding?[1]
A vicar, quoted in Private Eye

In September 2004 I began working as safeguarding advisor for the Church of England in the diocese of Bath and Wells; I was the first person formally to fill the post. Before my appointment, situations had been handled by a group of professionals, on a voluntary basis, occasionally advised by the safeguarding advisor for the Bristol diocese. I inherited this helpful group to act as support, but there was not much else to inherit. As I set about putting together guidelines, training and dealing with cases, I realised that no one else in the office knew anything about safeguarding and, more significantly, that no one really wanted to know about it – apart from the youth worker. Most would have preferred that I and the 'grubby' work I did were not there. Looking from my desk out of one of the beautiful mullioned windows of the twelfth-century building called the Old Deanery onto a corner of Wells Cathedral, the place seemed to me timeless and very peaceful. Everyone was always friendly and smiling and, regularly, there were cakes to celebrate someone's birthday. Six years later I left with exhaustion, partly due to Bishop Peter Ball. By then I understood that, below the veneer of pleasantries, were levels of complexity, deception and anxiety that made the NHS adolescent psychiatric unit where I had previously worked seem like a vicar's tea party.

This book then is about looking below the surface, about uncovering the layers of complexity, deception and anxiety, about analysing the underlying culture, and about looking to see what lies beneath once the veneer is stripped away. It is about exploring the reasons behind the culture of avoidance and denial found especially amongst those in positions of church leadership in their mishandling of disclosures. Whilst shocking examples of this that have occurred in the recent past and that are in the public domain are included in this book, the aim is to understand *why* the Church of England finds itself in such a crisis. The intention is to uncover and to understand *how* the Church's issues of power and control as exemplified in the hierarchical structure, in its theology and teaching, and underlying assumptions as an institution have contributed to the current mess and associated heartache. Whilst the focus is on the Church of England, much of what is discussed in the book could also apply to other denominations.

There have been plenty of good intentions about safeguarding in the Church of England. A policy was first put together in the early 1990s, by the then Bishop of Bath and Wells, Jim Thompson. Unfortunately, the emphasis was on 'responding to any allegation of clerical sexual abuse by contacting the Church's insurers as a matter of urgency'. As Josephine Stein writes[2] this laid the ground for a confrontational rather than a pastoral approach. A review of clergy discipline resulted in the Clergy Discipline Measure of 2003 (CDM) stating that the burden of proof of an ecclesiastical offence had to be 'beyond all reasonable doubt'. Survivors were then directed to this CDM, a procedure that invariably failed to deliver guilty verdicts. Direct contact with survivors was avoided and the aim was to avoid liability. Stein adds, 'The Church used avoidance behaviour, proceduralism and various barriers and obstacles to frustrate attempts by survivors to be heard.' Yet, when the Compensation Act came into force in 2006 (which included changes to the law of liability), then, as Stein notes, apologies began to be given and prayers offered for survivors, but mainly from senior clerics who knew neither the survivors nor any detail about the abuses that had occurred. The CDM was eventually amended in 2016 and placed in line with complying with safeguarding guidance, but such 'legalistic processes . . . tend to fail' because there is 'rarely unambiguous written evidence or witness testimony' and 'abusers use manipulation and deception as their main weapons in the grooming phase . . . not spotted by the target/survivor'.[3] Over the years more safeguarding policies were produced and new structures instigated – nationally and locally – but, as will be shown in this book, the Church's own policies were not being followed, rather they were being interpreted by the hierarchy. In 2002 *Time for Action* stated: 'If the Churches recognize that it is the time to act on the recommendations . . . then a new day will dawn for many people who have experienced great sadness and yet have somehow held on to hope.'[4] This proved to be a false dawn and, sadly, one of many.

However, widespread bad publicity has begun to achieve that which good intentions have not. The recent hearings of the Independent Inquiry into Child Sexual Abuse (IICSA) revealed much that is shameful and in February 2020 at a meeting of the General Synod of the Church of England some significant votes were passed to prioritise the needs of victims and survivors of clergy abuse. It was agreed that words of action must be followed by 'concrete actions' including accepting all the 2019 IICSA recommendations. Synod also agreed to give adequate financial compensation and support to survivors and to take an approach to safeguarding that saw things from the survivor's point of view. The Bishop of Huddersfield, Jonathan Gibb, the new lead safeguarding bishop, said that the response to sexual abuse should be guided by 'the righteousness and compassion of God's kingdom, and not by the short-term and short-sighted financial and reputational interests of the church'.[5] So, has the Church finally been forced to respond appropriately because of the persistence and resilience of survivors and their supporters, many of whose voices are included in this book? Or is it proving to be another false dawn? This remains, as yet, unclear but the immediate signs are not promising.

The basic point is that contemporary reporting in the media of sexual abuse by Anglican clergy arouses pity for the victim, and disgust and horror towards the perpetrator. It also raises anger towards the institutional Church that has been so quick to comment on and judge everyone else's sexuality, but so slow to control abusing priests and get its house in order. Whilst there have been many positive changes to safeguarding in the last decade, what has become increasingly clear is that the superficial following of procedures and good intentions, sadly, do not mean a change of perspective. Rosie Harper describes how everyone 'is working very hard to produce new systems and more training and issue more apologies. It is hard to see this as anything other than moving the chairs around on the deck of the Titanic.' This is because the underlying culture needs to change fundamentally through a deeper understanding of the problem: 'This is not a little local difficulty. This cuts to the heart of things. It is a test of the authenticity of the Christian faith.'[6]

As Simon Barrow, director of the think tank Ekklesia, writes:

> The Christian church supposedly witnesses to a God whose love changes lives, transcends tribal boundaries and puts the poorest and most vulnerable – not least the violated and abused – first. In practice, however, church bodies often behave in ways that flatly contradict this message, even rendering bureaucratic lack of concern, evasion and refusal of accountability in a language of piety that only adds insult to deep, life-long injury.[7]

This book shifts the context of sexual abuse in the Church away from surface policies and guidelines (important though they are). It also aims to look beyond the cycle of harrowing account of clergy abuse followed (eventually) by hand-wringing apologies and reviews of lessons learned by the Church, where someone or some people are blamed and assurances given that practices have changed, only to be – so often – followed by further horror stories. Where accounts are included in this book, it is with the focus of exploring the underlying attitudes, habits, traditions and structures – structures that can dominate ordinary human responses.

Any abuse, and especially sexual abuse, is always difficult to think about (so I could understand the reluctance in the diocesan office), partly because it 'disturbs our normal orientation to reality'. At a deep level it is a breach of one of the central foundations of social order, the maintenance of the sexual boundary between generations, and so it is 'an attack on generational difference', on the sexually vulnerable and immature child or young person by the adult.[8] In the Church sexual abuse by the ordained adds a further disturbing dimension, for it is betrayal by those who preach of love and kindness and moral standards. This book argues that it is almost inevitable to want to emotionally defend against these strong disturbing feelings by projection, denial and repression. These same defences are then used by the institutional church when faced with such disclosures and the distress of victims and survivors. In all forms of abuse issues of power and control are fundamental, so, again, perhaps it is not surprising to see these same issues replicated and repeated when the person who has experienced abuse either as a child, a young person or as an adult reports to those in authority about what has happened to them. It is suggested in this book that the secrecy and deception shown by the institutional church in this situation, results from a similar desire for power and control. It is further suggested that the Church has demonstrated an institutional narcissism not dissimilar to the narcissism and solipsism that characterises the self-justification of most perpetrators. The self-serving entitlement and renunciation of responsibility of the perpetrator, demonstrated by preoccupation, denial and lack of empathy, is then too frequently mirrored by the institution in its response.

The damage caused by such re-enactments which are often covert and insidious is shown to be almost as damaging to the person as the original abuse. The closed-system hierarchical thinking, which accompanies a closing of ranks and the protection of the institution, leaves the person who has been abused outside the so-called Church family; it's an 'us and them' – an exclusive rather than inclusive – response. The denial of the reality for the person who has been abused seems a reflection of an incapacity to emotionally understand or fully appreciate the implications of what has actually happened. Many children have been betrayed in what has been seen in the past as a safe setting, and this has left many distrustful of the Church.

The Extent of Sexual Abuse in the Church of England

In the context of the Church the findings of various reviews and accounts point out that the overwhelming majority of abusers are men, men usually in a position of authority such as clergy or church workers of some sort. In June 2019 the Church of

England released safeguarding statistics covering the time frame of 2015-17.[9] The published figures were compiled largely from parish and diocesan self-assessments and, as has been pointed out, this should be a consideration when trying to interpret them, as usually any person or institution who is asked to assess his or its own performance is likely to give a more favourable analysis than an independent and external assessor might. The report shows that in 2017 there were 3,287 safeguarding concerns or allegations recorded by diocesan safeguarding advisers (DSAs), twelve per cent of these related to clergy. These figures show significant increases from past surveys which may be linked to increased reporting. However, the total recorded cases only relate to those reports which reached the DSA and so it is impossible to tell whether concerns or allegations made at a local level made it up the chain in what is essentially a discretionary reporting policy. As the campaign group Minister and Clergy Sexual Abuse Survivors (MACSAS)[10] points out, another area of concern is that two thirds of those reports which did reach DSAs were not reported to the statutory authorities and so were dealt with internally or dismissed; this statistic is linked to the high threshold that the House of Bishops' guidance sets for reporting a case to the authorities. It also illustrates well the Church's tendency to deal with things in-house which has led to numerous serious safeguarding failures in the past. The same report notes that only 39 cases led to disciplinary action against clergy and only 33 cases led to disciplinary action against lay people, that is, only 2.2 per cent, and it is unclear and unpublished what the outcome of these procedures were.

Some Definitions

In this book I regularly use the term the 'institutional church'. As Andrew Brown and Linda Woodhead explain, the Church has always been both national and congregational, both are needed. By the institutional church I mean the national and diocesan organisation of the Church of England, where hierarchy, structure, systems and factions take precedence over relationship. Here the complexity that you find in any institution is 'multiplied by its antiquity, linkages with state and society, diocesan and parish system, connection to other churches in the Communion, and scale. . . . It's a recipe for paranoia, paralysis and multiplying complexity.' The institutional church is not the local church, 'which baptized, married, conducted funerals, organized fetes and pageants, ran schools, rang bells and looked after roofs'.[11] Local churches have their own formal and informal ways of organising, largely oblivious of decisions at synod, battles between factions and scandals. National projects trickle down via the dioceses through to the parish setting, where they are moulded to fit the setting – or not. The institutional church is the hierarchy of senior clerics and the structures and rules that surround them.

There's an ongoing debate about the use of the terms, 'victim' and 'survivor'. Some people identify as a victim, while others prefer the term survivor. Victim is often more appropriate when discussing a particular crime, especially if recently committed, or when linked to the criminal justice system. Generally, survivor has been the preferred term in this book where it refers to someone who has gone through a period of recovery. It's also appropriate when discussing the long-term effects of sexual violence.[12] Survivor is the term used by those campaigning and involved in church safeguarding. However, the value-laden idea of passive victim and strong survivor has led to a counter argument where survivor: 'paints a misleading picture of victimhood, and healing, while silently promoting a super-human response that encourages victims to "get over" an unspeakable violation. All so that those around them can feel more comfortable when faced with the realities of such a heinous act.'[13] The term victim can be reclaimed and reinterpreted as exemplifying fortitude and as a reminder of the reality of what happened. For, whilst time passes, trauma sadly does not; and this is discussed in Chapter 2. What changes is the person's ability to manage and deal with what happened to them.

I have tended to use the term perpetrator or abuser when discussing clergy abuse. As is explained in Chapter 3, there are different labels attached to those who are attracted to different ages, which is why the term paedophilia does not cover some of the clergy involved with adolescents and young people. The term perpetrator or abuser places the crime foremost with the man who has committed it, and in this book all the perpetrators are men. Research has shown that, when the word priest or vicar or clergy has been used, this is seen as a 'genderless term', even when the clergy person is male. This can then imply that somehow the desexualised man (because he is a man of God) was 'led on' by the sexualised child or young person.[14]

Psychoanalysis is one of the main perspectives used to uncover the reasons behind the ineptitude, the lack of urgency and the poor levels of empathy shown by the institutional church when dealing with situations of abuse and the people who report them. By this, I mean awareness of unconscious, as well as conscious, psychological processes and the belief that all people possess unconscious thoughts, feelings, desires and memories – some of which may cause anxiety if they emerge into consciousness and thus against which a person may react defensively. The idea of defence mechanisms has proved useful; these are the ways that an individual or an organisation avoids or resists having to think about something that causes anxiety. This might include denial or repression but, usually, projection, which involves unconsciously pushing onto others one's own unacceptable thoughts, motives or feelings. This can also take place at a collective level against groups or types of people that threaten the organisation's well-being. Interestingly, the Church has often been wary of or threatened by psychological insights and support unless it has the prefix 'Christian' – such as Christian counselling – which perhaps makes it sound a lot safer than psychoanalytic psychotherapy. Rather than enter further into this debate, I quote Carl Jung, who engaged in many a discussion with theologians and religious leaders. He saw analytic thinking as a tool rather than an end in itself: 'Analytical psychology only helps us to find the way to the religious experience that makes us whole . . . analytical psychology teaches us that *attitude* which meets a transcendent reality halfway.'[15] It is this psychological attitude that has been employed in this book to help understand 'why'.

Whilst this book is about a religious institution there is little if any theology included. Spiritual abuse is defined and discussed later in Chapter 10 but any abuse that takes place in a religious context will inevitably deeply alter and often damage the person's relationship with God, especially when religious rituals and theological justifications have been used. The work of Alistair McFadyen[16] is worth noting here; in *Bound to Sin* he traces how one of the after-effects of abuse is that the survivor is left with a constrained identity. Here he discusses the need for the person to hold himself together against any repetition of the chaos and disintegration that was experienced by the sexual abuse. He feels that this then blocks access to transcendent sources of meaning, energy, truth and value. There is an inevitable undercutting of genuine joy in oneself, others and God. However, therapy means that one's approach to the trauma can change and healing is ever possible and, for many, their personal belief system and a dependence on their faith can help. One further theological thought is on the ubiquitous 'ethic' of forgiveness which has been badly misused by the Church. It has been put forward endlessly as something demanded of the victims and survivors. For example, many survivors speak 'painfully of being exhorted to forgive their abuser, and of being blamed for their own suffering, for the abuser's suffering and for everyone else's suffering if they fail to do so'.[17] So much so that it has become a cliché, catchphrase theology and part of the propaganda, without any appreciation that recovery from abuse is a long-term and deeply personal process. The historic demotion of justice for forgiveness compromises insight, compassion and action and so the person who has been abused once again has his/her trust betrayed. The 'mission of forgiveness' is in this context simply poor theology.

THE CHAPTERS

Chapters 2, 3 and 4 cover recent experiences of abusive situations that have taken place in the Church. We turn immediately in Chapter 2 to the experiences of the survivors. Their voices are central to the book and need to be heard. It is emphasised that each person has a different story to tell and has been affected differently by what happened to him or her. Speaking out and challenging someone who has authority over one is enormously difficult, if not impossible, for most children and, indeed, for adults too. Victims are easily silenced and often remain silent, there are difficult feelings of fear, shame, guilt and uncertainty.[18] As one victim reported feeling: 'What happens to us does not happen to nice people who go to church.'[19] Those who do speak out are very brave and to be praised, but many are never able to speak about what happened to them, or only if their own mental health breaks down later in life. The after-effects of such abuse are life-long and can be deeply damaging for mental and physical health, in relationships, lost income and distress and this is also explored. Three accounts are given of clergy abuse; the third account is of someone whom I worked with in psychotherapy many years ago. The accounts are sad and at times horrific, but within each account there is also a sense of resilience.

In Chapter 3 the mind of the abuser is explored. The accounts included in this chapter have proved to be a contrast to the survivors, who were clearly aware of their feelings of distress, looking for ways to relieve this and get justice for or understanding about what had happened to them. When running training courses in the diocese of Bath and Wells, I sometimes used videos provided by the Lucy Faithfull Foundation. These included extracts from two priests. My experience of those film accounts was the same as that described by Alex Renton: 'watching the videos, there's a disturbing sense that they are performing in a scene of their own long life story, that this latest turn provides another outing for their egos'.[20] The bland accounts and the false lines learnt, contribute to colourless narratives. This seems to suggest that the inability to be able to reflect on what they have done reveals the extent of their psychological damage. In this chapter I attempt to understand what might have been going on in the mind of Peter Ball and also draw on material connected to three of the abusers from the diocese of Chichester. How did their role as priests and belief in God co-exist with being an abuser? The final part of this chapter includes the account of a paedophile who sought treatment so that he would not offend. I suggest that this is what taking responsibility, and being able to take responsibility, for your life and actions looks like.

Chapter 4 is based on three accounts of the way that the Church handled abuse allegations. The first is a situation from Bath and Wells during the time that I was working as safeguarding advisor. When one is in the middle of dealing with something it is often hard to understand what one has been caught up in but, in this case, and indeed in the other two that are discussed in this chapter, it becomes clear that the Church has responded using a pattern similar to that of the abuser. This means that secrecy is to the fore. The second case discussed shows how the Church engaged in avoidance, proceduralism and obfuscation. This was not only about handling the actual disclosure but also in the follow-up claim for compensation where litigation games were played in the name of the Church and caused further trauma for the survivor. The third situation explores the strange system whereby one bishop is investigating another bishop. It may appear anomalous but unfortunately reflects a great weakness in the way that the Church has dealt with allegations. The situations described have contributed to a sense of frustration, anger and betrayal within and towards the Church.

The next part of the book turns to look at why the Church has been unable to respond appropriately, despite all the apologies, the new policies and even new systems put in place, and the series of lessons-learned reviews and reports – including some that are currently in the pipeline. Chapter 5 explores how the superficial adoption of safeguarding guidelines and training programmes and the appearance that the problem is being tackled has failed to make inroads into what is a deeply embedded structure of power and control in the institutional church. Examples are included about how the guidelines have been interpreted or misinterpreted. There is also a look at the system of the church insurers and their relationship to the institution, and how this has impacted on post-abuse compensation claims. Whilst there is currently a renewed focus on survivors, the question remains whether this can translate into a meaningful real change, or whether it is merely, as before, window-dressing.

Chapter 6 gets to the heart of the problem which is that the organisation of the Church is more or less a closed hierarchical grouping, which by its explicit and implicit structures nurtures a culture of almost unchallengeable authority. The explicit structure is characterised by a division into the central 'subjects' and the 'others' whom one could call 'objects'. Using this split between 'us and them' means that the subject is the clergy and the object is the laity (those who attend). In the implicit mode, men, whether clergy or laity, are the subject and women laity and children (if seen at all) are the object or are absent (and, as the predominant discourse, this perspective is then unfortunately almost inevitably adopted where women are also clergy). Within the implicit mode, archbishops, bishops and archdeacons are 'super subjects'. Looking at instances of what has happened in the past and contemporary examples show that the 'victim' who discloses is neither 'subject' nor 'object' but rather placed in a liminal place, on the boundary of the Church as 'family', a 'special' category rather mirroring the 'special relationship' – a term that some perpetrators use to impose silence. The chapter discusses how the powerful central core and those on the margin interact. There is analysis of networks, those that are formally set up and those that have evolved informally. Finally, I look at the issue of class within the Church and how this emerged in a specific situation.

Chapter 7 looks at two specific examples of charismatic leaders who have gone on to abuse their power and prestige. The Church is excited by charisma and what seem to be especially 'holy' leaders – particularly when it leads to success in terms of increased church attendance or positive media publicity. However, such reflected glory came at a price in both these situations for the Church too was hoodwinked, or, perhaps, instead chose not to see what was happening, with dire consequences for the victims caught up in abusive practices. For when allegations were made the response of the Church was to deny and diminish those who came forward – until there was no alternative.

In Chapter 8 it is suggested that the tradition of the British public school system has influenced, and continues to influence, the institutional church and so continues to affect the way that the Church responds to child sexual abuse allegations against clergy. This chapter looks at boys' boarding schools and includes discussion on the long-term effects of the emotional damage done by removing children from their parents at a young age. The ethos of entitlement fostered by such schools continues to affect the institutional church and senior clerics. Such privilege and sense of entitlement comes at a cost, not only in the constricted emotional response found amongst those in the hierarchy who were sent away to school, but also in the rule-bound ethos and traditions that, as a result, have become embedded in church structures. The abuse experienced by a large number of public school boys at Christian summer camps is discussed.

Sex, sexism and gender are discussed in the context of power and control in Chapter 9. Divisions over who can become clergy in terms of their gender and sexual orientation have preoccupied and dominated the Church for many years. Sex and gender issues are also important to any understanding of the institution's response to child sexual abuse allegations. The dilemma of the ordination of women and the issue of gay clergy (married or not) have provided and continue to provide preoccupying diversions from tackling the inherent discomfort and reluctance to acknowledge that sexuality, in all its diverse manifestations, is an essential aspect of what makes us human and alive.

Finally, in Chapter 10 I define what has gone on as a deep spiritual sickness within the institution. The Church has in its mishandling further spiritually abused many survivors. As Rosie Harper writes, 'How the Church responds to survivors, how we as individuals respond to survivors, is an infallible indicator of the sort of God we believe in. . . . That sort of God is a tiny, religious, defensive God and I think that is where we are.'[21] It seems that there are possibilities of small changes but whether these can really take hold and affect the underlying culture remains in the balance. The much-vaunted survivor-led renewal that the Church is promising will turn out to be another avoidance or deception unless the whole Church takes on the responsibility.[22]

2.
Survivor Accounts

The response of the institutional church generally has been to show more concern for the reputation of the Church than for the individual survivor, and it has been slow and very reluctant to help to take responsibility for meeting the victims' needs. As we begin to examine the response of the Church to child sexual abuse perpetrated by clergy and other church officials, it is crucial to establish the centrality of the survivors' experiences. Theirs is the lens through which the subject is explored and so in this chapter the voices of three survivors are heard; as well as hearing about their story, they also represent the many others who have not been able to voice their trauma. In this chapter the focus is on sexual abuse, which in itself always includes emotional abuse, usually physical abuse, and in this context undoubtedly spiritual abuse.

The word 'trauma' is generally used to mean any experience that causes unbearable psychic pain or anxiety. An experience is 'unbearable' when it overwhelms the usual defences, which Freud described as a 'protective shield against stimuli'.[1] Trauma can begin with one highly-distressing event, a series of frightening and unusual events, or the cumulative experience of trauma over a long period that gradually undermines and overwhelms the child or adult. All traumatic experiences disrupt our well-being and, even if just in the short term, disturb the individual's psychological growth. How we react to trauma depends on our age, the specific nature of the events and the context within which they occur, as well as our inner resilience and psychological needs. The emotional trauma that results from the sexual abuse of children, young people and young adults has profound and lasting effects. Often it drives people 'inwards', although on the outside they may appear to have coped.[2] Writing in early 2020 Angharad Woolcott describes very well the lifelong ramifications for her of being sexually abused by a Church of England priest and her feelings of anguish and disbelief when finding out about others' experiences:

> There is barely a single part of my life that has not been affected by the abuse I experienced as a child: from the small things, such as the rules my abuser enforced about eating with my mouth closed, to the big things, such as questioning my ability to take care of my children, or putting trust in those around me. The impact of his actions has changed the way I look at the world.
> My abuser was not a figure of national prominence, but he was a pillar of our rural community. He was a family friend, and his wife was a primary-school teacher. His social status allowed him to abuse with impunity. . . . A priest is someone whom we should be able to trust – a person involved in marriages and christenings, ceremonies steeped in hope and love. If we can't put our faith in them, who can we?[3]

Trauma is of course always experienced uniquely by individual people, not collectively by dehumanised or numbered victims, and every victim and survivor has a different story to tell and, if the Church is to understand and 'own' the current crisis, then these accounts all need to be heard, valued and inwardly digested. The experiences also need to inform future practice and responses. The person who has been abused may need to recount what actually happened or may instead want to concentrate on the ramifications and effects of the abusive experiences in his or her life. He/she may need proper funding for long-term psychotherapy; he/she will certainly want recognition for the harm done in the context of the Church. To experience the anxiety caused by sexual abuse threatens the very centre of our sense of self. One of the distinguishing features of such trauma is 'called "disintegration anxiety", an unnameable dread associated with the threatened dissolution of a coherent self. . . . To experience such anxiety threatens the total annihilation of the human personality, the destruction of the personal spirit'.[4]

The three survivors whose stories are included in this chapter were, like Angharad Woolcott, damaged in this way by Church of England clergy. The essence of all abuse is the breaking of trust, usually by those who are in a position of authority. It is about the irresponsible exploitation of this trust, and often of obedience, and in the case of children and adolescents also an exploitation of their ignorance and innocence. No matter the age, the blood relationship or the work setting, the three central elements are: the betrayal of trust and responsibility; the inability for different reasons, and especially for children, to consent; and the abuse of power. As will be discussed in a later chapter, the Church has unerringly and possibly sometimes unconsciously repeated or at some level re-enacted these same aspects when they have been disclosed to and told about what has happened by the person who has been abused.

'Suffer the Little Children'

Janet Lord, the first survivor to speak in this chapter, gives an account in 'The Power of Purple',[5] of her abuse at the age of fourteen by Bishop Whitsey. Janet Lord's vicar father had left the family and so his future and the future of the family and the family home were in great doubt. There had been extensive media coverage, the family were anxious and the invitation to visit the bishop was seen as very important for their future. She and her brother arrived at the Bishop's Palace in Chester:

> I felt very small and insignificant, and I suspect my little brother felt even more so.

> Again I was surprised that my brother and I were asked to see the Bishop separately. I was terrified – I didn't know what I would say. The Bishop was very tall, very big, very purple. He said that physical comfort was the best kind. He said 'suffer the little children to come unto me'. And then he abused me.
>
> I was bewildered, confused, hurt, worried. I had tried to shy away from being comforted physically, but he was a big man, and this was difficult for me. I was so conscious that this purple monster held my family's future and our house in his gift, and I knew I couldn't do anything to upset that. I didn't tell anyone. I didn't know who I could have told anyway. The bishop was all seeing, all powerful, and I had thought, all loving.
>
> That was the beginning of the end of my relationship with the Church of England.[6]

Janet Lord goes on to describe how this sexual initiation based on power and exploitation stripped away her identity. Telling victims not to speak about what has happened is always the perpetrator's first line of defence,[7] leaving the victim under the spell cast by the abuser. This has been referred to as the 'nexus of unfreedom'.[8] However, years later, Janet Lord and her brother shared that both had been abused by Whitsey that same day; an experience that had also, and inevitably, deeply coloured her brother's adult life. When they did disclose and this was heard by a member of the clergy, that cleric did nothing for some months, even though by then Whitsey's record of perpetrating abuse had been recognised. Whitsey had fostered the impression that he would be a help or a support to both children and their mother. Both victims' expectations were radically contradicted by the assaults, and so reality was turned upside down and was not what it had appeared to be.

One of the reasons that such abuse affects other relationships is because it is experienced as a 'global betrayal'.[9] Looking at the account by Janet Lord, 'I was bewildered, confused, hurt, worried', the first moment of doubt arises when the child or young person realises that the adult, and, in this case, the revered and important bishop, someone previously trusted or assumed to be trustworthy, will not keep them safe. This is the breaking apart of all assumptions, the shattering of expectations of security and safety. As Donald Campbell writes in Cosimo Schinaia's *On Paedophilia*, because of what has happened, both the mind of the seducer becomes incomprehensible and the child's physical integrity is violated by the abusive act: 'The victim is left without a trusting orientation to the mind of the other within which to find a representation of itself.'[10] In other words, the breaking of this taboo deeply wounds the victim's own understanding of himself and his world. The second betrayal happens after abuse has occurred, if what has happened is ignored, or minimised or denied. In Janet Lord's situation she felt it impossible to say what had happened because of the precarious position that the family was in, so she and her brother would have been left feeling totally alone and fearful that what had happened could not be understood or in any way mitigated.

Working with those who have experienced child sexual abuse shows that, no matter who has abused them, the parent is at some level, and at different levels of consciousness, held as responsible for not protecting the child, protecting the body from pain and the child's mind from the confusion and doubt. If the adult abuser is not a parent, the child's rage is still directed at the parents – generally, the mother – for having 'allowed' the abuse to occur. 'When the parents, or another caring adult, fail to provide meaning for the abuse, motivation to conceptualize an abusive experience by the victim is undermined and replaced by reliance upon action to resolve traumatic experiences.'[11] The long-term implication of the abuse is a challenge to one's reliance upon the developed internal perception of experience and sense of self. The choice is then between the authenticity of what the victim 'knows' as the reality of what happened and the false reality shown by those who minimise, ignore or deny. This is why the response of the institutional church in many situations, which often amounts to neglect, perpetrates a further abuse on the psychological health of the victim/survivor.

Soul Murder

It is inevitable that some amount of neglect and even at times torment are present in everyone's childhood, but the wilful abuse and neglect by adults that are of enough intensity and sometimes also frequency to be called traumatic has been called 'soul murder'. It is one way of describing how the child or young person is left after damaging experiences, often feeling sad and perhaps less able to feel natural joy in being alive. It has been defined as the destruction of the love of life and as killing the capacity for joy in another human being. As a character in a play by Ibsen puts it:

> You have committed the one mortal sin. . . . You have killed the love of life in me. Do you understand what that means? The Bible speaks of a mysterious sin for which there is no forgiveness. I have never understood what it could be; but now I understand. The great unpardonable sin is to murder the love of life in a human soul. . . . You have killed all the joy of life in me.[12]

A leading psychoanalyst in the field, using the term 'soul murder', means by this that the child and young person's emotional development has been 'profoundly and predominantly negatively affected; what has happened to them has dominated their motivating unconscious fantasies'.[13] Clearly, it is a subject full of contradictions and complexities, and one where generalisations are not always helpful. People are not made homogenous by having undergone similar traumatic experiences, but analytic therapy with those who have can sometimes reveal tendencies. Deep within each of us who has been violated and left feeling helpless is traumatic anxiety and rage. For many adult survivors of childhood abuse the emotional work in resolving this bodily violation, and the resulting psychological preoccupation, was not and could not be done at the time. Disclosing the abuse later gives a second chance to alleviate the pain. People in the Church context, who are ignorant or in denial of the subject, sometimes question why children and young people were unable to stop the abuse when it was happening and why then it is sometimes many years before they disclose what has happened to them. The reason the child is usually unable to stop what is happening is partly because he or she has been 'groomed' by the abuser and also because he or she is in a state of powerlessness and often very afraid. The child is overwhelmed by what is happening to him/her and, because he or she cannot retain any control or give informed consent, the experience becomes an assault. Detachment can set in as a survival technique. This dissociation can be to such an extent so that neither the event nor the emotions are fully recollected. The person may later remember what happened but have no appropriate emotional responses. This is what happened to Sam whose account comes later in the chapter. This is because trauma acts as an overwhelming assault not just on the body but also on the mind, the person is psychologically overwhelmed by something unbearable and the psychological objective is to survive.

One useful way of thinking about and understanding why it may take years to recall and accept what happened is to look at research on post-traumatic stress syndrome and survivor theory, which was originally developed from work with those who survived warfare. This shows that often after a severe trauma a pattern of repression, denial and emotional avoidance emerges. This is really a form of self-protection; it is a form of survival. This denial-numbing phase can last for days or decades, but repression can only work for so long and inevitably what has been suppressed re-emerges or is triggered in one way or another, sometimes through associations and sometimes through what are called 'flashbacks'. Freud calls this 'the return of the repressed'.[14] We do remember everything somewhere in our psyche so, when images return, this can be deeply painful and upsetting and often leads people to somehow or other try to avoid this happening where at all possible. It also threatens to challenge the adaptation that has taken place and the way the person has managed to adjust within his/her psyche. Any change is difficult psychologically and, again, this process is exacerbated if there is prolonged questioning during disclosure and re-exposure to the events at the point when the person is trying to demand justice and restitution.

The second survivor account is from another person who was also abused by the Bishop of Chester, Victor Whitsey. The survivor recounts the lifelong effects of this trauma upon him and how the deep impact of the event re-emerged in adulthood. This survivor, who wishes to remain anonymous, had gone to meet the Bishop as a teenager to discuss his wish to become a clergyman.[15] He said:

> When I met Victor Whitsey I was young, innocent, and naïve. I longed for his blessing to achieve my wish of a future as a vicar, serving God and the community. He told me he agreed I had a calling from God. He also told me he

had the power to give me everything I wanted in life and the power to take it all away. He then proceeded to abuse me sexually and psychologically. I was powerless to stop him.

Twenty years later the trauma re-emerged in full strength and led to a complete mental breakdown and a suicide attempt. The survivor is quoted as saying:

> I blamed myself, thought I was the only victim and rationalised that it was my fault. If he was acting with God's will, I should have enjoyed and welcomed what he did but I didn't; if he was acting against God's will, I should have rejected and reported him but I didn't. Whichever way I rationalised it, I was a failure and not worthy of God's love. I told no one; who would believe a teenage boy's word against a Bishop of the Church of England? I became reclusive and came to the ultimate conclusion: the prospect of ever seeing Victor Whitsey again was so abhorrent to me that I turned my back on my beloved church and my calling to serve God. I self-harmed and have spent a lifetime focusing on resentment and bitterness.

Here the adult survivor was taking on the guilt of the crime – which incidentally Whitsey may or, more likely, may *not* have felt consciously. This is a sort of brainwashing where the survivor is carrying the guilt and responsibility for what took place. In the account, we read also of the spiritual abuse involved around the idea that this could in some way be 'God's will'. This religious guilt and disappointment compounded the trauma. In analytic thinking 'taking on the blame' is also a way of managing and defending against all the mixed feelings involved, including repressed rage about what has happened, and this can contribute, as it has in this situation, to a deeply ingrained but unconscious need for punishment. The survivor continues to describe further losses and damage from the abuse:

> Because of the sexual abuse I suffered at the hands of Victor Whitsey I lost my faith, my chosen life as a vicar, my self-belief, my freedom from worry and my dignity. Child sex abuse is a crime which stays with you for a lifetime. As a

child you don't understand why or what is happening, but as you grow older you realise the enormity of the abuse and it hurts you all over again – you blame yourself for allowing it – you hate yourself for being weak. Since my abuse, not a day has gone by that I have not thought about what happened to me. In my mind I have a high definition video of what I went through, that I cannot eradicate no matter how hard I try. I remember him coming at me with shaking hands, I remember the feel of him on me, and I remember the last time I closed the door on my parish church realising that Christ had left me and I was utterly alone with horrific memories I could share with no one.

When a complaint was made by another victim to the Church of England, whilst Whitsey was still Bishop of Chester, it was not passed to the police and, whilst the Church was believed to have been made aware of further allegations following Whitsey's retirement, no action was taken. Here are all the signs of another Church cover-up, this time involving at least eighteen victims, both men and women, including the person quoted above, dating from 1974 until Whitsey's death in 1987. An independent review commissioned by the Church of England was published in October 2020, rightly called *A Betrayal of Trust*, and inevitably many apologies given.[16]

The sexual abuse by Whitsey, described by this anonymised person, reminds us of both the physical and psychological pain following abuse. Something has happened to the body, there is an actuality to that event, and yet the victim is, to some extent, left alone with his pain and the imprint on the body that is left behind. There is an unknowability to another's pain that leaves the person suffering alone and, although over time the physical pain is history, as the victim recounts: 'as you grow older you realise the enormity of the abuse and it hurts you all over again'. The immediate bodily pain has long passed but the psychological imprint of the pain still overwhelms the victim's attempts to think about what has happened and how to conceptualise it. In other words, the experience, so deeply embedded into the body memory, prevents attempts to deal with it by representing and conceptualising it.

'Pain is often experienced as destroying a trustworthy, taken-for-granted, physically, sexually and narcissistically gratifying body and leaving us frightened, helpless and confused with an unpredictable, attacking, alien body.'[17] Hence, there is the need to relieve the trauma, by self-harm or suicidal attacks on the pain-bearing body. Dissociation or splitting, by disavowing the body or attacking it, avoids the mourning needed for what has been lost. Sometimes the survivor of abuse adopts instead what has been called 'traumatic progression of a precocious maturity'. One writes, 'I grew up when I was five. Not only because I lost my virginity then, but because I realised in that moment of pain and terror that I was on my own.'[18] This quote from a woman abused when she was very small shows how she had quickly to grow up, letting go of childhood and adopting instead some form of emotional and intellectual maturity like an adult, as a way to defend herself against hurtful and dangerous adults. 'The fear of the uninhibited, almost mad adult changes the child, so to speak, into a psychiatrist and, in order to become one and to defend himself against dangers coming from people without self-control, he must know how to identify with them completely.'[19] This is the wise child who paradoxically cannot be a normal child because he or she does not know what he/she thinks and cannot allow him- or herself time and space; neither can he/she find a trustworthy adult who can help to begin to work it all out. Analytic studies suggest that typically responding to the abuse in the inner world leads to various defences being used, but also, as in the example of the five year-old, that one part of the functioning ego of the child *regresses* to the infantile period and another part *shoots forward*; in other words, the child grows up too fast and often becomes a 'false self', a pretend psychiatrist, who can then adapt to taking care of the regressed part. It's a form of self-care in the absence of reliable adults.

Another tendency of the long-term effects of abuse, especially when trying to repress what has happened, is the potential for the person who has experienced abuse to 'adapt' to the abuse as a 'normal part of life' in the sense of the experience somehow or other becoming integrated into the ego. This then means 'a pattern of living with misfortune and mishaps that we call masochism.'[20] The masochism is in many ways a form of negative excitement that can become compulsive, and so situations are unconsciously sought to repeat and possibly also try to master the dreadful event. However, the difficulty is that in such an 'adaptation' the child or young person becomes compliant and, because of his or her need to be loved, wanted and protected, may attach him- or herself to people or situations that are sadistic. The dilemma is terrible as the abuse often has been perpetrated by the very person to whom the child is looking for love and protection, and so there can be no simple solution. If the child is very young, then there is no way out other than to adapt to the situation; older children and adolescents can begin to use defences such as repression, denial and rationalisation. The frightened and often helpless victim is continually placed in psychological conflict – who is trustworthy, who can be relied on, who can be confidently loved and is this safe? This can continue for a very long time and so inevitably can be compounded by responses to the abuse. In these situations, often the true self of the person has to take on a secret life and become hidden.

Trapped in the Power and Control Dynamic

The two survivor accounts described so far in this chapter are from people who felt able to share and write about what had happened to them; however, for many, if not most, people this feels almost impossible. When I worked as a psychoanalytic psychotherapist, I saw patients in an adolescent psychiatric department for a number of years; I also worked in private practice and for a charity. Over that long period of time I saw a large number of people who had experienced sexual abuse as children and who had not previously felt able to discuss the trauma. The effects of the abuse had stayed, sometimes repressed or dissociated from, but often contributing to anxiety and depression or more serious symptoms. I discovered this insight from the work with people deeply trapped by the trauma: 'In situations of captivity the perpetrator becomes the most powerful person in the life of the victim, and the psychology of the victim is shaped by the actions and beliefs of the perpetrator.'[21]

Many years ago I worked with someone I shall call Sam who in his mid-twenties was referred by his GP. At the time he agreed that I might use our work together to write about sexual abuse as long as all identifying details were removed.[22] Dylan Thomas[23] wrote that the memories of childhood have no order and no end – this seems especially so of a childhood that involved sexual abuse. Often the memories are 'out of sequence' as the traumatic event has been impossible to incorporate fully into a meaningful context and so is an unassimilated experience.

Conscious or partially repressed memories of the abuse often feel unbearable to think about and yet, despite that, feel ever present, so the memories may seem unmanageable and therefore can be destructive of present relationships. The survivors may regard what they have to say as 'thing like' or concretised, rather than as imagined or remembered so that the open-ended quality of fantasy life seems to be missing.

This was Sam's experience as the distressing symptom that he shared with me when we first met was his sudden terrifying visualisations of sexually harming an infant. This fear which felt very real was triggered if he saw any small child with their parent. The image seemed real rather than a fantasy and part of the work was to try to uncover this sexual aggression, acknowledge that to which it was linked and so reintegrate it back into his memory rather than continuing as a present terror of acting it out. Over the time we met, it emerged that Sam had been violently and sadistically abused over three years from the age of six by the local vicar who was a family friend. It only ended when the vicar suddenly moved away. Sam did not know why the vicar had left but he did know that now, although the vicar was physically dead, for Sam he was still very much alive. As an adult Sam described the abuse as brutal, sordid and often very painful. He was required to dress up and elaborate rituals preceded the actual abuse. Sometimes another man was present. Quite early on he said something to his mother after she saw that he was bleeding, but this was dismissed and his visits to the vicar encouraged. His family were formal and very traditional, so he later supposed it was because they could not imagine the vicar doing such things and would never talk about such subjects anyway.

The work was grim in the sense that the words spoken were always about the event; he returned again and again to the painful details of the abuse but there were no feelings about it. He asked: 'Why did I keep going back?' His own answer was, 'Well, I must have enjoyed it. I must have been excited by it.' He explained 'how' he, as a small child, had survived the abuse. It emerged that the vicar would tell him to go off and play and forget about what had happened until the next time. As a child, he had split apart his feelings. He would leave the vicarage and go and play 'as if' nothing had happened, and this was repeated in the dynamic between us in the psychotherapy where I experienced painful and uneasy feelings, including feeling seriously overwhelmed and sometimes physically sick. In the therapy we were trapped in the same power and control dynamic that Sam had experienced as a child, and it seemed almost impossible to get out of it. Sam was still half in the fantasy that nothing was really happening, which had become his way of defending against the terrible reality – he had had to identify with the abuser's instructions and story to survive. His life from the age of six had been about holding himself together as best he could, through boarding school and then college, and now an office job, until the terror of the sexual aggression inflicted against him had re-emerged in his symptom of visualising inflicting it on an innocent child. The work was partly about getting to an 'as if' place, where Sam could feel that his symptom was a metaphor for what had happened to him; 'as if' he might act out the fantasy, why this might be and then understanding that the baby part of him was still in shock and suffering – very upset and very angry. We had to begin to break the cycle of abuser/abused between us.

All child sexual abuse involves the submission of the abused to the abuser; this is mastery domination and so the therapy is partly about inverting the dynamic so the abused seeks inner mastery over the abuser within their psyche. The mastery domination places the abused in a position of passivity and weakness with a disregard for pain, denial and misery. The passive state is assigned by the abuser, as the vicar did to Sam. It is his wish and is forcefully enacted in a physical way that annihilates any idea of choice for the child. So, as Sam experienced, the child is penetrated in body and in mind. In the process of denying the needs of the child, however, there is an aspect of unification: 'this is what we both want', which is compounded by the idea of the secret, special and guilty relationship that excludes anyone else. This is why telling someone is such a breakthrough and an opportunity to open up the power and control dynamic. Therapy is about telling someone, who may help you as an adult to tell the police,[24] and it can then eventually become about creating enough room for developmental processes to begin and space for the fantasy to try in some way to re-emerge.

The guilt of what has happened that has been left with the victim can be conscious, partly conscious or unconscious – that is, repressed and not accessible. In such situations, and especially for children, victims usually feel a conscious sense of guilt around the wrong that has happened, although the responsibility always lies with the abuser who has exploited the victim. There can sometimes be a guilt linked to the sexuality involved and, if the body has physically responded in any way to the event, in spite of 'knowing' that this was something that was not consciously enjoyable, there can be a feeling of 'a betrayal' by the body. The unconscious guilt has been described as 'borrowed', where the boundaries between the abuser and abused are no longer evident. This idea can help to explain the relentless, and at times unforgiving, feeling of guilt often carried by survivors, where it is suggested that there is transgenerational transmission (that these feelings, if not brought out, can sometimes be passed on to children or grandchildren),[25] an adoption of the abuser's unconscious sense of guilt by 'borrowing'. What is kept unconscious is the fact of the borrowing and the guilty feelings of the abuser towards the victim, which will exist somewhere. The abuse may have taken place 'in secret' but it is the aspect of guilt in holding the 'secret' that the abuser passes on to the abused. What is also kept secret is the sacrifice that this adoption places on the victim. The abuse does not end with the cessation of the abuse, 'but continues unabated in the inner world of the trauma victim, whose dreams are often haunted by persecutory inner figures'. Moreover, the person may sometimes find him- or herself in similar situations where he or she is re-traumatised:

> As much as he or she wants to change, as hard as he or she tries to improve life or relationships, something more powerful than the ego continually undermines progress and destroys hope. It is as though the persecutory inner world somehow finds its outer mirror in repeated self-defeating 're-enactments' – almost as if the individual were possessed by some diabolical power or pursued by malignant fate.[26]

The humiliation Sam experienced over the dressing up, fostered further shame about what was happening. It was the analytical psychologist Carl Jung who wrote that shame is a soul-eating emotion and it certainly is something that lingers long on after the event. We want to hide and cover up what feels shameful, and then we also long to hide the fact that we are ashamed. Where shame about an external experience becomes translated into an inner experience, and this is what tends to stay with us, is the connection with a sense of being unacceptable, unlovable. In religious language this can confirm an inner sense of our unworthiness encapsulated by the thought: I don't deserve to be here – who do I think I am? There's no one to hide from, nothing to hide from, nowhere to go and certainly no going back. That person is mortified, dead. What do people say? 'I was so embarrassed/ashamed, I could have died.' This is existential shame that implies fear of total abandonment and a fear of psychic extinction. This shame was compounded when Sam tried to say something to his mother but was dismissed and his trust further betrayed. So here a bond of empathy was breached, and the experience was one of falling out of attunement and into a place of loneliness; any connection that could have been made was lost and communication was inhibited. This is the re-abuse that occurs when victims and survivors disclose what happened to them to church authorities and they are ignored and their allegations mishandled.

The After-effects

In one sense the after-effects of any trauma always remain in the psyche. The aim is to manage and master it so that the person is no longer overwhelmed in the present or subject to self-harming behaviour.[27] There would appear to be a correlation between the depth of the trauma and the degree of powerlessness experienced by the child or young person whilst the sexual abuse was taking place. No child or young person can integrate such a mind/body assault at the time, though it may be grasped or interpreted by the child some time later if it can be put into words, but the resonances remain in the mind and often there are body memories. The task is to create some sense of inner order so that what happened moves from 'here and now' and stays as 'there and then'; it is about allowing creativity a chance.

The institutional church is not a therapeutic community and does not have the capability or the empathy needed for such pastoral work, but it does have the money to pay for professional, good and long-term therapeutic work when it is asked to do so by survivors. The Church has a moral responsibility to provide this; it also has a spiritual responsibility. The Church has a duty to treat survivors with respect and with an awareness of their needs. In their book *To Heal and not to Hurt*,[28] Rosie Harper and Alan

Wilson detail how the Church's response needs to be driven by the needs of each survivor, taking into account four dimensions: the first is the 'psychological harm and the ongoing support needed'; secondly, 'life chances that have been changed by the abuse, and possibilities for retraining, coaching and career support'; thirdly, taking into account 'financial hardship, including loss of income and lack of pension provision'; and, finally, the spiritual deficit, 'if the survivor so wishes, a spiritual friend could help detoxify faith as a resource for living'. Before moving to look at what the response of the institutional church has been, we turn in the next chapter to look at what is going on in the mind of the clergy perpetrator – the mind of the abuser.

3.
The Mind of the Abuser

The perpetrators of sexual abuse can be extraordinarily devious, presenting a carapace of piety and respectability to the outside world; and ... adverse facts can be concealed skilfully.[1]

Lord Carlile of Berriew

When I first worked as a psychoanalytic psychotherapist, I agreed to have an assessment meeting with a man who had recently been charged with child sexual abuse. This had involved a nine-year-old girl, the daughter of his current partner. This very reasonable and respectable looking middle-aged man wanted me to write a report for the trial to show that he was taking the crime seriously and looking to understand and change his behaviour. Except that he was not, for what I experienced was not genuine; it felt like a performance and an attempt to groom me into emotional collaboration. I realised that I could not continue with the process when he assured me in all seriousness that the sexual acts had not been his idea, but rather that he had been 'led on' by the child. He had been an unwilling partner to her seduction, and I needed to feel sorry for him. As a result of this meeting I came to understand that not only does the offender usually have distorted thinking, but also often a completely self-absorbed sense of reality. In my work in the diocese of Bath and Wells, I met a number of men, including some clergy, who had previous convictions for sexual offences against children and were required to sign up to what was called a written agreement that they would have no contact with or access to children and young people at church. This was only a voluntary agreement and the information was shared with the incumbent, church wardens and the person monitoring safeguarding in the parish. The clergy were always more reluctant and difficult to engage than the others. They seemed to find it hard to think that they could still be considered a risk and found the procedure demeaning.

Clearly each perpetrator is an individual and unique, although he shares certain characteristics with other abusers. Searching for accounts that help one to understand the mind of the clergy abuser shows that similar dynamics exist in the so-called 'confessions' that one can find in the public domain. This means that the descriptions feel two-dimensional, with bland attempts at explaining behaviour, whilst the details of each man's modus operandi are shocking. There is narcissism, but also solipsism. For the solipsist the self – his self – is all that exists at any present moment where there is a concern with the self at the expense of social relationships. In the novel *Lolita* by Vladimir Nabokov, the term 'solipsism' is a key word and when, in the book, the abuser Humbert states that 'Lolita had been safely solipsized', he is speaking of the power of his ruthless desire to create an object for his own pleasure.[2] There is also often self-justification and the blaming of others in such confessions. Take, for example, two extraordinary accounts, one by a North American priest and another by a French priest – both Roman Catholic. Between them they appear to have abused over one hundred children. The available accounts give details about how they went about selecting vulnerable children, those to whom they were most attracted and why, and the way that parents, families and communities were groomed. Both men seem entranced by their crimes. Whilst it may be easy to confess from the prison cell, the words used have no real feelings attached. In the case of Robert Van Handel the North American, his reasons put forward for offending were a domineering and controlling father, plus the Catholic teaching on the sin of masturbation, compounded by an assault on him that took place when he was fifteen.[3]

Paul-André Harvey, the French priest, writes that the reason he abused was that he had 'emotional needs that were not being met'. 'Mistakes were made, but not by me.'[4] Justifying his actions thus, he seems to extricate himself from responsibility by blaming everyone else.[5] He writes, 'I am convinced that the parish environment itself contributed to my crimes. Being in contact constantly with women and mostly the status enjoyed by the clergy greatly contributed to my wanderings.' He also casts blame on the police for not stopping him (he was questioned four times by the police) and blames his superiors for not getting him help. Harvey also 'blames' the victims for enjoying his assaults and returning for further abuse. He marvels at his ability to be both abuser and priest, wondering how he could have led such a double life for over twenty years, 'without it being a stain on the quality of my ministry'. He muses that there were perhaps two different beings within him: 'There was the pervert who was constantly looking for thrills. There was also a devoted priest who knew how to be appreciated and who gave all of himself to his mission.' He offers one reason: 'I knew what I was doing was wrong, but I was enjoying it like I had never enjoyed anything like it before.' These accounts make it seem as if searching to understand the mind of the abuser is almost naïve, as if their desire sweeps aside any reflective process and certainly any moral or religious prohibitions. However, such accounts demonstrate deep psychological damage and arrested emotional development. They reveal the power of being possessed by a compulsion to repeat and act out damage through sado-masochistic behaviour, and, thus, an inability to reflect sufficiently to see that there is a choice – the choice to seek help and treatment.

In 2018 Pope Francis, using language that owed much to medieval theology, blamed the devil, 'the great accuser', as a malign force tempting otherwise good priests to sexually abuse children and young people.[6] Decades before, when the first shocking disclosures of clerical abuse emerged in the 1990s, Pope John Paul II referred to those clerics who abused children as a 'few bad apples'. He stigmatised the offence with some angry words, in reply to pressing accusations which could have undermined the ecclesiastical institution, especially in the United

States. This seemed a thoughtless though unsurprising response, for he offered no reflections on why so many priests had abused children and young people and he made no attempt to consider why the Church appeared to harbour so many abusers. His successor, Benedict XVI, pointed an accusing finger, instead, at the high number of closeted gay men in the clergy, thereby confusing things by insinuating wrongly that those who are homosexual are also, almost by definition, paedophiles.[7] The demonisation of the paedophiliac is an understandable and relatively easy way to handle the distaste and revulsion that such behaviour engenders. However, it is basically a form of psychological division, in other words, separating crudely into black or white, victim or villain, good or bad, which is in itself anti-thought. This can be satisfying in the short term but is seriously limiting, for, if the perpetrator is 'just' demonised, then we are no further forward in our understanding, nor guided by how adequately to respond. Ironically, and disturbingly, the Church's response to abuse frequently is to support the clergy abuser, by rushing to defend him, and thus the Church compromises its authority and accountability.[8] In turn, the abuser becomes the victim, while, against all odds, the complainant – the person who has been abused – is then seen as the villain. This 'taking sides' does not lead to any understanding.

The Church of England has been largely of the 'few bad apples' school of thought, reluctant to enquire too deeply into what may be going on in the mind of the abuser. Quite naturally, there is inevitably resistance to understanding why someone abuses in this way and why it happens particularly in certain contexts. Yet the behaviour demands explanation, both for victim and for perpetrator, and for the institutions where this is happening. Like St Augustine, who said that we should hate the sin but love the sinner, Schinaia suggests, 'we also should show loathing for this kind of behaviour from an ethical and social point of view, while . . . we should find a way to get closer to the paedophile's world respectfully, in order to help him modify his behaviour'.[9]

This chapter initially looks at the relevant definitions of those attracted to what has been termed an 'asymmetrical relationship'. Extracts are then taken from Peter Ball's witness statement to try to understand him a little more. I have also included some findings from the investigations that took place in the diocese of Chichester. In the final section I include the account of a man who was attracted to boys but did not want to act this out. Why? Because his account stands in contrast to the other cases as it demonstrates that he wanted to understand why he had these feelings and wanted to change them so that he would never be a risk to children.

Asymmetrical Relationships

Unlike other behaviours classified as perversions, the sexual contact between the abuser and the child or young person is an attack on generational difference – one of the basic aspects of how society is organised and thereby all the more disturbing. It is doubtful whether one can use the term 'relationship' authentically in the context of what happens when one person abuses another, but, nonetheless, the two people are connected through the event or events, and the striking characteristic is always that this connection is asymmetrical. This means that there is usually inequality in age, size and status and so unequal power relations between participants, where one is superior and the other is very much subordinate. The implication of this unequal power relationship is that control lies firmly with the superior, and so expectations and behaviour are largely non-reciprocal (in contrast to symmetrical relationships). This will affect the way that the interaction develops, and what is initiated and the form that it takes. There are complications in using the word 'paedophile' as this strictly refers to attraction to a group not biologically capable of sexual reproduction, in other words, pre-pubertal children. The technical term for those attracted to early adolescent children is hebephilia; whilst ephebophilia is used for those whose primary sexual interest is mid-to-late adolescents, generally ages fifteen to nineteen. In terms of categorisation as a mental illness, there is, additionally, the odd situation in which the illegal act is a diagnostic factor, rather than merely an indicator of severity; in other words, the distinction is between an offending or a non-offending paedophile.[10] The general consensus on whether or not the sexual interest in children and adolescents is a mental illness is that it is a sign of disorder, but that, in committing an abusive act, it then becomes also a crime.[11]

The research work by David Finkelhor on why someone sexually abuses has influenced much contemporary policy and treatment.[12] He argues that sexual offending against children and young people is a multi-faceted phenomenon and is related to a variety of the person's needs (usually a man), as well as other variables to do with the context and the specific situation. He is very careful to highlight that quite different combinations of needs can motivate different offenders. Finkelhor proposes a four-step model of the preconditions that need to be present before abuse takes place. The first is that the potential abuser needs to have some motivation to abuse sexually and Finkelhor suggests three fundamental components to this: *emotional congruence,* in which sexual contact with a child satisfies profound emotional needs; *sexual arousal,* in which the child represents the source of sexual gratification for the abuser; and, thirdly, *blockage,* in which alternative sources of sexual gratification are either not available or are less satisfactory. The second precondition is that the potential abuser must overcome internal inhibitions that may act against his motivation to sexually abuse. No matter how strong the sexual interest in children might be, if the abuser is inhibited by taboos, then he will not abuse. Next, the potential abuser must overcome external obstacles and inhibitions prior to sexual abuse – this would include access to children, dealing with parents and any safeguards that are in place. Finally, the fourth step of the model is where the potential abuser has to overcome the child's possible resistance to being sexually abused, and this means grooming the child or young person, or overcoming their resistance by manipulation or force.

Research on the reasons that those convicted of child sexual abuse have given include unfulfilled sexual needs, the influence of drugs, ignorance of the law, learning difficulties, impulse disorder, alcohol, senility, the urge to feel in control and powerful, or the identification with young children as a result of arrested emotional development. It has been asserted that men are generally socialised to prefer sexual experiences with partners that are smaller, weaker and younger. This may also increase the likelihood for potential abusers to be motivated to sexually offend children. Therefore, individuals unable to meet their sexual and emotional needs in acceptable ways for a number of reasons, like fear of adult females or adult males, inadequate social skills, castration anxiety and/or mental problems, may be drawn to sexually abuse children.[13] One psychoanalytical case study, in which the abuser chose to enter treatment, suggests the need to access the paedophile's child world and his infantile anxieties. In the case described, this was a sexual trauma to which the paedophile as a child had been subjected and had never discussed, plus all the unspeakable feelings attached to the event. The therapy was able to trigger a process of identification with the victim, which meant that the victim was no longer experienced as a consenting partner, but rather as a traumatised and suffering person in his own right. It is then important 'for a paedophile to realize the psychological damage his behaviour has caused to his victim'.[14]

If the premise of arrested emotional development is explored in the case of Peter Ball, it could be suggested that his 'privileged' upbringing with a nanny and 'remote' parents, plus many years at boarding school, might have contributed to his mental ill health, as demonstrated in his perverted sado-masochistic interest in late adolescents. There are many accounts of the everyday cruelty of British boarding schools, and the implications of this ethos are fully discussed in a later chapter. However, it is worth remembering what the theologian and writer C.S. Lewis, in his account of life at Malvern College,[15] describes as 'the Greek Tradition', in which older boys picked a younger one for sexual comfort. This was fully accepted and understood as just what happened. There was also a tradition of fagging and the punishment for wrongdoing was beating administered by the older boys on the younger. Fifty years later, accounts of life at boarding school reveal that not much has changed. The playwright David Hare remembers how at Lancing College (attended by the twin brothers Peter and Michael Ball) boys were ordered to swim naked 'on the unlikely pretext that if we wore trunks, the fibres from our garments would clog up the filters'.[16] Peter Ball described how as an adolescent he had looked like a Greek god, 'an Adonis'.[17] His later behaviour then surely suggests arrested emotional development from a time when sexual desire and the need for affection was locked into adolescence and the school culture of abuse and beatings. In this next section we look at what Peter Ball had to say in his witness statement to the IICSA inquiry.

Shining a Light into the Dark Parts – the Narcissist

> I had been wrestling with my own sinful behaviour for such a time that it was genuinely (initially at least) a relief that a light was now being shone into the dark parts of my life.
>
> *Peter Ball*

There is some slight evidence that, when Peter Ball was arrested in December 1992, he recognised that he had problems.

Unfortunately, the light that shone into 'the dark parts' lasted only a very short time and, despite his many apologies, Ball's witness statement to the IICSA shows no evidence that he was really able to understand his own actions and experience genuine remorse.[18] The following account is taken from this witness statement. After his arrest, and on the guidance of Lambeth Palace, Ball was sent to an Anglican retreat house Ty Mawr in Monmouth. Here he had a number of long conversations with Sister Una Kroll. In his witness statement Ball calls her a psychiatrist but she was in fact previously a GP who had led the campaign for the ordination of women. Ball describes these meetings as mentally exhausting, detailing his shock, anxiety and bewilderment at the allegations and the involvement of the police. Kroll has referred to this time as 'a long journey through a dark night'. Ball also complains about being lonely: 'I described this time as representing a living hell. . . . I went, on occasion, ten hours a day without seeing or speaking to anyone.' This would possibly have been the time for Ball, feeling so vulnerable, to begin to acknowledge psychologically and spiritually what he had been doing. However, he was much bolstered by a supportive letter from the then Archbishop of Canterbury, George Carey, who, despite his knowledge of what is coyly referred to as the 'matter', went on to say that Ball was greatly loved by so many in the Church. Carey's admiration was in no way diminished; indeed, he was advocating Ball's return to 'the Episcopal bench'. Ball states: 'To know that the Archbishop had faith in me and my ministry, despite my sinful ways and my weakness and that there would potentially be a way back for me into ministry gave me the strength to persevere through this most difficult of times.'[19] This letter restored Ball's self-esteem and so, in effect, the door was shut on any real change and understanding that could have taken place; instead, his wounded pride was energised into a campaign to reinstate his ministry and vilify the complainants. Indeed, in one of Ball's own letters to George Carey, he seems to see Carey as the father who deeply understands; perhaps a further indication of Ball's arrested emotional state. He comments on the letter by saying that George's support 'were the rays of light which penetrated the darkness at that time'. In other words, he was too immature to search for inner awareness to understand the 'dark parts', instead relying on external intervention by the head of the Church.[20]

His account of events demonstrates self-justification, denial and distorted thinking. To really accept the ramifications of his devious sexual behaviour would have required Ball's acknowledgement that his normal human desires for love and affection had become badly perverted. This would have needed a genuine interest in exploring his own motivations and behaviour, through long-term therapeutic work, and immediate acceptance of why it was inappropriate for him to continue in any form of public ministry or spiritual direction. The later vilification of those he had abused shows how Ball's denial, and his own division into good and bad, led to the projection onto the young man Neil Todd as being someone who was irrational and mentally ill, whilst leaving Ball seeing himself as the sane and rational one. This is explored further in Chapter 10. An element of paranoia does emerge in Ball's statement: he initially believed that there was 'some sort of conspiracy against me' to remove him from the episcopal office. This is bolstered by Ball's perception of his 'hostile reception' on his appointment as Bishop of Gloucester, 'particularly from senior members of staff'. He attributes this to his views on the ordination of women.[21] (It would be interesting to speculate what Sister Kroll might have made of this.) In the following months Ball did receive some psychiatric treatment from Dr Angela Rouncefield in Truro; this was for depression and she concluded Ball was unfit for work.[22] Interestingly, fifteen years later she was part of the campaign orchestrated by Ball against me to prevent him having a risk assessment in the diocese of Bath and Wells and so any curtailment of his ministry.

In the available extracts from the risk assessment made in 2009, Peter Ball admits that he was primarily attracted to post-pubertal adolescents and young adults (although, importantly, one of the allegations in his trial of 2015 was from a child). What is disheartening, though perhaps unsurprising, is the comment that 'he displays a concerning lack of awareness of the impact of his behaviour on victims'. This mirrors Ball's general lack of curiosity about why he might have behaved in what he himself calls 'sinful' behaviour motivated by what he recognises as lust. The reviewer continues in his conclusion that:

> Bishop Peter Ball presents, in interview, as a very personable, polite and generally co-operative person. However there are aspects of his behaviour which may

be seen as highly manipulative and controlling. This is evident in the efforts he has made to thwart this assessment, including his lack of honesty in reporting the opinion of his GP concerning the appropriateness of completing a psychological inventory. One has to wonder what it is that he is fearful of disclosing.[23]

A psychoanalytic perspective might suggest that the perverted sexual behaviour displayed by Ball because of his arrested psychological development was a form of mental illness that he was at times both reluctant and unable to control. Donald Campbell describes how a paedophile whom he was seeing for psychoanalytic treatment described his abusive behaviour as the terror and manic triumph of an omnipotent infant. He reported, 'No one can stop my abuse. The abuse is out of control. I'm a baby.'[24] Ball's unhealthy narcissism, evident in his behaviour and indeed in his witness statement, suggests a personality where there is no concern for the wellbeing of the other, who merely exists to fulfil Ball's need for sexual gratification – albeit of a perverted kind. The work by Daniel Shaw on the traumatising narcissist is helpful here and his thinking is explored further in Chapter 7. In his book Shaw writes about how the heightened sadistic tendencies of the traumatising narcissist may be masked in some cases by charisma and seductive charm and how the victim is often induced into the role of an admirer.[25] Sexual abusers have a conviction that sexuality is the best way to express love and caring: 'Paedophiles state how easy it is to find victims by looking for unhappy, lonely, unprotected children who will respond to offers of care and attention.'[26] The abusers are also often unhappy and lonely themselves and, though outwardly presenting a strong, supportive façade, 'may be starved for affection and symbiotically dependent'. This leads to the need for omnipotent control over the victim.[27]

Ball, in his later years, when questioned by police, during his trial and to IICSA, was keen to apologise, offering 'sincere penitence', seeking to 'deepen penitence' and recognising that he 'had defiled my ministry' and was 'sorry and sad' for the hurt caused. Many letters were written to the victims, in which Ball 'apologised', but these were largely experienced as harassing. His defence against the charges was that his abuse was in fact consensual, denying the power and control of the asymmetrical relationships involving young people attending his community. Other aspects that were known to have occurred Ball denied. The details of the abuse perpetrated by Ball shows plenty of sexual experience but, like that of all sexual predators, it is shallow. Sex for Ball was a control operation; he ordained the time and place of the encounter and the seeking of a conquest was the overriding aspect. As evidenced in his denial of the abuse and insistence on its consensual nature, Ball cared little about what the young men experienced. As is clear from his available statements, Ball's aim was to achieve what he calls 'an emission' through the conquering of another person's body; it was not to have a relationship.

Normalising – What Went on in the Diocese of Chichester

The idea of the normalisation of sexual abuse emerged as one of the central aspects of what happened in the diocese of Chichester, as a result of which a large number of clergy went to prison for the abuse of children and young people (eleven are mentioned).[28] Peter Ball was one of those convicted, with strong connections to some of the others. He was Suffragan Bishop of Lewes (part of Chichester diocese) from 1977-92, before moving to become Bishop of Gloucester shortly before his arrest. The IICSA hearings and report details a long history of offences including the abuse committed by Colin Pritchard and Roy Cotton.[29] John Hind, Bishop of Chichester from 2001-12, told the inquiry that abuse can involve collusion between different people and that a climate can develop in certain areas in which people's normal inhibitions against bad behaviour can get reduced: 'When you are in an environment in which a number of other people are abusing as well, there can be a tendency to normalise what's happening.' Interestingly, part of this process of making what was criminal normal was the attitude of the senior clergy, who gave their concern to the two perpetrators rather than to the victims. They also did not follow the correct safeguarding procedures. The old virtue of forgiveness was used as part of the normalising process. In 2011 the Meekings Report was published online and then taken down. A redacted version came out in 2012. Then Baroness Butler-Sloss released her comments on the Meekings Report.[30] The chaos surrounding these two reports is outlined by the then Archdeacon of Lewes and Hastings in his witness statement to IICSA.[31] The Shemmings Report, published later in 2019, looked at patterns of victimisation and offending behaviour and factors within the diocese of Chichester which possibly contributed to the initiation and maintenance of the abuse. This thorough report included an analysis of the normalisation of certain cultural values linked to abusive practices. The authors use the phrase 'social network' as a more accurate term to describe what happened and give the example of how:

> one senior priest met with a new member of the clergy in his room, while sitting with a boy on his lap, with his hand on the boy's thigh. This is, we believe, a powerful example of how cultural values, beliefs, opportunities and even expectations could have been transmitted, in a 'deniable' way.[32]

The earlier Meekings and Butler-Sloss reports cover the behaviour of Cotton and his co-perpetrator Pritchard and the response of the diocese of Chichester. In 1954 Cotton as an ordinand in training was convicted of an indecent assault against a young boy. There were further unsubstantiated allegations of abuse at a school in 1966 but he was taken back into ordination training where he met Colin Pritchard. In a letter to the then Archbishop of Canterbury Michael Ramsey dated 13 May 1966, the Bishop of Portsmouth outlined Cotton's history, including the earlier criminal offence, and Cotton's repeated requests to be considered for ordination. He said: 'At the time he protested his innocence, and he has done ever since, and in fact from that time has been teaching.' Seeing him as a man of 'considerable ability' and 'free of any trouble for twelve years', he is quoted as saying, 'Roy was more sinned against than sinning'. He added, 'He pleaded guilty at the time to spare the boys concerned having to appear in court. There has been no breath of suspicion of trouble since.' Cotton continually denied that the earlier conviction of sexual abuse had taken place. In one document presented to the enquiry,[33] Cotton is reported to have been 'staggered' that this old conviction should have been raised again. He suggests in 1968 that he is justified in his interest in becoming further involved in the Scout Association and is quoted as saying, 'am I to be continually dogged by an incident in which I still assert my innocence'. Cotton was supported by an earlier bishop of Chichester, Eric Kemp, who told a fellow bishop: 'In my opinion, it is all right. He's been badly handled by the police. You can give him permission to take church services again.'[34]

Cotton denied what he had done and what he was doing. His deception extended to the senior clergy who supported him. The fault of and any guilt about the earlier conviction was projected onto the 'persecutory' police. There is evidence also of this being pushed onto the victim(s) where Cotton convinced himself and others of his having been 'more sinned against than sinning'. The inverting of this guilt is, as Schinaia writes, 'very common, and is the foundation of a vast, explicit, propagandistic literature defending paedophiles'. Sometimes this includes the belief in an altruistic motivation. Here Cotton's interest in rejoining the Scout Association sounds similar to a paedophile who stated, 'My interest in children is linked with a pedagogic motivation – I only want to help them and do them a world of good.'[35] Cotton's victims, of whom there were believed to be at least ten, would not have agreed.

Colin Pritchard also served as a vicar in the diocese of Chichester until arrested in 2007. In 2008 he pleaded guilty to sexually abusing two boys in the 1970s and 1980s and was jailed for five years. Cotton had also been involved, but died in 2006, two weeks before Pritchard was arrested. At his trial Pritchard pleaded not guilty to conspiracy with Cotton to sexually assault one of the boys and to a serious sexual offence, and those charges were ordered to lie on the court file. After his release from jail Pritchard changed his name by deed poll to Ifor Whittaker. However, in 2018, after being rearrested, he was given a sixteen-year sentence for sexually abusing a boy and conspiring with Cotton to do so in the 1980s and 1990s in East Sussex. The judge spoke of Pritchard's (Whittaker's) manipulation of the boy and also of his attempts 'to bamboozle, cheat and mislead the jury'. He said the abuser had 'plied the victim with alcohol' and 'emotionally blackmailed the boy by saying "no one would believe you over a priest"'. The boy is quoted as saying that Cotton had been the main abuser and had 'just passed me over like a toy to be borrowed by a friend'.[36] Deception and cover-up were the hallmarks of what happened, and also in the response of the Church. It is worth noting that Pritchard was granted permission to conduct services in February 2007, upon his retirement, despite having been rearrested at that time for sexual offences against children. Bishop Benn (then responsible) told the IICSA that, without any instruction from him, his personal assistant had '*issued the PTO* [Permission to Officiate] believing that she was supposed to do so and using a signature stamp . . . it was an error on her part'. In other words, once again, mistakes were made – but not by me.[37] In 2013 the bishop of Chichester Dr Martin Warner wrote to one man who had been abused as a choirboy that, 'There has been deception and cover-up here.' To another victim he also apologised and visited him privately at home.[38]

One of the issues raised by the crimes of these two men is how their abuse towards children was reconciled with their apparent vocation and faith in God. Or was the role of priest merely a useful cover to access children? In the videos from the Lucy Faithfull Foundation, mentioned in Chapter 1, one of the abuser priests is asked this same question. He answers with confidence:

> The bottom line would be, this was a weakness in me – and God really understood it. But look at all the hard work, and all the good people were getting. . . . God was using me as a broken reed, really. God knows me, he understands where I am coming from. It's up to him to do everything and me to do nothing.

Renton comments on this arrogance, which is spoken with an over-layer of self-pity, that it is as if the hard work counted as mitigating circumstances.[39]

In 2013 Gordon Rideout, also from Chichester, was sentenced to ten years' imprisonment for systematically abusing sixteen vulnerable children. In 2016 he pleaded guilty to a further charge for which he received an additional nine months. In the early 1960s, as a curate, he visited a Barnardo's Children's Home and then in 1967 he moved to become chaplain at an English army base in 1967 where he was accused of abusing children but acquitted after a court martial. Following his resignation in 1973, he returned to the diocese of Chichester as a clergyman. He was later appointed as a rural dean, a senior role in which he acted as the eyes and ears of the bishop.[40] Rideout resisted any suggestion that he was a risk to children and believed that in either way all was forgiven by God and his slate was therefore wiped clean. This was confirmed by Rideout's close friendship with the then bishop, Wallace Benn, who entirely believed in Rideout's assertions that he was innocent and 'sought to intervene in due process by seeking to prevent a referral of Gordon Rideout's blemished Criminal Records Bureau (CRB) check to the DSA.

Philip Jones (archdeacon of Lewes and Hastings at the time and now retired) explained in his IICSA witness statement that Benn was a conservative evangelical, fundamentally concerned with forgiveness, who sought to apply New Testament strictures to dealing with those who 'erred'.[41]

The view of Cotton, Rideout and indeed many other clergy perpetrators, including Peter Ball, is that it is almost as though the events for which they are or were under investigation have not happened. Psychologically, they believe that forgiveness means the sin has gone. This fits with the idea of antinomianism where, under the Gospel dispensation of grace, only faith is necessary for salvation and so the person remains outside socially established morality and no longer subject to the law. In other words, true believers, because they are already chosen, can do no wrong. Such self-justification may have been bolstered by interpretations of the Bible on forgiveness but it is driven by cognitive dissonance. There has to have been a state of tension between the two psychologically and morally inconsistent parts of being both an abuser and a priest. In his theory of cognitive dissonance, Leon Festinger describes how the individual strives to make sense out of contradictory ideas to do with his or her behaviour.[42] It becomes imperative to manage these contradictions so realities can be denied: 'So powerful is the need for consonance that when people are forced to look at disconfirming evidence, they will find a way to criticize, distort or dismiss it.'[43] This leads to passing the blame onto others and seeking refuge in dubious reasoning on forgiveness, rather than taking responsibility and seeking proper help and control for dissonant actions.

The Church of England has also found it very difficult, if not impossible, to say: 'We were wrong; we made terrible mistakes.' It seems that dioceses such as Chichester are driven to make apologies only after devastating publicity. Another example of this pattern would be the apology made by the diocese of Lincoln, following pressure from a television documentary that revealed a systemic failure within the diocese to handle past allegations of 'appalling' abuse. The diocese had taken years to refer more than 50 names of clergy and staff to the police. The Bishop of Grantham, Dr Nicholas Chamberlain, responded that: 'the diocese of Lincoln wishes to acknowledge that past matters have not been handled well. The diocese is committed to learn from its mistakes. I am very sorry that it took so long for justice to be served.'[44]

Taking Responsibility Looks Like This...

None of the abusers discussed in this chapter took any responsibility for their abusive behaviour, seemingly believing that they had the right to satisfy their sexual interest in children and young people. However, this example shows how one man overcame his shame and sought help at the Portman Clinic in London.[45] His account offers insight into his feelings of despair at his condition, but also some understanding of how this developed. He writes of paedophilia as a disorder and a deeply distressing sexual orientation, which, for him, was triggered by traumatic experiences in childhood:

> I'm in my sixties now, but when I was a young boy my mother used to sit me on her lap while she dried me off after my bath, and she would fondle my genitals. Her behaviour never felt sexual but, looking back, of course it was. I can't remember exactly how long that went on but it was a long time. By the time it was over, I was self-harming.
>
> I think my attraction to young boys came from what my mother did to me.

The writer first acknowledged what he calls his 'abnormality' at the age of fifteen when he was not developing sexual interests with others of his age:

> They were taking an interest in women or, in one or two cases, in men. But I never did. I remained fixated on pre-adolescent boys, which was the age at which I had been sexually interfered with. It was horrible.
>
> I never even contemplated abusing a child. It was a million miles away from what I wanted to be – which was a normal adult man . . . but it was like my development had stalled. It was completely terrifying, and I felt revolted with myself.

At university he was eventually forced to face the fact as his interest was seen by a housemate who had noticed his discomfort around children:

> I was sitting in the front room. All my mates were cooking the evening meal and I don't think they realised I'd come

downstairs. They were chatting away and I heard my friend say something like: 'I think Jack's interested in young boys.' I put my coat on and quietly walked out of the house. . . . I went to the university GP the next day. I said, 'I'm a paedophile. Can this be cured?' The conventional view of paedophilia is that it's an incurable condition. But this doctor laughed – he laughed! And he said, 'Of course it's curable.' It was an absolutely huge relief. The doctor didn't challenge my identification with paedophilia; he just accepted it and said: 'No problem, we'll sort it.'

During the long-term treatment – this was in 1972 – he was able to explore the past trauma through talking freely and so, together with the therapist, construct a picture of what was happening in his mind:

After treatment, I was a very different person. I even developed a sexual interest in women, which felt extraordinarily liberating. But there was a lot about me that was shy, inexperienced and naïve. In a sense, I had to experience my adolescence years after all my peers. I'd had minimal sexual experience, all my friendships had been warped by my self-hatred and I had a huge lack of self-esteem. . . . I'm now in a good relationship, and have been for a long time with a woman whom I love. She has always known about my former orientation, which will always be something I carry with me. No one else knows, not even my family.

Paedophilia is not understood. . . . People think paedophilia is synonymous with child sexual abuse. But I would never have abused a child. Most paedophiles have two warring drives within them: the urge to offend, and the urge to be normal. Most paedophiles are desperate for those desires to go away.

The interesting aspect of this account is this man's awareness and moral responsibility alongside his ability to link events in his childhood with his adult interest in children. This is just one person's account and does not imply an inevitable progression; certainly, there are many who were abused in childhood and do not go on to develop a sexual orientation towards children and, conversely, people who abuse and are not able to link this back to specific traumatic events in their own past. Nonetheless, there is a suggestion that the person attracted to non-adults has suffered some sort of arrested emotional development that can be explored, accepted and integrated rather than acted out as a crime.

In the next chapter we look further at the response of the institutional church to three cases of sexual abuse.

4.
How the Church Has Responded

Any case in which the Church has failed to prove itself a safe place for children is deplorable.[1]
Archbishop Rowan Williams

When you try to speak out, and you go to the people that should be there to protect you, and they call you liars and mischief-makers, and make out that you're the one that's stirring up a load of rubbish, you have to go through the ordeal all over again.[2]
Neil Todd's sister, quoted in Church Times

In the previous chapter aspects of the behaviour of three perpetrators were highlighted: narcissism, solipsism and self-justification. When we look at the way that the institutional church has responded to allegations, it becomes clear that there has been a similar pattern of defensive and deceptive processes used as a way of combating the anxiety evoked by disclosure. This is a deception fuelled by power and control and underpinned by institutional narcissism. In this chapter several cases are used to explore this further.

Secrecy as a Defence

In the Church one defence has been to act secretly. Secrecy is not only a central dynamic between the sexual abuser and the child;

this same dynamic has permeated the way that the Church has responded over decades to disclosures, especially those involving clergy and priests and those in religious orders. Churches tend to mirror aspects of family life and relationships, so the abusive possibilities of one may be replicated in the other. It appears that secrecy, similar to that fashioned by abusers, can be seen to be revealed in the way that decisions about responding to incidents of abuse have been made and the way that the church hierarchy has operated. The secrecy and deception in the response were for many years efficiently pursued within the organisation of the Church through internal and arcane legal systems, such as canon law, or managed discreetly within the church hierarchy. Secrecy was one of the central aspects to emerge from the case of the Reverend David Smith from Clevedon in Somerset, who first came to the attention of the public in 2007; it later emerged that his paedophilic interest had been well known for a number of years, but *only* to the church hierarchy. This case is significant because, as a result of what came out at his trial in 2007, the Church of England instituted the Past Cases Review (PCR) where all old files were to be assessed for safeguarding concerns. Whilst later findings would reveal that this review was inadequate and in itself 'a cover-up', it was still an important moment of recognition that situations had always been managed with scant regard for victims and survivors.

This case emerged whilst I was working as safeguarding advisor for the diocese of Bath and Wells (2004-10) and I had first-hand experience of the secrecy. I shall use the first person in my account and include my commentary of what happened alongside the events. The first I knew of the Reverend David Smith was when the then bishop's chaplain came to my house on a Saturday in May 2005 to tell me that 'the worst has happened'. I was told that a vicar from Clevedon had been taken in for questioning and then arrested, following the disclosure of sexual abuse of a thirteen-year-old altar boy, who had spoken to a trusted female member of the congregation, who, to her credit, then took this further by informing the police. The bishop's chaplain explained to me what action had been taken and, as this was to do with clergy, seemed to assume that it would be handled centrally and that my role would be limited to support and the offer of resources. There was immediately for me a sense that the hierarchy was closing ranks by rallying around one another to minimise the damage that this might cause in the diocese. The hierarchy clearly did not include me as the safeguarding advisor, despite the fact that it was a child protection issue; I was seen as peripheral (not ordained and female and not, as it turned out, 'in the know' about what had been going on). Here was the 'closed system' in operation, for I then found out that there was a long history to this case and that Smith had been under the pastoral care of the then bishop of Taunton because of previous allegations. This pastoral care consisted of infrequent meetings which did not touch on safeguarding concerns other than in the most superficial of ways. In other words, it was already centrally known within the hierarchy that Smith was a sexual predator, but this had been handled internally as a pastoral, not a safeguarding, issue. As the safeguarding advisor, I had not been told about Smith's history and knew nothing about past allegations. Indeed, I only learnt at this point (about eighteen months into my work) that there was indeed a 'special' file which contained details of clergy who had in one way or another 'transgressed'. This file I was not permitted to see (apparently because I was outside the closed system). In fact, it was only once the PCR got well underway sometime later that I was allowed to view the file. Only the church hierarchy within the diocese, and presumably beyond, could have access to and know about this file. The dynamic of secrecy and obfuscation held sway.

Despite pressure from the bishop's chaplain, I insisted on trying to take some control of what had happened and this involved an early visit to St John the Evangelist Church in Clevedon on the Sunday following the vicar's arrest. I arranged to meet the church wardens and some members of the parochial church council (PCC). There I found out that the majority of the congregation seemed to be taking the side of the arrested vicar, and there was anger and dislike towards the altar boy who had spoken out. Indeed, there were even some suggestions that he should be asked to leave the church and there was criticism voiced about what the boy had done wrong, rather than concern about the abuser. It seemed that the idea that the 'good' vicar could be wrong or 'bad' was intolerable in the minds of those who had trusted and liked him. So, the 'bad' was split off and projected instead onto the troublesome boy who had caused the problem. This certainly showed how powerful emotions and opinions are in such situations, where often the 'victim' is rejected in favour of the established vicar. This is a good example of the victim becoming the villain and the predator villain becoming the victim, hounded by the complainants and persecuted by the safeguarding advisor. On this same occasion I met the then bishop of Ebbsfleet. He was acting as a 'flying bishop' to provide episcopal oversight for parishes, such as St John the Evangelist, that do not accept the sacramental ministry of bishops who have participated in the ordination of women. The bishop of Ebbsfleet had come to lead the service during the immediate crisis following the arrest. I spoke to him but he was determined not to listen to me and stated strongly that he believed people were innocent until proved guilty, that he was confident that Smith's innocence would become clear, and that he would be vindicated and soon back in the church. Presumably rather like the victim, I was left feeling that I was in the wrong, that my concerns were dismissed and that it would be very much 'business as usual'. I was also left with the feeling that my presence was not at all welcome. From this I understood the power of this network – bolstered by control and by connections within the church establishment. Once again, little concern was shown for the thirteen-year-old victim.

I only learnt of Smith's history of sexual predation once it came out at the trial in 2007 and luckily this was extensively reported so I could find out more.[3] It turned out that concerns about Smith had been raised with the Church of England in 1983 and again in 2001 and, on both occasions, the complainants said they had been assured that their concerns had been 'dealt with'. However, clearly, as it emerged, Smith was able to continue to abuse boys. His pattern of behaviour began when he was appointed assistant housemaster at the Douai Abbey monastic boarding school in Berkshire in 1975, where he abused three boys after inviting them to his room. It was almost a quarter of a century later that one of the people he had abused saw Smith speaking on television about the death of Smith's cousin in the 11 September 2001 attacks in America. Amazed to see that Smith was still a vicar, the survivor wrote to the church authorities. He was reassured by the then bishop of Bath and Wells, Jim Thompson, that the problem had 'effectively been dealt with'. The accounts state that no charges were brought because the victim declined to make a formal complaint. After Smith left the school, he was appointed as curate in Wotton-under-Edge, in Gloucestershire in 1981, where he formed a close relationship with another boy. In this setting Smith 'befriended' a family and was entrusted to look after their twelve-year-old boy while his parents were on holiday for a week. However, he used the opportunity to indecently assault the boy. At his trial it was reported that the boy's parents had become so concerned about Smith's relationship with their son that they contacted the police. His mother said she was left with the impression that the Church was going 'to deal with the problem'. In response to this, a diocesan spokesman said that the concerns at the time centred on Smith lending the boy money rather than sexual abuse. The charge was dropped during the trial on a legal technicality and the vicar was cleared of abusing the boy.

Here is what one might call wilful blindness or a denial of awareness towards the victims and, indeed, the perpetrator. There is no sense of concern, empathy or understanding about the damage inflicted on these boys. The Church had no interest in them, only in turning away and blocking action that might cause difficulties. The Church also demonstrated here total ignorance about abusive behaviour, about grooming by the perpetrator and the way that Smith could manipulate and 'normalise' his activities. It showed not only disregard, but an abdication of responsibility by not following its own procedures, and refusing to involve outside authorities.

Following his acquittal, after becoming vicar at St John the Evangelist, Clevedon, in 1993, Smith went on to abuse three more boys. As part of his work, he visited schools recruiting for the church choir and gained boys' trust by inviting them to the vicarage to help with homework or by taking them on trips to the seaside. Some stayed for 'sleepovers'. Victims, other than the thirteen-year-old altar boy mentioned above, were traced through church records, some giving vivid testimony in court. One described how he had joined the choir aged eight or nine and said he had become close friends with the priest. He recounted how he had once gone to the vicarage to dog-sit for the priest and had fallen asleep on the sofa. He said: 'David [Smith] had come back from a service at the church. It was quite late. . . . I woke up and sort of saw David next to the sofa. I knew something wasn't right. I knew I was being touched. I knew it was wrong and couldn't say anything.' He said he was terrified of being branded a liar if he exposed the abuse. Another described his feelings of fear: 'I was terrified. I didn't know what was going to happen. If I'd said anything, would David have got violent? But people knew I was there. I was terrified for my own life. . . . I didn't know what to do . . .' On a holiday in Malta, the alleged victim said he had woken one night to find the priest in his bed again touching him. Smith had told the boy that he loved him. Smith's defence team attacked the witnesses, one still a teenager, the others young men, by suggesting that they were fantasists and that one had only come forward after learning that his older brother had made a complaint. Smith denied all fourteen charges involving seven boys under the age of sixteen and claimed that all the offences were a 'figment of someone's imagination'.[4]

Smith's denials, lies and cover-ups mirror those of the institutional church over the 30 years that the abuse had taken place. Smith showed solipsism with no concern for the witnesses, forcing all, including the thirteen year-old to give evidence and be subjected to aggressive questioning. In this case not only was there corroborating forensic evidence, but also a sequence of similar stories, styles of grooming behaviour and ways of operating. The jury unanimously found him guilty of ten charges of indecent assault, one sexual assault of a child under thirteen and one of sexual activities with a child under sixteen. The then bishop of Bath and Wells said after the trial that he was 'shocked and horrified' by the crimes and apologised to the victims and their families. He made an unequivocal apology for the failure of the Church to follow its own guidelines on sexual abuse and declared: 'We're very sorry that these offences were committed by a man in a position of trust. We have taken all necessary steps to do all in our power to ensure there is no repetition of this situation.'[5]

After the trial, the bishop held what he referred to as a 'washing-up' meeting with his chaplain, the safeguarding administrator and me to discuss what had happened. At this meeting there was some criticism about the difficult position that the bishop had been put in by the broadcast media and the press, including questions raised about 'sleepovers' at the Clevedon vicarage; the bishop said that he never wanted to be put in that position again. My response was that I was not personally able to stop the abuse, but better safeguarding measures might help. His plea was understandable as the media attention was most obviously unwelcome to the diocese, but his request to me was also disingenuous as the church hierarchy already knew about concerns over Smith's behaviour which it had kept secret. The bishop's reaction suggested to me that the shock and horror he was experiencing was rather because he had been put in a difficult position. I had been asked to do my job but with one hand tied behind my back; I had been placed in an impossible position, in that I was excluded from knowing what was going on. Interestingly, and somewhat inevitably, despite this, it still seemed somehow to be 'my fault', firstly, for the bad publicity and, secondly, for not being able to extricate the bishop from being confronted by some uncomfortable truths – and this was from a bishop who positively supported safeguarding. Clearly the blame and shame were being deflected onto someone else. Interestingly, this is the same dynamic experienced by the victim, who often carries the responsibility of what has been done to him or her with the associated guilt and shame, including the 'borrowed' unconscious guilt discussed earlier in Chapter 2.

The case of David Smith prompted serious concern in the established Church. There had been criticism of complacency within the Church on the subject of safeguarding[6] and pressure was put on the church hierarchy to re-examine historic cases of alleged abuse and refer them to the authorities if necessary. A further high-profile conviction of a choir master, Peter Halliday, which happened around the same time as Smith's trial, added weight to the request for a review. Again, this conviction revealed that the diocesan authorities were still hiding files containing allegations of child sexual abuse against clergy and others in positions of trust, allowing them to continue working with children and young people, and affording them the opportunity for further abuse. It was commented by the judge in that case that the Church's decision to keep the allegations made against Halliday secret and so not inform the police had been 'unfortunate, but procedures were different then'.[7] A diocesan spokesman, offered the self-justification that:

> we are completely satisfied that what was done at the time was the way things happened in those days when child protection awareness was on the cusp of serious change. Church officers at every level acted in good faith in accordance with what they perceived to be in the best interests of child and family at that time, in that setting – before the law and government guidelines were as they are today.

This statement was rebutted by David Pearson, who at the time ran the Church's Child Protection Advisory Service (CCPAS, now known as Thirtyone: Eight) and who said: 'It has been stated that the law was different back then. This is, I am afraid to say, a complete red herring.'[8] The Church had a clear responsibility to take effective action to ensure that both Halliday and Smith as known risks to children were prevented from having any further contact with children or young people, but this was ignored, minimised and mishandled. To deflect the criticism, the Church of England's answer was to set up the Past Cases Review which would be 'thorough and consistent'.[9] Sadly, however, the PCR was neither thorough nor consistent, and in 2018 the report of an independent review headed by Sir Roger Singleton, former chief executive of Barnardo's, stated:

> While we found no evidence of a planned and deliberate attempt to conceal information, there were shortcomings in the Church's public statement, which failed to reflect the true extent of the concerns which needed to be addressed. Victims and survivors were not involved, and there were gaps in relevant files and records. The Church has improved its practices in the past ten years and I hope that the lessons learnt will mean that it can move onto important preventative work in the area of safeguarding, which is vital for all institutions.[10]

A second PCR (known as PCR2) was announced in the summer of 2019.[11] Anxiety-provoking institutional dilemmas give rise to defensive projective processes[12] and in these manoeuvres around past cases reviews we can see the tension between wanting and not wanting to know, and between open transparent processes and discreet, more deceptive ways of managing. The difficulty in not resolving the tension results in a 'fudge', which, for the first Past Cases Review, was the worst of both possible options. The difficulty in finding out the truth is that it might expose shadow aspects of the institution and uncover deeper malaise (which I discuss in the second half of this book). One way of managing and avoiding this discovery is repeatedly to reframe the presenting problem by commissioning the reports, inquiries and reviews.

Deceptive Practices – Avoidance, Proceduralism and Obfuscation

In February 2020, Meirion Griffiths, an 81-year-old former Church of England priest, extradited from Australia, was given an eight-year sentence for sexual offences against a girl and a woman in Sussex during the 1970s and 1980s. The two victims had independently approached the police in 2014, but it took time to bring Griffiths to trial as he claimed ill health and employed various delaying tactics. During his trial he denied all charges and said: 'I went around trying to heal people.' He admitted being sexually attracted to members of his congregation, but insisted he had done nothing wrong, saying that, as a professional, he had curbed his instincts. One of his victims was Julia Macfarlane, now a law professor, who campaigned for many years for the Church to be held to account for what had happened to her as a teenager. This was a campaign that began before the court case and continued as she sought compensation. It is this campaign that further illustrates so well the deceptive tactics employed by the Church through the Church's insurers.[13]

Macfarlane told her story in an article in *Church Times*, 11 December 2015. She explained that as a teenager she was a member of her church youth group and an enthusiastic evangelical.[14] In 1975, aged sixteen, she worried that her enthusiasm was waning and her faith fading, so she asked the rector of her church in the Chichester diocese for advice. She writes:

> He told me that God wanted me to kneel and perform oral sex on him. This was the start of more than twelve months of constant sexual abuse by the priest. He continued to make me perform fellatio on him, and masturbated on me, in multiple locations. He waited for me in dark alleyways as I walked home from the restaurant where I worked as a dishwasher in the evenings. I told no one. I thought that no one would believe me. But more than this, I had no idea how I could tell anyone what was happening to me, what I could possibly say. I had zero sexual experience. I knew only that it felt dirty, disgusting, surreal, and terrifying.

The added confusion was linked to the powerful spiritually abusive nature of the abuse:

> The priest . . . my spiritual mentor, a man of God whom everyone else in my church treated as authoritative on spiritual matters – told me that God wanted me to do this . . . I thought he was a man of God, so he was able to do that to me over and over again.

Finally, leaving to go to University, Macfarlane tried to forget, but a decade later she confided in someone about what had happened. She continued to worry about whether the priest was repeating his behaviour with other victims:

> I knew that in order to come forward with any type of complaint, I would have to write a detailed statement about what took place in 1975-76. The problem was not that I couldn't remember the details of what had taken place – the problem was that I could. And remembering was very painful.

In 1999 Macfarlane went to the church authorities, Griffiths was then working in Australia, but immediately resigned once he knew that a full hearing was to be held within the Church. Macfarlane continues: 'The Archbishop of the province wrote to me, and explained that his [Griffiths'] file would be marked "Not for employment", to prevent his working in ministry in the future.' Macfarlane initially felt relieved as she assumed that he would no longer work as clergy, though she wished she had acted sooner. She later discovered that in fact Griffiths had continued to minister for a different, non-Anglican church.

In 2013 she brought a civil suit against the diocese seeking compensation for the impact on her life and as a way of holding the Church to account. Macfarlane writes about, what she describes as, 'the litigation games that are being played in the name of the Church, which further traumatise survivors like me – even as the Church claims publicly to be sorry for these crimes. This is a breathtaking hypocrisy.' Whilst the diocese was not refuting the facts, her case was clear, fully documented and corroborated, the litigation process involving the insurers revealed a dramatic undermining and contradiction of the public statements made by the Church. Assured in a letter of December 2014, from the Archbishop of Canterbury's solicitors, that 'the whole Church' was concerned and apologised for what had happened, Macfarlane wryly comments that this did not appear to include the litigators retained by the insurers for the diocese who were acting to defend sex abuse claims.

She identifies the three strategies used by those acting for the insurers. The first litigation strategy perpetuated 'discredited and offensive myths about sexual assault', insinuating in 2015 that, whilst there might have been inappropriate touching, this might not have been unwelcome. As Macfarlane writes, 'there is not a shred of evidence for this disgusting assertion', which she also sees as an all-too-familiar rape myth, often used against a complainant: 'I was a child, being played with by a powerful adult. Moreover, "touching" is not how most people would describe forced fellatio.' The statement of defence from the litigation team then proceeded to deny that the inappropriate touching would have caused harm. Macfarlane sees this as a continuation of the rape myth, where long-term harm is minimised or dismissed: 'These are the very same myths that made it possible for the actions of this priest to remain hidden for so many years.'

The second strategy she notes is for 'the Church and its insurer's representatives to hide behind archaic legal defences', arguing that her claim was barred by the statute of limitations and that, as a law student, Macfarlane should have got on with suing the Church at an earlier stage, even although she had not at this point told anyone about the abuse. She rightly sees this as a barrier to survivor claims, but points out that:

> Lawyers in England and Wales, including my own solicitor, have drawn on evidence assembled by psychologists, trauma specialists, and other professionals, and successfully argued against this technicality in historic sexual-abuse cases, where the details are not in doubt but it has taken many years for the complainant to find the courage and will to come forward.

Thirdly, 'the Church claims that it cannot control how legal claims brought against it are handled'. Macfarlane quotes the Archbishop of Canterbury's solicitors in 2014 who said: 'You will be very aware of the constraints under which we in the profession have to work in dealing with these miserable matters. The scope for personal and sensitive engagement is very limited.' Again, she points out, a disconnection between the Church's public face and the actions of the litigators acting for the Church's insurers:

> The problem is that the Church appears to have signed away all responsibility for relations with survivors when it agreed to the terms of its insurance policy. The pretence that things are otherwise is perhaps the most shockingly

hypocritical aspect of the Church's strategy towards abuse victims. By permitting the lawyers, instructed by their insurers, to play games on their behalf, the Church is complicit in both their behaviour and its impact.

The Church reveals here a split within itself, whereby the litigators and insurers become the villain whilst the Church officials present a good and sympathetic persona or front, and so become almost a victim of the insurers. Yet, of course, the Church is 'morally responsible for the aggressive and technical contestation of legal liability put forward by its insurers through the tactics of the insurer's lawyers', who importantly act on the *wishes* of their client. Macfarlane comments:

> While it is, of course, important to ensure that claims brought against the Church are legitimate, this neither requires nor justifies church complicity in an aggressively adversarial process that they must recognise both re-traumatises survivors like myself, and discourages others from coming forward. Neither can the Church credibly hide behind its insurers and their lawyers. Its publicly expressed goal of atonement is incompatible with the goal of limiting financial responsibility using any tactic, however low, and regardless of the impact on complainants.

Pressured not to publish her concerns about this process, Macfarlane aimed to show the split between the public face of the Church and its complicity in 'this immoral approach to sex-abuse litigation'. In fact, her article in *Church Times* galvanised the Church insurers to settle the claim in 2016, although at great personal cost. She commented recently to the Portsmouth newspaper, *The News* (15 January 2020), 'I look like a strong person but this took me decades to do this.' The imprisonment of Griffiths and the rejection of his appeal confirmed both his guilt and the obfuscation of the Church in bringing him to justice and the claim to be resolved.[15]

Josephine Stein calls the legal confrontational approach that Macfarlane encountered a barrier of hostility and defensiveness, originally erected in part by the Church's insurers and legal advisers, which prevents survivors of past abuse getting help and support and discourages a pastoral approach. (The relationship between the institutional church and its insurers is explored further in a later chapter.) Macfarlane did not get compassion or understanding, rather, once again, the victim and the one needing help becomes the villain. Stein traces this process noting that, 'The Church used avoidance behaviour, proceduralism and various barriers and obstacles to frustrate attempts by survivors to be heard.' The result from a financial perspective was successful, but the approach by the Church has meant that many would-be complainants have simply given up at an early stage. Some disappeared and the Church has been able to wash its hands of them, legally and pastorally. With this disappearance, potential financial burdens for the Church have also decreased. 'Those survivors who persist in seeking to have the matter investigated . . . may encounter ever more officious, manipulative and threatening behaviour.' This means that it is a brutal business to try and achieve compensation let alone justice. This struggle has been generally acknowledged as re-abusing but Stein says that a more accurate term would be 'institutional grooming and abuse'. Once again, the dynamics of the original trauma of abuse are repeated at a time when, following disclosure, support and compassion is needed.[16]

Clearly, the very dynamics of deception that characterise and are embodied by the behaviour of the perpetrator are not dissimilar to these underlying dynamics. These are personal and institutional dynamics that involve denial, projection, suppression, repression and oppression – even if of the most subtle natures. In both the individual abuser and in the institutional church the psychodynamics present involve an abuse of power and an abuse of trust. In both there are the isolation of some and the elevation of others. In both there are issues of control. In this third example all these dynamics are present in the way that the Church has responded. Matthew Ineson has also, like Julia Macfarlane, waived his anonymity in an attempt to get justice.

Collusion in High Places – 'Bishop Investigates Bishop'

Matthew Ineson was sixteen years old in 1984 when he was raped by a Church of England vicar, the Reverend Trevor Devamanikkam, who had taken the boy in when the boy's home life collapsed. After the abuse happened various interventions meant that Ineson was initially left homeless. He made a suicide attempt and then was rehoused and found a job in hospitality to support himself. Ineson became ordained in 2000 and tried to put the abuse behind him. However, in 2012 various events made it hard to suppress and so, between 2012 and 2013, he spoke out about the abuse to various church officials (he made eight disclosures in total) and also to the police. On the basis of the evidence, Devamanikkam was charged with three counts of rape and three counts of indecent assault of a child. He committed suicide on the day before his trial in 2017. At his hearing before IICSA in July 2019, Ineson testified that he had disclosed his abuse to Archbishop John Sentamu and then to Bishop Steven Croft, Bishop Peter Burrows, Bishop Martyn Snow and Bishop Glyn Webster. However, none of them took appropriate action about the disclosure. As Ineson states, 'the re-abuse I have suffered as a result of the negligence of some of these bishops since my disclosures can only be described as wicked'. Ineson later wrote to Bishop Stephen Croft, quoted at the IICSA hearing, 'You will never know what it took to tell you, but you will also never know the hurt you and your suffragan have caused me by doing absolutely nothing about it.'[17] Ineson explains that the 'only person who did respond was the Archbishop of York, who wrote back and said, "Thank you for copying me into the letter, which I have read. Please be assured of my prayers and best wishes during this testing time", and he did nothing'. At the IICSA hearing John Sentamu, then the Archbishop of York, admitted that the Church's treatment of Ineson had been 'shabby and shambolic' but denied he had made personal mistakes in the case. Ineson wrote to Justin Welby, the Archbishop of Canterbury, for the thirteenth time, in 2017, saying:

> The Church of England has made me fight at every step to try to achieve both justice and the further prevention of abuse by my abuser. By doing this, you have added to my abuse. The bishops have actively colluded together to attempt to ignore, discredit and get rid of me.[18]

Unsurprisingly, Ineson lost trust in the church.

Following inaction by the senior bishops and before the planned trial Ineson made a number of complaints under the Clergy Discipline Measure against the senior bishops to whom he had disclosed and who had taken no action. These were dismissed by the Church for being filed outside a time limit of one year. Astonishingly, those against whom Ineson made a complaint were consulted to see if they upheld the objection to the time limit to bring a complaint. Inevitably, they would object. Even more astonishingly, the Church also wrote to the Reverend Trevor Devamanikkam asking his opinion of the one-year rule and whether he thought he should be investigated, he did not reply. Ineson commented: 'They consulted my rapist about asking him whether he thought he should be investigated or not. And that hurt. That really hurt.'[19] According to the IICSA transcripts, the police, who were also involved, contacted the legal office at Church House; Ineson reported at the inquiry, that the police 'said, basically, "Who in their right minds thinks it's acceptable to write to a priest who is under investigation by the police for historic child sexual abuse and give him the opportunity to object to being investigated?", and the reply was, "That is church procedure."' The one-year rule was in fact amended after this. Not only did it appear that the Church brought up such procedures to prevent justice, but it also seemed reluctant to pursue complaints involving untruths and seemed endlessly to rely on the defence that church officials could not remember or did not recall what had or had not happened.

One incident worth highlighting here was an admission by the then bishop of Doncaster, who in November 2017 was heard by a number of people in a café discussing and laughing about Ineson's abuse. This became a CDM complaint under a breach of the Data Protection Act but the Archbishop of Canterbury decided to take no further action. In his admission, Peter Burrows, the then bishop of Doncaster, blamed everybody but himself. As Ineson reports:

> He actually blamed me and said that he'd – his words were, 'I had made a momentary lapse of judgement', and it was because I'd waived my anonymity, it had been in the papers and on the television and that had put him under stress. So it was all my fault.[20]

The IICSA transcripts reveal a number of conflicts of interests. For example, not only the procedure of, in this case, 'bishops investigating bishops', but also in the situation where the registrar to the Archbishop of Canterbury turned out also to be the registrar to one of the bishops complained against.[21] When another person took over, the same registrar was still involved in offering consultations to his replacement. It was later found that the original registrar was also an ordained priest and his training incumbent had been the perpetrator of the abuse against Ineson. A further flaw was uncovered within a core group set up by the National Safeguarding Team when Ineson exposed the conflict of interest in a number of the members of that group. Ineson stated: 'You can't investigate yourself. There's too much bias there. There's too much conflict of interest.'[22] He added:

> It's the re-abuse by the bishops and the archbishops themselves, and I think, if any shame wants applying, it needs to be applied to the Archbishop of Canterbury and the Archbishop of York and the House of Bishops, and not all the bishops, but the vast majority of them. . . . I think they are cruel . . . it's the old story: abuse is about power. . . . That abuse of power is used again, and again, and again. . . . And why? Because bishops sit on thrones. They live in fine houses and palaces, they wear the finest robes and garments, which cost the earth. . . . They bully people. . . . Who would give that up? They don't want to, and that's why they're protecting themselves.[23]

In November 2019 the Church of England announced a review over its handling of its response to the allegations relating to Devamanikkam. Ineson, reported in *The Guardian*, commented, 'I don't believe the Church should be appointing anyone to investigate it – it should be truly independent, which it isn't. The Church, the ones who are being investigated, are trying to control the whole thing.'[24] The way the Church responded to this situation reveals the power and control dynamics that characterise the mind of the perpetrator discussed in the previous chapter. The narcissism of the abuser is reflected in institutional narcissism; the individual solipsism of the abuser is replicated in episcopal solipsism; and overall there is a fall-back position of self-justification. In each of the situations discussed the institutional narcissism displayed meant that the Church became dominated by its own internal self-preoccupations, which meant there was an absence of love for others – especially those threatening the Church's image of itself. Another characteristic of both solipsism and narcissism is that of an arrogant response when asked to engage with issues outside the immediate preoccupation. From this it is easy to see how institutional secrecy and the dynamics of deception for the purpose of power and control became a way of reacting to unwanted interruptions about clergy abuse.

In the next chapter we explore how the superficial adoption of safeguarding guidelines and training programmes and the appearance that the problem is being tackled have failed to make inroads into this deeply embedded hierarchical and patriarchal structure of power and control.

5.
Surface Awareness – Policies, Guidelines and Training

> The Church has learned to tolerate and accept dangerous safeguarding practices, believing that all that is needed is the creation of a safeguarding policy framework and a raft of new posts which carry the label 'safeguarding', and that these will be sufficient to keep the wolf pack away from the door of the Church. They will not achieve that objective.[1]
> *Ian Elliott*

The safeguarding policy and the associated training that are run by all dioceses in the Church of England provide a framework of guidance and procedures for how those in the Church are to respond when an allegation is made or when they become aware of something that raises suspicion.[2] The Church of England statement of safeguarding has six principles:

1. Promote a safer environment and culture.
2. Safely recruit and support all those with any responsibility related to children and vulnerable adults within the Church.
3. Respond promptly to every safeguarding concern or allegation.

4. Care pastorally for victims/survivors of abuse and other affected persons.
5. Care pastorally for those who are the subject of concerns or allegations of abuse and other affected persons.
6. Respond to those that may pose a present risk to others.

The national and diocesan safeguarding manuals based on these principles are aimed at everyone involved in the Church, and especially those in leadership positions, those dealing with safeguarding or in children's activities, or with vulnerable adults. The policy handbooks and the training courses cover what is abuse and how to recognise it, what to do and what not to do if you have suspicions or someone discloses, what to say and what not to say when this happens, and whom to inform. There are lists of 'dos and don'ts', clear guidelines and sound explanations. The training days and online courses that also cover the same guidance give an opportunity for people to share concerns and practise appropriate responses and, from my own experience of both being trained and working as a safeguarding advisor running these courses, those who attend in the parishes are almost all eager and anxious to learn.

In 2015 Ian Elliott, an independent safeguarding consultant, was commissioned to undertake a critical case review for the Church of England. Prior to this he had little knowledge of or contact with the Church and in his witness statement to IICSA in July 2019 he explained that his way of briefing himself in the role was to read the policies of the Church: 'I was very impressed by the document . . . and I felt, this is good, this is great, we have an enlightened approach, that's excellent.'[3] However, two years later he had learned that, despite the surface veneer of acceptance of good safeguarding practice, 'when it comes to holding people accountable for bad practice, nothing much has been done'.[4]

In this chapter we look more closely at the reasons for the apparent discrepancy between the comprehensive policies and training on offer and the reality of how allegations are handled within the hierarchy. It is suggested that policies and guidelines are approached with different levels of emotional awareness and, in some cases, this includes ambivalence and, at times, resistance. This attitude leads directly to difficulties with taking responsibility and then owning accountability for the decisions that have been made, or, as will be demonstrated on many occasions, not made.

Elliott described it as being almost as if the policy was in one place and the practice in another, leaving the subject somewhere in the middle. The discrepancy appears to be located not amongst the laity and those handling situations at the local level, who are aware and know what to do, but located firmly within the upper levels of the hierarchy who are then involved in further decision making.

My time in the diocese of Bath and Wells can provide two examples of these different levels of awareness, ambivalence and resistance. The first took place at a training course given to the then bishop's staff group, which included two bishops, three archdeacons, the diocesan secretary, the deputy diocesan secretary and the bishop's chaplain. The training course was scheduled to last a couple of hours and included some film extracts of the after-effects of sexual abuse on survivors. One clip featured a middle-aged woman who was still dealing with the trauma of a serious sexual assault by her vicar when she was a girl. This was a powerful witness statement so I was taken aback to note some of the senior clergy laughing and talking about it both during and afterwards. When I asked why, they said that they could not take it seriously: 'can't understand why she doesn't pull herself together' was one comment; 'she had such a boring voice and went on and on' was another. It seemed that there was a disconnection, a dismissal of this woman, perhaps even embarrassment about her raw emotion, but no embarrassment about their own response, which revealed as much about the emotional illiteracy of these men and their own repressed emotions. Worryingly, it also showed their inability to hear and value the survivor's actual experience and thus, probably, their inability to make the correct decisions when dealing with a disclosure. It was necessary for the senior clergy to be seen attending the training session, but they clearly had very mixed feelings about so doing, in part, perhaps, wanting to dismiss such training as irrelevant to their position in the hierarchy and, I also now think, to them personally.

This response is in contrast with my second example which took place at a training course in a small rural parish, where I showed the same film extracts. Afterwards I was approached by two older women who wanted to disclose their own abusive experiences as children. I listened to their stories and heard the relief that they experienced in being able to share and be heard, and see that the subject was now recognised and being discussed. They had empathy with other survivors and an emotional awareness of the need to follow guidelines. As will be discussed in a later chapter, it is not that the senior clerics are not aware of the trauma of child sexual abuse, indeed they may have experienced aspects of it themselves especially if sent away to boarding school, but their denial of awareness is part of an emotional defence, a resistance that seems to go with the power structures of the institutional church. There was clearly reluctance for these church leaders to acknowledge their own vulnerabilities and past experiences; it was so much easier for the senior clergy on that training course to project their own weakness and damage onto the survivor and then ridicule both.

'They're Guidelines, and so They Have to Be Interpreted' – Issues of Accountability and the Example of Bishop Dr Peter Forster

If you are part of a power elite, then your vulnerabilities have to be disowned; it is also essential that you maintain control of the decision making, that you do not appear to be told how to respond by others – especially those that at one level are deemed inferior. This may mean that you consciously choose to exercise this right by seeing things differently from others, even from the 'experts' whom you may see as 'below' you in terms of the hierarchy. Elliott, in his report and the discussion of it at IICSA,[5] locates bad practice in the church hierarchy in its reaction to dangerous safeguarding policies which appear to be firmly woven into its very fabric. The hierarchy maintains a deliberate blindness to what most other reasonable people in society can appreciate, namely, that the Church does not hold clerical offenders or those who cover for them to account. Elliott was asked why he thought this was happening – did those in positions of power and control not know about the policies or had they forgotten them? His reply was that this group, of mostly powerful men, seemed to see that any implementation of policy was up to them; as if they were somehow outside or above the agreed guidelines that everyone else was expected to follow:

> *Elliott:* Deference exists at many different levels, but nobody should be contributing to safeguarding decisions unless they have the experience and knowledge that is required in order to make informed decisions.

> *Questioner:* Is it your view, from your experience, that senior clergy may, in practice, be the ultimate decision makers?
>
> *Elliott:* Yes. That would be very much my experience, and also that the decisions that they would take would not be informed by dialogue with other people; that they would tend to retain the information, consider the information themselves, and make a decision which they considered to be the right or appropriate decision, taking into consideration matters which were totally inappropriate.[6]

In July 2019 there was an interesting example at the IICSA hearings of the episcopal attitude in these matters. This involved the questioning at the inquiry of Bishop Dr Peter Forster, then bishop of Chester. He was asked about three situations: his mishandling of the case of Victor Whitsey, the previous bishop of Chester, discussed in Chapter 2; his 'misjudgement' in not following the guidelines in the case of the Reverend Gordon Dickenson; and his interpretation of the guidelines in the case of the Reverend Ian Hughes. In the examination of the third case, Forster was questioned about the Church's guidelines under the CDM where a cleric who is imprisoned for a child sexual offence is prohibited for life from further ministry and about his interpretation of the guidelines.[7] The examination by Ms McNeill (Questioner) followed Forster's reason for departing from the guidelines which in summary was that he, Forster, felt that he knew best. This extract illustrates well this attitude of 'being above the law':

> *Questioner:* But in the case of the Reverend Ian Hughes, you wanted to depart from those guidelines; is that right?
>
> *Forster:* I wanted to discuss with the President of Tribunals the possibility of departing in a small degree. [Forster wanted a 20-year rather than a lifetime ban.] They're guidelines, and so they have to be interpreted, and I felt that in his [Hughes'] case, given his relative youth, the fact that he was entirely penitent from

the outset as to what had happened, and his previous record of ministry was excellent, that it was worth raising with the President of Tribunals....

Questioner: How can we know that that penitence is really genuine? It's somebody who has just been convicted of a sexual offence and imprisoned. It is pretty likely that, at that time, they're sorry that they're in prison, but how can you make any real assessment as to whether this is genuine penitence?

Forster: The penitence arose at the moment of his arrest, before he was, you know, put in prison or anything....

Questioner: You say that he had an exemplary record in ministry to date. I would ask you to question, really, what the relevance of that is. Because, almost universally within the cases we have seen in this inquiry of clerics who have been convicted of a child sexual offence, they had an exemplary record in ministry until they were convicted of something. So, really, what's the relevance in that in deciding what the appropriate penalty is following that conviction?

Forster: Well, I mean, I take that point. It is a game changer if somebody is arrested – and he admitted his guilt, and so forth. Twenty years living out penitently.... It simply kept open a possibility which otherwise would have been ruled out altogether by the lifetime ban....

Questioner: But my question was, and I'm not sure it's really been answered, is, is it really relevant, when you're making these decisions, to say, 'Well, somebody has been a really good priest or cleric to date, they have an exemplary record, they are really liked within the parish.' Once they have been convicted of a child sexual offence, is that really relevant?

Forster: Well, it's part of the background picture. One makes a judgement against all sorts of things in the background. There's also – again, I don't

	want to make too much of this, but his own self-confessed sexual orientation probably – I think he was somebody who had been wrestling a great deal with that, and maybe that . . . you have to form an overall judgement. . . .
Questioner:	Do you think the fact that you were relying on your knowledge of him and your experience of his ministry demonstrates exactly that difficulty I flagged up at the beginning, which is the conflict for diocesan bishop to be judge, jury and sentencer, in disciplinary terms, of a cleric whom they might know?
Forster:	The decision to approach Sir Andrew about the possibility of a 20-year ban was discussed with my sixteen colleagues, and not just a decision taken by me.
Questioner:	Yes.
Forster:	That would bring different perspectives, but I don't believe it compromised my fundamental juridical responsibility, which is what I had to consider. I mean, this was a synoptic decision which left open a possibility, it did no more than that. . . .
	(The inquiry looks again at the guidelines.)
Questioner:	Essentially, the guidance is saying, is it not, that the child pornography offences should not be considered any less serious than child sexual abuse of itself, because the individual must be considered complicit within the original offending?
Forster:	I accept that that's how things are viewed, and this is 'guidance' and 'normally'. 'Guidance' and 'normally' are words which leave open the possibility of looking at the particular circumstances. . . . I suppose I would also, in my own mind, regard the fact that pornography is so ubiquitously available and viewed . . . could it be the case that some people would be easily misled into viewing child pornography, who themselves would not dream of abusing a child? . . .

Questioner: First of all, you said that pornography is, of itself, ubiquitous at the moment, but there must be, mustn't there, a very clear distinction between pornography and child pornography, indecent images of children?

Forster: In my mind, completely, absolutely, yes. But I think in the case of people who do get drawn into this sick desire to download, maybe the two are not. . . . I have heard that in direct testimony from people, you know, working late at night on their computer, and whatever. . . .

Questioner: [quoting from a news report on the details of Ian Hughes conviction] What it says is: 'An Anglican vicar was caught with more than 8,000 images of child sexual abuse, including 800 of the worst kind. He admitted 17 offences.' That would sound like, wouldn't it, very different to somebody who is, as you have said, working late at night and has been inadvertently, or sort of, drawn into downloading these images. It was 8,000 of the most serious kind. What I'm trying to explore is why, knowing that, you chose to write . . . to the President of the Tribunals?

Forster: Because of the overall circumstances of Mr Hughes, who [sic] I knew well. I think he had got drawn into a very sick and unsatisfactory situation. The question was whether . . . penitently coming to terms with what had happened, whether at least the door could be left open.[8]

Here is a bishop in the unusual position of having his authority questioned, in public, outside the diocesan culture of deference and, significantly, by a woman, a young woman. It is then not surprising that both in his words and by his body movements (revealed in the available video of the proceedings), he demonstrates his discomfort and his underlying anxiety. His main defence is to rationalise and then justify his action of seeking the advice of another member of the establishment, the senior judicial figure, Sir Andrew McFarlane, then Chairman of the Church of England Clergy Discipline Commission and President of Clergy Discipline Tribunals. There is in this an implicit and perhaps even unconscious pulling of rank over the junior barrister Nikita McNeill, who cuts through this to the heart of the matter, which is Forster's belief that his own personal judgement of the perpetrator is the default position rather than the guidelines. This backed up the report produced by the Social Care Institute of Excellence (SCIE) that stated: 'The Bishop of Chester does not delegate any of his safeguarding responsibilities and takes all decisions about if and when the threshold for referral to statutory agencies takes place.'[9]

This illustrates the difficulty of the episcopal hierarchy interpreting and controlling what referrals and advice are taken on safeguarding cases. Interestingly, until 2016 awareness and understanding of safeguarding had not played much or any part in ordination training, those training to be clerics or for those in lay ministry or training to be readers; after 2016 it became compulsory. This means that those who currently hold the role of bishop would not have been subject to thinking seriously about safeguarding during their early ministry. This then raises the inevitable and logical question as to why the decision of whether or not to refer a safeguarding matter to a statutory body is not left with a trained and experienced safeguarding professional rather than with a cleric.

Discussion of the SCIE report at the IICSA hearings brought up the issue of the division between line management and professional supervision: for example, where the professional experience of the safeguarding advisor, supported by a supervisor from outside the diocesan structure, may differ with the stance of the diocesan line manager – even though that line manager is untrained and unqualified to make such professional safeguarding decisions. This report also highlighted concerns about the ultimate responsibility for safeguarding lying with a diocesan bishop, who is not a safeguarding professional. Furthermore, it raised concerns that the current guidance must clearly differentiate between what is obligatory and what is good practice, and that the professionals need to be able to make decisions, as opposed to recommendations. Bishop Alan Wilson, questioned how somebody who is a mid-range employee of the bishop can hold the bishop to account, commented:

It simply doesn't work that way. There is no way that that would ever happen adequately and structurally. It's quite odd to expect that to work. I mean, the point was made earlier . . . that advice is given, but advice is just advice. That's what it is. But bishops have a responsibility for how they handle that advice and how they respond to it. Now, if they respond badly, who is to hold them accountable for having responded badly? And the answer is, probably not one of their mid-range employees.[10]

A Culture of 'Casual and Systemic Inertia'

As Ian Elliott summarises in his report, the central concern is the reluctance to hold people accountable for bad practice: 'Those who have committed abuse or failed to report it, have not been challenged, even when they have brought the Church into disrepute and, in some cases, are thought to have committed crimes.'[11] The church hierarchy cannot be held to account because there are no guardians of their responses. This is not necessarily to do with individual bishops but is linked to the culture of deference to the episcopate. In the following chapters, the power dynamics embedded in the institutional church will be further explored. In this chapter, however, the following example of bad practice suggests that for a whole number and range of senior clerics the issue of their responsibility for safeguarding, whether through adherence to policies and good practice, or pastoral care and concern appear as if irrelevant to them.

Dangerous safeguarding practices and the failure of the hierarchy to respond appropriately is well illustrated by the case that Ian Elliott was asked to review in 2016. 'Joe' – not his real name – was seriously abused by the Reverend Garth Moore at the age of fifteen. Garth Moore was the chancellor of the dioceses of Southwark, Durham and Gloucester, and the vicar of St Mary's Abchurch in the City of London. He was also an expert in canon law. He was a friend of Joe's family and the boy was asked to serve in St Mary's Abchurch and, with his family's blessing and encouragement, was invited to stay overnight occasionally in Moore's flat in Gray's Inn. He describes Moore as his 'spiritual mentor, very solicitous. He treated me as special.'[12]

We can get a good sense of Moore, remembered as a highly esteemed church lawyer and very much part of the church establishment, and, indeed, his own sense of being 'above' ordinary life, by this postscript to his obituary written in 1990 in the Ecclesiastical Law Journal.[13] It includes this vignette:

> Garth was – well, Garth was Garth. He called me over at the first E.L.S. conference to tell me, 'Rupert, the clergy don't wear brown shoes.' He was wearing a white tie ('entirely acceptable instead of a dog collar'). Garth was like that, but he never expected people to give in to his foibles. He once boasted – and I am still inclined to believe it – that he was the only person in England unaffected by advertising. He had a great gift for friendship and, once a protégé (and there were many), he never forgot to give you a helping hand or a word of encouragement. His passion was the Church and its canon law.

Unfortunately, Joe was one of Moore's protégés and with later understanding could see that Moore had groomed him. Moore's sinister interest culminated in a violent and sadistic serious sexual assault. The boy considered reporting the attack: 'But I knew no one would believe me. Moore was a very senior figure in the establishment. My feeling was that I would get into trouble. Something bad had happened, and it would be worse if I told anyone.' It was a couple of years before Joe was able to speak about the episode, and then he told mostly Church of England priests but none took any action.[14] One of the earliest was Michael Fisher, the highly regarded leader of the Society of St Francis and later the suffragan bishop of St Germans in Cornwall. Fisher, who was then in his 60s, was acquainted with Moore and was a close associate of Peter Ball. According to Joe, then aged eighteen, Fisher 'drew the full story out of me in confession. Immediately afterwards, he led me into an intensely romantic friendship with him' – kissing and caressing but no penetrative sex – which lasted eighteen months. At no point did Fisher record or act on Joe's disclosure of the earlier abuse. 'This was not the right response to a young man who was seeking help,' says Joe. It 'added another layer to the complexity of abuse. At the time, it didn't occur to me that this charismatic figure [Fisher] was abusing me spiritually and emotionally.'

Over the years, among the senior figures whom Joe told about the abuse were three bishops and a senior clergyman who was later appointed a bishop. What has emerged is that not a single senior church figure admitted any recollection of the disclosure, and certainly none took any action. Joe says: 'There was casual and systemic inertia all the way through. These were not bad people themselves – they were people working in a profoundly dysfunctional structure.' In 2014, finally, with the support of a local parish priest, the assault was formally reported to the police and the Church of England safeguarding team. Two years later following investigation, and what has been called unseemly 'horse-trading' between Joe's solicitor and the Church's insurers, the Church of England publicly apologised and paid £35,000 in compensation. While the insurance claim was underway, the Church dropped its pastoral care of Joe, which halted vital professional therapeutic help. The Church afterwards did launch an independent review into its handling of the case.[15]

The Elliott report[16] on the hopeless handling of this case was published in March 2016. Elliott notes 'a tragic catalogue of exploitation and harm' leading to serious mental health issues and a loss of faith for Joe. What Elliott found was that practice did not comply with the policy documents: 'It falls short of it in that it did not place the pastoral needs of the survivor in a position of priority. Financial interests were allowed to impact practice.' It rightly seemed extraordinary to him that those to whom Joe had disclosed details of the abuse later claimed not to remember. The basic guidance in all the safeguarding handbooks and manuals is to write down and make a record of a disclosure; apparently this did not happen. Some expressed concern but not sufficient enough to do anything about it:

> Practice of this nature is simply not acceptable and must be addressed. All who find themselves to be in this position must know what to do and must have some understanding of how they should respond. To have no records and to rely entirely on memory is simply not good enough.

Elliott advised that safeguarding practice be monitored by an outside body, from outside the diocese but within the church and with the power to intervene and seek change if needed – in other words, a body that can move from an advisory capacity to a decision-making one. Elliott points out that in the case he reviewed it was alleged that:

Two of the abusers were senior members of the hierarchy which would suggest that they would be unlikely to make sound safeguarding decisions. Similarly, if a bishop is unable to recall a disclosure of a serious sexual assault occurring, this would cause the reviewer to doubt their ability to respond appropriately to identified risk in their diocese. These are not trivial issues. Behind every disclosure that is received lies human pain and suffering that can be so intense as to be life threatening. It deserves everyone's close attention.

Whilst recognising the Church is to be commended for creating the policies that it has, this is not enough. What matters is that the policies are followed and complied with. What matters are the actions that are taken to implement those policies and deliver high quality safeguarding services to those who require them. The recommendations in the report emphasised appropriate training and recording of disclosures:

> Those in positions of seniority in the church are more likely to be approached by a survivor of abuse to report what has happened to them. It is particularly important that these people have a comprehensive understanding of the policies of the church, and also have an ability to implement those policies.

The input of the experiences of survivors has to be crucial for real change and this will affect compliance with the stated policies. Elliott also recommended that the Church does not give priority to financial considerations while dealing with claims, so that pastoral help is not compromised and an adversarial approach is avoided. When speaking to his report at the IICSA hearings, Elliott agreed that the summary might be:

> *Questioner:* So if you are going to have a policy, follow it. If that policy isn't practical, please say so, essentially?
> *Elliott:* Exactly. That's the critical point.
> *Questioner:* [quoting Elliott's report] 'If it has committed itself [which it has] to the provision of

	"informed pastoral care and support to anyone who has suffered abuse". It has to find a way of delivering this. . . .'
Elliott:	Correct. There is no other option, as far as I'm concerned: it either dispenses with the policy or it abides by the policy.[17]

What is very clear is that the culture of irresponsibility means that, despite having the policies and training in place, implementation of the policy in practice can be affected by other factors which include deference to the hierarchy. Bishop Alan Wilson,[18] who has expressed concern about inconsistency between bishops, has been critical of the level of record keeping about disclosures and the sharing of the central list (previously called the Lambeth List, and now called the Archbishops' List) of those clergy who should not be employed because they are thought to be a danger. This information may not always be up to date and there may be issues about confidentiality linked to it. It is worth noting that Peter Ball was not on the Lambeth List, so there seems an element of choice about whom and what may be included.[19] This is part of what Bishop Alan Wilson refers to as operational difficulty in which bishops are placed in the extraordinary role, 'where they are both expected to be judges, which they have no particular training or yen for being or experience of doing, and also pastors at the same time. I think that that is, in itself, very problematic indeed.'[20]

The Church of England document called 'Policy for Bishops and Their Staff',[21] approved by the House of Bishops in 2018, is designated as 'policy' and 'best practice' rather than 'legislation', though it is 'legally sanctioned', and in this document the power of the episcopate is further demonstrated. What is usually included in the personal files of the clergy, commonly referred to as 'blue files', is listed in the policy with the diocesan bishop as 'data controller'; the bishops' personal files are managed by the relevant archbishop. The bishop processes data according to his or her 'legitimate interest and activities'; any sharing of data is weighed up according to 'necessity and proportionality' and based on 'a reasonable judgement as to whether the proposed sharing is likely to make an effective contribution to preventing or reducing a risk (e.g. of malpractice or incompetence) to which the public would otherwise be subjected'. Admittedly, it is now deemed essential to record safeguarding allegations and concerns and how these were handled, but it still appears to be the bishop who determines how the information is held and managed.

It has been pointed out that inevitably the Archbishops' List has been used, aside from safeguarding concerns, in a discretionary way against clergy who may have been seen 'in the opinion of the Archbishops, [to] have acted in a manner (not amounting to misconduct) which might affect their suitability for holding preferment' – in other words, used against clergy who might deviate from the pastoral guidance, for example, on same sex marriage.[22] What this demonstrates is the power of an episcopate that in the past has shown undue haste in removing the permission to officiate from clergy in a same sex marriage or 'blacklisted' them, but acted a great deal more slowly to withdraw PTO from fellow bishops, such as Peter Ball, about whom there were serious safeguarding concerns. Which actions are taken remains discretionary, given the variety of views in the House of Bishops, so there are problems in achieving a consistent approach. This seems especially the case when bishops, rather than lower-grade clerics, are involved in complaints. Again, Bishop Alan Wilson notes this lack of clarity: 'people who have entered CDMs against bishops feel that they get lost in a dense fog where everything takes twice as long and, at the end of it, nothing very much happens and, if it did happen, you wouldn't know it had happened because nothing is reported anyway.'[23]

Elliott's report on Joe's case raised the important issue of how financial liability can interfere with the safeguarding policy of responding with compassion to the victim. When Joe entered his claim for compensation, the Church shut down communication with him on the instruction of its insurers, who wanted to avoid liability. This sudden total withdrawal deepened Joe's difficulties and removed any church support. Here we see the Church working closely with the Ecclesiastical Insurance Group (EIG), a business that insures the majority of Church of England properties and organisations, but also schools and heritage properties: 'a specialist insurance and financial services company with over 130 years of experience offering honest advice, deep expertise and caring protection. We exist to contribute to the greater good of society.'[24] Joe, who writes under the name of Gilo, has researched the 'deep-rooted affiliation between the Church of England and its insurer EIG'.[25] He writes that their shared history and interests date back to 1887, but in 1972 the Church created Allchurches Trust Ltd (ATL) and EIG became a wholly-owned subsidiary of ATL. Therefore, profits made by the insurers are given to ATL, which then gives grants to the Church of England and other religious organisations; so, for example, between 2014 and 2017 EIG gave just over £100 million to ATL. This included grants to small charities (a system referred to by the then ATL chairman Sir Philip Mawer as a 'virtuous circle') but 80-92 per cent of the donated profits went to the dioceses and Anglican churches. This, as Gilo notes, 'is a major cash cow for the Church of England'. Whilst the separation between the Church, EIG and ATL may be legally accurate, the reality is somewhat different as high-ranking clerics have been on the EIG board of directors for decades. For example, Mawer, who was chairman of ATL for six and a half years until the end of 2019 and a trustee for nine years, has also occupied roles as the Secretary General of the General Synod of the Church of England (1990-2002) and of the Archbishops' Council.[26]

As Gilo notes, during a decade of cover-up the board had three or four senior church figures at a time: 'It's not hard to imagine the embedded deference, spheres of loyalty, patronage, and mutual interest that have accompanied so much hierarchy.' Indeed, as he personally experienced, the pastoral care for the victim would be lost in this powerful nexus in which the two organisations are morally and institutionally 'joined at the hip. . . . EIG regularly attended the Church's central safeguarding committee from the mid 1990s right through to 2015.'[27] Here is the fusion of the pastoral and legal, which makes following guidelines about compassion and concern for the victim highly contaminated by legal and financial priorities. At the IICSA hearings ATL was asked what money has been directly given to fund or develop projects concerning child sexual abuse since 2014: the company presented evidence that it has given £292,000 to the Safe Spaces project (mentioned again in Chapter 10). It was also noted that some survivors have been concerned that an organisation which ultimately funds the Church, and over which there is significant clerical presence, does not act in a way which is consistent with the Church's values and statements in respect of child protection and safeguarding.

The question of financial support for legal action reflects the ongoing support for the clergy against whom allegations have been made. Ironically, and not surprisingly, the perpetrator may be offered legal aid by the Church, but the complainant is not. As has been noted, institutions with deep pockets have a huge advantage here over the individual. Stephen Parsons writes, 'An institution will, when feeling under any kind of threat, always be able to outspend an individual.' He quotes, 'In one case I heard of a bishop, questioned under caution by the police about a safeguarding failure, who was accompanied to the interview by a top London QC. No doubt the bill for this QC was paid for by the central funds of the Church of England.'[28] Again, as Parsons points out, the Church or its insurers can use aggressive questioning of witnesses, or offer so-called expert witnesses to cast doubt on the mental state of the survivor, and so reduce the compensation claim. Usually, compensation claims are settled out of court and are extremely modest given the long-term effects of abuse and the re-abusive experiences of the Church. Dr Josephine Stein has carried out independent research and she estimates that the Church pays £55,000 towards the cost of therapy for survivors of abuse out of an estimated annual spend of £20 million on safeguarding. This is less than the cost of supporting a single 'alleged clerical perpetrator who has been suspended' which 'would cost on average £60,000, including a stipend, housing, upkeep, and insurance costs'.[29] So why is the Church so mean? Part of the reasoning for this is its defensive culture which reacts to anxiety-provoking situations. The anxiety about being sued, being seen as party to abusive practices, all contribute to the church hierarchy holding tightly to the rule of law, where survivors are seen as legal problems rather than as members of its flock. Parsons sees this culture of legal protectionism as so deeply embedded that it inhibits any spontaneous pastoral response.

In light of so many critical reports and evident failings, the Church appears eager to offer new structures to deliver safeguarding. One of these is the National Safeguarding Steering Group (NSSG) which met for the first time in October 2016. Yet, it seems that it may merely be part of the same structure as before. This group, established by the archbishops, is a successor to the House of Bishops Safeguarding Monitoring and Reference Group.[30] The terms of reference show that membership is appointed by the archbishops and should include both lay and clerical representation and the lead bishop for safeguarding (chairman), deputy bishop for safeguarding (vice-chairman), up to five members of the House of Bishops appointed by the archbishops – to include bishops from the Northern and Southern provinces and to include (where possible) bishops having experience of the religious communities and theological education institutions, one to two members of the Archbishops' Council, one to two members of the Board of the Church Commissioners, one cathedral dean, the chairman of the National Safeguarding Panel, the Bishop at Lambeth and the chiefs of staff to the archbishops. This reads as another hierarchical group within the church, predominantly made up of those whose status rather than knowledge privileges them to membership. A quote from 'The Rise of the Bluffocracy' seems relevant here, where safeguarding is predominantly being run by people whose knowledge:

> Extends a mile wide but an inch deep; who know how to grasp the generalities of any topic in minutes, and how never to bother themselves with the specifics. Who place their confidence in their ability to talk themselves out of trouble, rather than learning how to run things carefully.[31]

This confident group of people is accountable to the archbishops and the national church governance bodies and the dioceses and is required to issue an annual report at the end of each calendar year. Yet this group has oversight of the National Safeguarding Team, has oversight of national safeguarding activity and 'considers' the recommendations and advice of the independently-chaired (chair appointed by the church from outside the church) National Safeguarding Panel. It also vets reports and comments on recommendations from case reviews and scrutinises draft safeguarding policy, legislation and practice guidance prior to final approval by the House of Bishops.

In the 2019 Annual Report the National Safeguarding Panel rightly stressed the importance of changing the culture within the Church: 'Key elements are the requirement to be proactive in safeguarding, that inaction in response to concerns is unacceptable and that protecting the reputation of the church by concealing safeguarding issues is wrong. Only openness and transparency can restore the church's reputation.'[32] In the next chapter we start to look more carefully at this culture in terms of institutional and structural power and control.

6.
Dynamics of Power and Control in the Institutional Church

I think that the rotten apple theory is always nonsense. There is never just one person involved in abuse. It always happens in a context. And the context is what makes it possible and what makes cover-up possible. Unless you understand that context, you won't be understanding what actually happened and understanding what actually happened is the beginning of anything else you may then want to do by way of response.[1]

Bishop Alan Wilson

However genuine and caring individuals are, the system is flawed and built on sand. It's a perpetrator-centred system, essentially risk management. The survivor is essentially a trigger and then an afterthought.[2]

Jane Chevous

The structural dynamics of the institutional power and control of the Church have tended to maintain a form of 'group think', which is about knowing and accepting one's place within what is almost a closed system, admitting only those who adhere to maintaining the power and control of the structure. Here, power rests with a group of predominantly white men who exercise their will and control over others, with or without resistance, in order to obtain their target or promote their interests. Power is everywhere in human relations, and that includes the Church.[3] For many, it probably seems as if the business of safeguarding and the cases that have reached the public domain are nothing to do with the core function and business of the Church – indeed, seen as a diversion from the main business. It may seem that it only involves a handful of 'rotten apples', a few rogue clergy, and can in no way detract from the far more important mission of the Church's religious and social purpose. The survivors who seek justice are seen as people on the margins, peripheral and, thus, as has been shown, are often marginalised. In the first part of this chapter we look at the relationship between the two: powerless on the margins and the powerful at the core – because there always is a relationship. The reports and reviews published so far on the Church's mishandling of clergy abuse cases are a useful way of looking at this; as each report and review shines 'a considerable light on how the relationship between the margins and the core is understood, misunderstood, assumed, accepted and all too often unacknowledged'.[4] Later in the chapter, there is analysis of two power networks, one formal, the other informal. The final section explores the general effect of the British class system.

The Margins and the Core

The report on the case of Robert Waddington serves as an example of this structural dynamic. Waddington was dean of Manchester Cathedral from 1984-93 and then held permission to officiate until 2004. In 2013 the Church commissioned an internal review headed by Sally Cahill QC, who, in her report published in 2014, identified systemic failure within the church hierarchy over allegations of Waddington's sexual abuse of a number of boys over many years.[5] The report details that between 1956 and 2013 almost twenty people, including a number of Waddington's victims, reported allegations to church officials in both the UK and in Australia (where Waddington had also worked). None of the church officials reported the allegations to the police. At the time of the review crimes against at least nine children and one adult over five decades were known about, allegations had been made in 1999, 2003 and 2004, and the Archbishop of York, then David Hope, was found to have breached child protection policies eighteen times in his responses to these allegations, despite having presided himself over the writing of the Church's child protection policy, 'Protecting All God's Children', and having contributed to the earlier policy, 'Children First'.

However, when it actually came to adhering to policies in a specific situation, Archbishop Hope failed to abide by the basics on all three occasions when allegations were made. In the context of considering the power and control dynamic, it is relevant that Hope prioritised the perpetrator as in his mind belonging like him to the core. This is shown in his actions or rather inaction and in his responses. For example, on one occasion he excused the dean in a letter to the Australian Bishop of North Queensland, citing Waddington's ill health. His letter also persuaded the Australian victim to drop his civil action. Sally Cahill's report gives details of health records and letters, which show that in fact at this time Waddington was healthy and fit enough to have been investigated. When further allegations came to light in 2003, once again Hope breached the guidelines by taking no action at all; he failed to consider the risk at that time to children and young people and he did not suspend Waddington's PTO. Finally, in 2004 after further allegations this was suspended. However, again Hope acted inappropriately by sending the complainants' statements to Waddington in advance of an interview by a diocesan member of staff that should not have taken place. This decision Hope termed 'natural justice'. Furthermore, Hope made no record of the actions he took. When the Australian investigation was dropped due to 'insufficient evidence', Hope told Waddington, who replied that he was doing some entertaining and would be able to do so 'with a much more cheerful countenance'. Waddington died in 2007 with his reputation intact; not so the Church which received a lot of critical media coverage.

As is evidenced by the report what happened to the victims helps our understanding of what the core represents. Those on the margins and those at the centre 'are not only inextricably linked – they are logically symbiotic'.[6] There is an inherent tension in such relationships where resources and opportunity are all in play. The institutional church is founded on structural distinctions, based on power and control, between different parts of the system, so that within the core there are levels of differing power and control, as indeed there is within each diocese and benefice. The clearest power distinction for those outside the Church is that between clergy and laity. Explicitly, the clergy are those 'called' by God to divine ministry, whose vocation is tested before ordination training, which is the process by which individuals are consecrated and so set apart and elevated from the laity to the clergy. The status implies that clergy know more about God and the divine mysteries as they are 'allowed' to minister the sacraments and so channel the love and gifts of God. The reverend is one to be revered. Within the clergy there are further categories which set them apart and the more each cleric progresses up the hierarchy, the further distanced he or she becomes from the laity. Implicitly, senior clergy become even 'holier' and more powerful and, in the case of bishops, closest to apostolic succession and to Jesus Christ, increasingly reverent and thus even more powerful. Amongst those who are bishops there are further distinctions to do with power: the Lords Spiritual with *ex officio* seniority; the Lords Spiritual with seniority of service (those who serve in the House of Lords); other diocesan bishops, and the suffragan bishops. The furthest away from the powerless on the margins are the two archbishops, who implicitly, as in the 'holy of holies' (c.f. Hebrews 9:2), are the closest to God and by definition are the most powerful with the greatest control within the structure.

In contrast, the laity is by definition made up of those *not* chosen for such 'divine' ministry. Explicitly, they are the furthest away from the apostolic succession and, implicitly, need to be ministered to, to be forgiven and absolved of sins by the clergy. The implicit meaning (which would be denied) is that the laity is therefore more sinful than the clergy, though less sinful than all those who do not go to church. (That is partly why so much importance is placed on mission and evangelism, as well as the need to maintain the institution.) Of course, amongst the laity there are those who are more powerful and who have more control than others such as readers, the music director or choir master, those on the parochial church council. The children are usually at the bottom of this pyramid.

As Bishop Alan Wilson expressed it at the IICSA hearings on the Anglican Church:

> In many church contexts, people are, for religious purposes, unequal in the power they hold in particular situations, whether that is a young server serving the altar at mass for a clergyman or whether that's a clergyman with her or his bishop, and there are many, many inequalities nested within the life of the church . . . it is very difficult for people to know what to do when somebody who you're supposed to look up to behaves in a way that is extremely discreditable.[7]

The Church thrives on power, although much is made of ministering to and praying for the powerless. Wilson calls it 'the geometry of the church' which by definition 'sets up a large number of kind of iconic figures and inequalities of one sort or another'.[8] Undue deference happens at all levels of the Church from the parish up. The power that is found in the local church has been referred to as 'soft power' or 'influence' and it is often found within the (over 40) dioceses which can be seen to function as little fiefdoms with their different routines and family flavour and particular obsessions. This also means that there is little consistency about the way with which some things are dealt. In a system where the fundamental differential is of who is 'holy' and who is not, abuse, perpetrated by a 'holy' cleric, begins to threaten the social fabric. Often, when allegations of abuse are made, the powerful core includes not only the senior clerics and a majority of clergy, but also many of the laity who attend church. Then the victims and their supporters become very much the few on the margin. It often seems that, after the reports and reviews are published, bringing associated bad publicity for the Church, then the distinctions briefly become fluid. The perpetrator and supporters become more central, as apologies from the hierarchy come to include, or appear to include, the survivors and their supporters. Thus, when the extent of a clergy perpetrator's abuse is publicly revealed, his 'reverence' is quickly recalibrated to 'rotten apple', though the reverential title (mostly) stays. Importantly, as the Waddington review revealed, this is not to do with numbers, but everything to do with power, privilege and control of resources. Decisions are made at the core; consequences are felt at the margin.

Because of his power and privilege at the core of the institutional church, Waddington, who was close to Robert Runcie (Archbishop of Canterbury, 1980-91), was able to groom the boys to whom he had access, often through the cathedral choir, whilst at the same time cultivating the illusion of his propriety and the view of him by other senior clergy as someone with 'a special gift with boys'. This 'special gift' could not be seen for what it was – sexual grooming and abuse. Here we come up against the concept of denial of awareness. Denial is a central defence mechanism but, in the context of Waddington, it can also be seen to operate in conjunction with unconscious bias. In other words, some decided to deny what they might have seen – they turned a blind eye, but others did see. For example, in the 1980s, Manchester Cathedral choirmaster Stuart Beer reported his concerns about the then dean's relationship with the victim Eli Ward to the cathedral organist and choir director Gordon Stuart, who reported to the cathedral chapter. However, no report was made to the police and Waddington forced Eli Ward to resign from the choir.[9]

In this instance, the cathedral chapter (which usually comprises, among others, the dean, the precentor, the canons and the cathedral administrator) chose to deny the information they were being given about 'one of their own'. Hashi Mohamed, who initially found himself very much on the margins of British society but then as a professional entered into the heart of it, writes of the power of the fixed mindset which is partly made up of direct prejudice and partly by unconscious bias: 'The kind of direct prejudice that Britain is steeped in . . . compounded by the fact that we are naturally drawn to people who we perceive to be like us, something that is known as homophily or affinity bias.' Both denial of awareness and affinity bias are largely unconscious processes, and Mohamed notes how the idea that we hold prejudices and opinions that we might act on without being consciously aware of them has now been legally established.[10] Overall, unsurprisingly, biases tend to be in favour of the kind of people well-represented in positions of power. Affinity bias, the preference for 'people like us', that comes into play in interviews, promotions and networking, reinforces the status quo. In other words, thinking that someone is like you often means choosing to believe or be on the side of someone who sounds just like you, even if his behaviour may cause concern; it also means preferring him when it comes to interviews. This may partly explain why the chapter of Manchester Cathedral took no action and, incidentally, perhaps why so many of the male members of the House of Bishops look and sound the same.

Unconscious bias is often the result of learned biases, the type we pick up during the course of our lives; in a later chapter the embedded cultural ethos of the public school and boarding school which permeates the church hierarchy will be explored. The failure of the hierarchy to respond appropriately to the allegations against Waddington may have been a result partly of affinity bias and partly of the set of preconceptions that they held: 'it's a fundamental fact of life that those in a position of power . . . can end up penalising people on the grounds of gender, class or race, or on any other irrational basis, without ever really grappling with *why*'[11] and, conversely, not penalising those like them. Most people deny that they have an unconscious bias, although research has shown a link between self-perceived objectivity and judgemental bias.[12] In other words, 'when people feel that they are objective, rational actors, they act on their group-based biases *more* rather than less'. This goes some way towards explaining why, despite personal and institutional pressures towards avoiding bias, it still flourishes. The implication is that, despite all the safeguarding training and policies, the reports and reviews, what matters is that those involved take personal responsibility not only for their individual actions, but also for their unconscious motivations.

At the same time as unconscious bias, another type of bias emerges from the information about Robert Waddington's years of abusing boys and this is conscious bias. Waddington left to work in Australia following an allegation of abuse and, during his time at St Barnabas boarding school in North Queensland, not only was Waddington said to have beaten and sexually abused at least three boys, but two teachers hired by both Waddington and his 1970 replacement as headmaster, Barry Greaves, were later themselves convicted of child abuse at other Australian schools and parishes. Some intuitive sense or information meant that Waddington realised that these men were 'like him' or could be 'like him' and so he appointed them. In one case, a teacher, Peter Gilbert, who faced an allegation that he abused whilst at St Barnabas, claimed in his defence that Waddington directly encouraged him to become interested in children. 'Prior to joining St Barnabas, I hadn't the slightest interest in children . . . now they were the centre of my life,' Gilbert wrote, 'He misled me . . . while being in a position of special power and influence. He encouraged and facilitated my romantic love for children directly and indirectly through ideology, through literature, by example and through specific guidance and advice in response to my concerns.'[13] Gilbert was appointed by conscious bias.

A further example of this is shown in Waddington's involvement in Chetham's School of Music. While Waddington was dean in Manchester, he was also chairman of the diocesan education committee. Obituaries from 2007 draw attention to his great interest in the choirs at the cathedral and at Chetham's School of Music (opposite Manchester Cathedral) and the connections between the institutions are strong. Waddington was also a close personal friend of John Vallins, headmaster of Chetham's School from 1974 to 1992 during the period of some of the worst allegations of sexual abuse. In the context of conscious bias, Waddington was also a school governor of Chetham's and a 'Feoffee', or trustee, of its charitable foundation Chetham's Hospital School and Library between 1984 and 1993. This was at the time when a number of concerns and allegations were being made by victims and when no action was taken, although presumably these concerns were raised at governors' meetings or between Vallins and Waddington. For example, when a Chetham's pupil, a man who attended between 1983 and 1988, raised the alarm about one teacher to a staff member, he was told by the housemaster that he was being a 'vulgar, smutty schoolboy spreading rumours' and no action was taken. As Ian Pace, a student at Chetham's from 1978-86, who has researched the prevalence of abuse at music schools and the involvement of Waddington, states: 'At the time when some of the worst abuse is alleged to have gone on at the school, the school board contained someone who has been outed as an abuser himself.' Seven individuals were either convicted, were likely to have been convicted if alive, or have admitted to sexual relationships with pupils while Mr Vallins was head teacher. Vallins said he was unaware of any misconduct.[14]

Powerful Networks, Formal and Informal

As conscious bias reveals, people in power foster powerful networks and thereby maintain control. One example of a formal, apparently powerful, network is the General Synod of the Church of England. In Bishop Alan Wilson's discussion at the IICSA hearings on deference, he pointed out how this goes on at every level in the Church and refers to what happens at General Synod where the power dynamics are encapsulated in the three houses: the House of Bishops, the House of Clergy and the House of Laity. It is at these meetings that legislation, finance, policy and forms of worship are discussed and voted on, but power and control issues frame the body. Wilson gives the example where, 'a business committee will just say, "Well, we weren't allowed to ask to talk about what we wanted to talk about because we have been told that we can't"'.[15]

Martin Sewell, who has been a member of the General Synod for many years, has written about the Church's response to child sexual abuse allegations, highlighting how control has played a major negative part in church culture, contributing to safeguarding deficiencies in the cases of Peter Ball, John Smyth and Jonathan Fletcher (the latter two men are discussed in Chapter 8).[16] He writes that, perhaps 'unwittingly', the way in which the agenda is controlled at synod has been a contributing factor to the inadequate response of the Church. When reports and reviews have been published, they have been considered and debated in a variety of settings, such as Church House, Lambeth Palace and in the House of Bishops, but never brought to discussion at General Synod. Commenting on the reviews, Sewell writes, 'Gibb, Elliott, Carmi, Carlile and the Past Cases Review were treated like a D.H. Lawrence novel: they were scandalous and not to be discussed in polite society. One would not want one's servants to read them.' When the interim IICSA report on Peter Ball and the Chichester diocese was published in 2018, members were offered what Sewell describes as a bland motion rather than being enabled to endorse the response to the five recommendations made by IICSA. Sewell was part of a group that tried to challenge, 'the control that was being exercised to channel the General Synod of the Church of England into safe and moderate modes of thought. After consultation across the church, we introduced amendments which attempted to put responses of real substance up for debate.'

This had happened previously and both times the suggestions and amendments were rejected. The first time the archbishops thought it premature, the second time sentiments of repentance and endorsing a good pastoral response 'were ruled technically out of order'. The group involved thought it important that such an initiative 'should come from below' as distinct from above, that is, the House of Bishops, 'Archbishop Justin has previously acknowledged that a change to the culture of deference is needed. We were taking him seriously.' General Synod was the place to discuss this and the group urged a prompt acceptance of the IICSA proposals, 'on the basis that it was inconceivable that we would pretend to know better after all the embarrassment of the IICSA evidence and submissions. Our track record does not merit once again wandering off on a safeguarding frolic of our own.'

Pressure from the group seems to have worked, especially after IICSA's final report was published in May 2019. When the synod met in February 2020 important new amendments were debated and discussed and the result was that, 'General Synod voted unanimously today [12 February 2020] to endorse the

Church's response to the five recommendations from IICSA and urged its national safeguarding steering group to work towards a more fully survivor-centred approach to safeguarding, including arrangements for redress for survivors.'[17] Sewell welcomed the fulfilment of 'the primary purpose of our original initiative . . . to bring a fully engaged Synod behind a proper and resourced project to "Rebuild my House" as a place of safety, and a place of reconciliation' and called it 'an important acceptance of bona fides'.

The significance of the vote in synod was the acceptance that earlier responses had been inadequate and the recognition of the 'survivor-centred approach'. Indeed, during the debate, the issue of power and control was voiced by the Bishop of Burnley, Philip North, who said that, following his reading of the IICSA report, 'I found myself more and more reflecting on power, its use and abuse and on how I perceive the power I hold myself. . . . Hidden power, opaque structures of power, ill-defined patterns of accountability are very easy to abuse.' While his comments (noted as main points) hold much relevance, his theological view against the ordination of women to the priesthood seems to temper his insights. The contribution of the Bishop of London, Sarah Mullally, offered a small ray of light when she stated that a change in culture was needed. Her statement says that, 'Culture change does not happen and the "way we do things around here" does not change unless . . . owned by those that are part of the culture. Anything less would turn what are behaviours at the heart of the gospel into something which is seen as a bureaucratic checklist.'[18]

The shift in the power and control dynamics at General Synod in February 2020 meant that the issue of how the Church deals with allegations moved away from being 'a problem', defined by Campbell and Groenback as an 'activity which is outside dialogue', to becoming a topic or an issue.[19] Previously there was no theological space for the members of synod to think about the issues or begin to discuss their implications. Of course, it may be that it re-emerges as a problem because it cannot continue to be thought about and freely discussed across the organisation, or because the appropriate discourses may not be seen as available or suitable within the organisation itself. The tendency could be for it to become an issue only within the relevant safeguarding groups and their remit and so still remain 'a problem' (outside dialogue) for the rest of the Church. Unfortunately, the signs are that this may happen for, in the following July 2020 synod, the Church appeared to have returned to the familiar cultural repertoire of keeping distanced from the agreed-on survivor-focused position.[20] This sort of change of position can be understood through complexity theory whereby the relationships forged in the large meeting of the General Synod might then become supplanted by a spontaneously self-organising network of shadow relationships. Here the term 'shadow relationships' refers to those that were in play long before synod met, relationships embedded in the history of the hierarchical church culture found, for example, in Church House, Lambeth Palace, the Archbishops' Council and the House of Bishops. The motions agreed at General Synod may be given lip service but the changes are merely superficial because the shadow relationships function as a way of 'subverting or undermining existing legitimate relationships'.[21] The interest in changing what has taken place would be to avoid what is then deemed to be threatening. This is linked with the idea of conceptual repertoire, for it is possible to see that the action taken, in unanimously passing the motion and the accompanying dialogue at the General Synod, cannot remain as part of the conceptual repertoire of the institutional church outside the synod. The survivor focus agreed to is outside this culture, and in some ways outside the fantasy of the organisation and how it sees itself (and this despite the conscious affirmation of the action taken). The positioning that took place at synod brought the survivors in from the margins but, away from their influence, and as a result of 'reflective positioning', the repositioning back to the familiar male hierarchy may feel more comfortable.[22]

An example of an informal powerful network, firmly positioned as part of the male hierarchy in the institutional church, is Nobody's Friends, which was described at the IICSA hearings by Lord Lloyd as 'simply a club, half consisting of the clergy, members of the clergy, and half consisting of members of the laity, which [sic] dine together probably twice a year, very often in Lambeth Palace'. The IICSA counsel pointed out that, on the other hand, it had been described by one newspaper as 'centred on a strong core of bishops, ex-Tory ministers and former military top brass, a highly secretive, all-male group representing Britain's most entrenched professions and institutions'. It began as a private dining club for thirteen members but has since expanded and meets quarterly.[23]

Following the IICSA hearing, Stephen Parsons commented that the forum Nobody's Friends suggested a 'toxic masculinity' in the Church of England: 'The club provides an opportunity for a privileged church group to network and sometimes lobby those in authority in the Church . . . an exclusive world of male privilege within the heart of the Anglican establishment.'[24] In 2015 the president of the club was Sir Philip Mawer, the former Secretary General of the Church of England Synod and the chairman of the All Churches Trust, who was on the board of Ecclesiastical Insurance Group (discussed in the previous chapter). As the club is 'secret', it is not known whether he has been replaced. As Gilo, who has also written about this club, writes, this informal powerful network, 'has or aspires to a role in shaping the public life of the Established Church and the country at large'.[25] Membership of the club has included many bishops and archbishops, headmasters from a sprinkling of top schools, various archbishops' appointments secretaries, prime ministers' appointments secretaries, leaders of the House of Commons and House of Lords, Tory peers, Admiralty figures, judicial figures and church lawyers. All are safe pairs of hands; they are 'one of us'. Gilo writes that abuse in various forms has been rife in many of the institutions represented in this private dining club, and this informal and 'secret' powerful network has either failed to address this important inconvenient truth or, worse, succeeded in keeping the lid on it for many years.

Gilo also draws our attention to another incident in which privilege and protection of an abuser took place and which drew into its ambit yet another Church of England dining club – on this occasion, the Nikaean Club that exists to promote the Archbishop of Canterbury's ecumenical mission and whose members pay to dine with him and other senior clergy.[26] In 1993 Patrick Gilbert, a former chairman of the Nikaean Club, head of the Society for Promoting Christian Knowledge for many years and, incidentally, secretary of the Athenaeum Club's wine committee, was prosecuted for abusing a boy between the ages of fourteen and sixteen. Canon (later Bishop) Christopher Hill, also a member of the Nikaean Club, accompanied Patrick Gilbert to court and a character witness letter was given by another Nikaean member, the former Archbishop of Canterbury, Donald Coggan. Gilbert, who had a previous conviction for the indecent assault of two thirteen-year-old schoolboys received a suspended sentence and sympathy from the judge for the considerable stress he had endured. As the judge explained, he decided not to jail the bachelor because of his health and the 'very severe punishment' he had already undergone through loss of reputation.[27]

Power and Class

> England is the most class-ridden country under the sun. It is a land of snobbery and privilege, ruled largely by the old and silly.[28]
>
> *George Orwell*

The dining clubs and the powerful informal networks linked to them are clear examples of the way in which class permeates the hierarchy of the Church of England. For class pervades every aspect of British society, shaping all of us from our life expectancy to the brand of teabags we use. It is both strictly codified and somewhat vague, although as Hashi Mohamed notes, many British people will have internalised it to such an extent that they will reflectively be able to 'sort' a stranger by such details as where they live, what they order in the pub and what sort of dog they have.[29] Mohamed writes, 'the best way to define class . . . is . . . in terms of access to privilege, opportunities, and representation in elites, institutions and professions'. He looks at the cultural capital accrued in terms of access to art, music and literature as values and attitudes underpinned by centuries-old customs and mindsets, which are for the most part designed and meticulously maintained to ensure that everyone 'knows their place'. This wealth of experience, reference points and taste leads to what has been called 'an emerging sense of entitlement', further discussed in Chapter 8. In contrast, working-class children, whose parents are less likely to have positive experiences with authority, develop 'an emerging sense of constraint', a feeling that places, roles and opportunities 'aren't for the likes of us'. Class barriers are consciously and unconsciously enforced by most people, who then conform to certain rules and stick to codes on how 'people like them' ought to behave, look or even think. In this way, class is one of the markers of power and control in the Church.

This divide is illustrated by some of the exchanges quoted in the independent report by Lord Carlile into the way that the Church of England dealt with a complaint of sexual abuse made by a woman known as 'Carol' against the late bishop George Bell. The report was published in 2017 but the documentation includes the following comment from 1995, after Carol had written to Bishop Eric Kemp, then the bishop of Chichester, alleging sexual abuse by Bell when she was between eight and ten years old. The bishop's response was to ask for further information: 'Try to find out more about this lady.' Carlile notes that written on the same copy was: '[. . .'s] parish. [He] does not know her. This is where the council houses problem people.' Carlile rightly adds, 'In my view this was an inappropriate comment to have written.'[30] In his reply to Carol's first letter, Kemp said that, whilst he was 'sorry that you have such distressing memories', he could suggest some counsellors and advised her to visit her parish priest. In the context of class, what is relevant here is that Carol told the review she felt daunted by this letter, especially as her complaint was against a powerful senior clergyman, and the suggestion that she might approach another clergyman. Further enquiries did confirm the basic facts that Carol had outlined in her allegation but no further action was taken. In the autumn of 2012, Carol sent a number of e-mails to Lambeth Palace, in which she reiterated her complaint of 1995. She did not receive the first reply, because her e-mail address had been compromised, but the second included the following dismissal:

> Unfortunately, other than the most recently retired bishop, the former bishops of Chichester are all now dead so there is nothing we can do to take your story forward and deal with it. If you feel the need to talk to someone about it however, please let me know and I will put you in touch with someone. Meanwhile please be assured of the Archbishop's prayers and concern. And thank you for telling us of this difficult and distressing episode.

Carlile saw the response as inadequate, and, one might add, patronising. On 4 April 2013 Carol e-mailed Lambeth Palace again but, when there was no reply, sent a further e-mail on 8 April, which Carlile quotes with the original spelling:

> Didant think I would get a reply. It figers. I'm elderly so all through my life I was blighted by my abuse and being

a woman Im to be ignored. It is the two faced way of the church you hope by ignoring it will go away but I won't I will keep reminding you.

On 9 April Carol received a short holding reply and on 24 April a longer message that began: 'I am really sorry that it has taken so long to reply to your message. We have been inundated with correspondence since Archbishop Justin's Enthronement.' Again, the lack of sensitivity and the implicit message about the importance of the enthronement, for the one class, and the unimportance of Carol, who is clearly not part of this, demonstrates the privilege of one and not of the other. Offered some time with a specialist safeguarding advisor, Carol's response included explaining why it had taken her so long to speak out:

> the longer I left it it became harder to say anything besides who would of believed me I do want to speak to the lady you spoke of but it will be hard it took years to tell my husband why I was fridged and was not keen on personal contact.

Following the work with the independent safeguarding advisor, the Church reached a settlement in October 2015 in a civil claim, an announcement that caused much indignation and outrage from many of the powerful and privileged supporters of Bishop Bell, who said that the Church had been too quick to condemn a highly revered man who, because he had died decades earlier, could not defend himself.[31]

Within the church hierarchy, different vestments reflect the different levels of power and the 'class system' within the institution. There is the separation of those called to be clergy from those who are not and, within that, there are different garments to denote status. For example, different stoles denote different signs of order and office; and the way they are worn distinguishes deacons from priests. Anglican bishops wear purple shirts, officially, violet, as a sign of their office (surely the equivalent of 'blue blood'); in Chapter 2, Janet Lord is quoted remembering Bishop Whitsey as 'very tall, very big, very purple'. Along with the pectoral cross and episcopal ring, this marks their status; bishops also have a mitre that matches their cope and often carry a crozier to symbolise their leadership. These clothes are representations of 'group think' and a form of classification. The hierarchical and rather rigid power structure of the Church of England means that it is a very 'congested system'; it lacks the fluidity needed for the culture significantly to change. The tone of the controversy over the George Bell compensation settlement (whatever its rights or wrongs) exemplifies the demonisation of those forces intruding from the margins, including the poor, in this case, female, those 'sullied by sexual abuse' and their 'politically correct' agitating supporters as somehow an attack on the pure, the holy and the good, the traditional, powerful, white male core, who have so many resources to call upon, including a great deal of money.

One of the resources of the powerful classes has been called 'opportunity hoarding', this is about opening up opportunities to your children by conferring advantage on them so that they are on the inside track to success, wealth and status. Many of these senior clerics in the Church of England have had educational opportunities that Carol for many reasons had difficulty in taking. Opportunity hoarding includes both cultural and social capital where social capital is connections, friendships and networks, and cultural capital is knowledge, behaviour and skills. It is what you know and whom you know, where and with whom you dine, to which club you belong and then the right person believing in you and promoting you. For the most powerful have a monopoly of cultural and social capital and, in the context of the church hierarchy, this includes many raised in environments and schooled in institutions that closely mirror the institutional church. They have set the tone, defined the culture and shaped the parameters for what is institutionally permissible. Future deans, archdeacons and bishops are carefully sought and nurtured, in order that they can be shaped to fit the existing culture and social world of the episcopate; they are supported and given space to develop along acceptable lines through a vast range of resources and opportunities. Women in church leadership and those from black or ethnic minority backgrounds may begin to influence this culture but this would need a critical mass to tip the balance and move from the current tendency of a self-involved clique that has rewarded group membership above competence and self-confidence above expertise.[32] This is less about individuals, who cannot help where they are born or how they are educated, and more about a system of power and control which seems only to

6. Dynamics of Power and Control in the Institutional Church

reward white, middle-class and middle-aged men (preferably Oxford or Cambridge graduates). Findings about racism in the Church confirm this: 'the one-colour nature of the senior leadership of the Church of England begins to look perilously archaic'.[33]

Inevitably, alongside access to power and control, there is the existential fear of power being taken away or control overrun, in this context by survivors. How else can one explain the dogged persistence of various senior clerics to make meaningful changes? Perhaps it is more to do with what Lynsey Hanley describes, 'The further up the social ladder you are, the more external influences are set up to favour you and your kind, to the extent that privilege becomes invisible and so weightless that – literally – you don't know how lucky you are.' The failure to acknowledge the role of luck in our lives often damages peoples' true understanding of where others are actually starting from.[34] In the next chapter we look at individual power and charisma and how this has affected the way the Church has responded to abuse.

7.
Charismatic Power and Control

> Well, a large amount of abuse in church is what I think is now being termed spiritual abuse . . . you are dealing with people on the level of identity and their very deepest convictions about themselves and their lives and who they are and the communities that give them value in their lives and circles of friendship that they rely on from day to day. This is a very powerful web in which to find yourself, and when that web becomes a means of exculpating somebody who has done something wrong or covering up wrongdoing, it's remarkably difficult for people to blow the whistle on that.[1]
>
> *Bishop Alan Wilson*

In I Corinthians chapter 12 St Paul writes of 'spiritual gifts', 'gifts of grace' determined by God and divinely ordained; the word 'charisma' is taken from the Greek meaning 'favour freely given' or a 'gift of grace'. It is generally used about people who convey some sort of compelling attraction or charm that can inspire devotion in others and this can lead to power over others within a relationship of authority. The better word for this type of power is domination which usually implies some sort of voluntary compliance from those involved with the charismatic person. As the sociologist and political economist Max Weber wrote, in *Economy and Society*, the followers are influenced by devotion to what seems the exceptional sanctity or the exemplary character of the person whose mission and vision inspires others.[2] A much quoted version of Weber's definition of power is: 'An actor called A has power over another actor, B, to the extent that A can make B do something that B would not otherwise have done.' That the repression of B's needs becomes a necessary part of power is first shown when, 'A exercises power over B, when A affects B in a manner contrary to B's interest.'[3] Weber thought that charismatic authority founded on faith and belief in someone lasts only as long as the person can preserve moral influence, for the relationship depends on recognition by the followers and their enthusiasm, hope or faith. Initially, the duty of the followers is to trust the leader and obey his orders and thus the followers become dependent on the authority or domination of the leader. Another aspect is the acceptance by the followers that usual ways of behaving or normative standards can be dissolved and traditional controls abandoned as guided by the leader. Once the trust and the acceptance of new ways are set up, then the followers and the leader form an emotional community centred on his or her charismatic leadership. Weber also stressed the indifference of the group to rational economic activities and to the everyday routine world. There is a new orientation of all attitudes towards the different problems of the world. If the charismatic leader 'appears deserted by his god or his magical or heroic powers, above all, if his leadership fails to benefit his followers, it is likely that his charismatic authority will disappear'.[4] This may take time as people may still hold onto the belief, reinterpreting what has happened even if it looks very negative. Earlier, in the chapter on the mind of the abuser, we discussed how cognitive dissonance can be used to resolve two opposing beliefs and this can hold true around communities of followers when emotional enthusiasm is still aroused or an alternative course of action seems too difficult to be pursued.

In this chapter charismatic domination and control and the way in which this has led to sexual and spiritual abuse is explored and illustrated through the examples of Peter Ball and Chris Brain, both of whom inspired followers through their charisma. In both situations the church hierarchy was also caught up in the charisma and illusion of the priests' holiness and so benefited through reflected glory. The response of the institutional church when allegations were made was to deny and diminish those who came forward – until there was no alternative.

Sexual and Spiritual Domination in the Case of Peter Ball

> Bishop Peter seemed to want me to be more obedient to himself than to God.[5]
>
> *Neil Todd*

In 2002 Bishop Peter Ball led a much-heralded Good Friday service at Bath Abbey which I attended. He was dressed in his monk's robe, carried a staff and spoke in a rather ethereal but penetrating manner about spiritual truths. He looked the real deal and, as a new convert, I was enthralled. Here seemed a truly holy person. The only jarring note came after he had quoted from John Keats, 'Ode to a Nightingale':

> Charm'd magic casements, opening on the foam
>   Of perilous seas, in faery lands forlorn.
> Forlorn! the very word is like a bell
>   To toll me back from thee to my sole self![6]

Ball said that even the most ordinary and uneducated 'lads' would spiritually respond to hearing these words and for a time turn away from their 'floozies' (an old-fashioned and pejorative word implying promiscuous women). I put his use of this down to a rather otherworldly and out-of-touch approach to women, noting that he thought only young men would respond, but excusing him as a monk, because he so clearly presented as a genuine spiritual leader. This personal anecdote is used to explain not only the persona that Ball had developed, but also the charm he conveyed; wise after the event, I soon found that this charisma was only part of him and very much the surface.

In his evidence at the IICSA hearing on Peter Ball one of the 'lads', who was also deceived by this charisma and joined the quasi-monastic 'scheme' that Ball set up in Sussex, commented:

> I remember seeing a film about St Francis which was about him giving up everything to follow the life of Christ. As far as I was concerned Peter Ball fitted in to that mould with vows of chastity and obedience and he was a very respected man in the church. He had a huge presence and seemed to have wisdom and a deep spiritual

understanding. With regard to my fears of my sexuality and the devil I thought that he would have the answers and the lifestyle to address these issues.[7]

This victim's evidence shows how gradually and carefully Ball groomed the young man, initially by his discussion early on about cold showers and praying naked in front of an open window for an hour on a Thursday, whatever the weather, and with other men, which Ball linked to Christ's suffering in the garden of Gethsemane:

I was aware that what Peter was suggesting was not mainstream practice, although I did not know it was not usual monastic practice. However, he appeared to be an unusually saintly man with a very distinct and real relationship with God. He impressed upon me the idea that I could be a modern-day saint, that Christ demanded great sacrifices from those who wanted a real relationship with God . . . he implied that I was special and somehow chosen by God for a monastic lifestyle.

When Ball discussed erections during the first talks, the victim, whilst feeling uncomfortable said, 'he spoke about them naturally and in context of overcoming one's reservations and egoism as part of understanding Christ's humiliation'. Throughout the victim's time with him, Ball imbued suggestions and expectations of abusive behaviour with spiritual meaning. He demanded the cold showers and so the victim not only felt that the cold showers were expected, but that it was also a holy thing to do. In this context the presence of Ball watching him voyeuristically in the shower was introduced as part of being 'vulnerable' and 'open to each other': 'Bishop Peter himself was a holy man, and I accepted that cold showers were part of the holy life.' The witness found this deeply uncomfortable and in the shower turned his back on Ball, as the thought of being watched made him feel very uneasy. The longer that the victim stayed, the more lewd the conversations became. There were regular questions about masturbation, though the term used by Ball was 'misbehaved': 'He asked me how I would like to "rid myself" and "overcome this" and used biblical quotes to back up what he said.' Ball's 'immense personality' made it hard for the victim even to consider saying anything to anyone. He says:

Even when he was not there, he was there. I know it is difficult for people outside of such dynamics to understand, but I felt beholden and loyal to him. I believed that he had recognised something spiritually unique in me. To even imagine that there was something improper in his behaviour was a form of disloyalty, so it was not something I consciously considered.

The account shows the highly controlling nature of the relationships that Ball encouraged. These relationships were based on subjugation with the understanding that Ball was superior and entitled to rule over those who followed him; these were master/disciple relationships. The mutual beatings and abuse that took place Ball linked to a spiritual discipline of 'entering into the sufferings of Christ'. Again, this felt deeply uncomfortable but the victim was 'being told by a saintly man that it was natural to feel uncomfortable because otherwise it would not be a sacrifice'. This he was told was the path to God: 'I felt that this must be right and identified his [Ball's] will with God's will.' Furthermore, 'It was a slow process with me as to how much of what happened to me with Bishop Peter was abuse and how much was just religious and spiritual life.' Later the victim realised how much he had been excusing Ball and the true extent of the abuse – physical, sexual, emotional and spiritual – that had been perpetrated against him.

In the report, 'An Abuse of Faith', Ball's method of grooming boys and young men is discussed and it is noted how his abuse was 'charged with religious intensity' and the way in which he exploited the Anglo-Catholic tradition of the significance of ritual. These religious rites became 'a mask for abuse, and theology [was] used as a way of justifying abuse' and, indeed, the message that being abused in this way made 'the victims more special and more holy'.[8] Some men, who reported Ball anointing their penis while they were naked, were told by him that it was a way of enabling every part of their body to be part of God. When one victim who was abused for many years tried to leave, Ball persuaded him that his unhappiness was appropriate, that it evidenced the sacrifices he was making for God. This man described how there was some awareness in their community of how controlling and deceitful Ball was – he was referred to (covertly) as 'Snidey Pete'. However, he was skilled in exploiting an ethic of forgiveness – he would express contrition and, in that religious environment, it was always expected that he should be forgiven for what he had done. The Gibb report accepts that Ball was undoubtedly a man with charisma and a powerful orator, who through his eloquence commanded trust and commitment and influenced many people. However, he was also highly manipulative and a 'master of self-deceit' and, as someone with a narcissistic personality, he failed to consider anyone other than himself. The report highlights the contradiction between Ball's professed dedication to a monastic way of life and his reluctance to submit to the authority of the Church. Alongside this was his desire for recognition from the establishment. By founding and leading a religious community, he created, 'a cohort of devoted disciples. He actively sought high office and elicited the support of well-connected individuals to further his cause. A picture emerges of a man driven by a desire both for followers and for the endorsement of the establishment.'

Charismatic Power and Mental Illness

The Christian Church has a long history of charismatic and inspiring leaders, as indeed do other religions. These leaders exert a powerful influence and domination over their followers, so a 'cult of personality' and 'high-profile names' develops. If this cult of personality is accentuated by positive media attention, then the Church is very happy to be associated with this 'success' and benefit from it. For example, Peter Ball was interviewed in his monk's outfit on the Terry Wogan show and supported over years by many well-known people, including royalty. However, charisma is very often linked, as in the case of Ball, with mental illness, such as a narcissistic personality disorder, and the domination of followers and supporters can quickly become abusive and corrupt. The movement or the religious organisation that the charismatic leader has set up can be seen as an extension of his personality, though this may initially be obscured by his teachings. In the case of Ball this included a perverted form of sexual excitement based on sado-masochism, which he camouflaged in the form of different religious rituals that would bring him and the victim closer to God. The sado-masochism became all-embracing over time, and thus prescriptions for belief and daily behaviours – such as the cold showers and praying naked – became permitted and prescribed acts, whereas masturbation became the route into sexual aggression and punishment beatings. For some of those who stayed in his scheme and the so-called 'monastic' order, the rules may initially have seemed a relief as coming from an outside adult authority, an auxiliary superego, and so a way of someone else dealing with the young person's difficult sexual feelings and their problems. Leaders who move firmly away from the established way of doing things can very much appeal to those looking for a vehicle for rebellion and outsmarting tradition.[9]

Looking further at the delusional nature of Ball's charisma, it can be seen that because of the narcissistic nature of his relationships, and what can be seen as the permeability of his ego boundaries, he experienced others and dealt with them as part of his self. So those important figures in the establishment who admired him, such as Prince Charles, Lord Lloyd and Archbishop George Carey, provided a boost to Ball's persona and his clearly fragile ego and self-regard. However, for Ball, aware at some level of his own perversion, those living with him who admitted their desire for masturbation came to represent the unacceptable shadow part of himself, and so punishing them by beatings and so on, and encouraging them to beat him, relieved Ball sexually and satisfied his sado-masochism. Ball's demand to take on the punishment he was inflicting on others might have been presented on the surface as Christ-like, and so rationalised theologically, but ultimately his control over others represented his unconscious attempts to control himself.

The psychoanalytical psychotherapist Daniel Shaw offers some helpful thinking about the traumatising narcissist – and one could indeed see that almost all the perpetrators discussed in this book fall into this category because they are either sadistic and/or sociopathic, and their relationships are characterised by a striking incapacity to tolerate a subjective authentic voice in those around them. The traumatising narcissist's disavowal of his own feelings of vulnerability and dependence takes place in a relational system in which the victim is often induced into a role of worshipful admirer: 'The heightened sadistic tendencies of the traumatizing narcissist may be masked in some cases by charisma and seductive charm.' By projecting his or her own dependency needs and vulnerabilities (needs that were never met in his childhood, because they were themselves the object of a parent's narcissistic strivings) onto others, 'the traumatizing narcissist achieves a complete super-idealisation of him- or herself'.[10] This leads to delusional feelings of infallibility and entitlement. To keep this false state of mind intact demands that all the badness is projected into others and all the good is kept within. It is notable that the statements issued by Ball, from the time of accepting the caution in Gloucestershire until, and after, his trial in 2015, demonstrate his aggressive defence of his own righteousness (in order to keep his own shame away), which can make sense as a psychotic delusion.

Charisma is undoubtedly power but it is power of a particular nature, which is the ability to create an illusion. The charismatic personality gives an appearance of exceptional self-confidence and of strength and authority, which inspires trust, confidence and adulation in others, but the psychological drive behind this is actually a profound insecurity, expressed in the overwhelming need to win adoration from and control over others. Church leaders who are charismatic have the power to affect others through awe and this has been used for a variety of purposes but inevitably, because of the person's narcissism, leads to ongoing demands for praise and special treatment, with associated grandiosity and arrogance often rationalised by feelings of entitlement. Again, this originates in childhood, where meeting the demands of a parent, whose interest and approval was desperately wanted, can lead to an adulthood in which others are manipulated to fulfil these unmet needs and used to fill the emotional void left by childhood neglect and abandonment. Often sexual compulsivity combined with the drive for power and control can be part of the charismatic personality. The leader needs the follower almost more than the other way round, and the need is ultimately for so-called relationships in which the other person is subjugated and dependent; defeating and controlling the follower keeps the leader from insanity. The effect on the follower over time is the gradual loss of his ability to know who he is. The follower's subjectivity is hijacked and (as discussed in Chapter 3) successfully solipsised. Each one of us is potentially vulnerable to being drawn in by a charismatic church leader, indeed most people long to be inspired. Similarly, each charismatic church leader has the potential to become corrupted by power, excited by self-aggrandisement, then for the universal potentialities of sadism and masochism to become activated, and the use of power to seduce, coerce, belittle, humiliate and intimidate others for the ultimate purpose of psychological enslavement and parasitic exploitation.

Power, once one has it, seems very attractive both psychologically and materially. Yet, once power is attained, there comes the shadow fear of losing it and, with the loss, also all the benefits. Ironically, the fear of loss of power may prompt increasingly abusive and self-serving behaviour. Before falling herself, Aung San Suu Kyi presciently said: 'It is not power that corrupts but fear. Fear of losing power corrupts those who wield it and fear of the scourge of power corrupts those who are subject to it.'[11] If charismatic power is based on psychological deficits, as was the case of the two men discussed in this chapter, then the fear of losing power threatens the innermost part of the person. It is this fear of psychological collapse that then heightens the need to dominate and control those whom one influences. As explored earlier, in the religious context this deep psychological need becomes dressed up in religious justifications. The leader by claiming closeness to God (or even unity with God) can therefore claim to be exempt from the usual social or moral restrictions. Followers, crucial for the leader, are offered salvation, noble and sweeping goals, and structure and certainty and to be part of a community. Once again, here is the traumatising narcissist, discussed earlier, often with paranoid and megalomaniacal tendencies who needs to seduce and manipulate followers into submission. However, that which is presented as surrender to God is really a demand for submission to the leader, and the follower becomes increasingly concerned about approval and unclear whether disapproval from the leader is then also disapproval from God.[12]

Over time the fear that develops in cult followers and in victims of ongoing sexual abuse has been likened to what happens to victims of terrorism and domestic violence. The ultimate effect is to convince the victim that the perpetrator is omnipotent, that resistance is futile and that the victim's life depends upon winning the perpetrator's indulgence through absolute compliance. The goal of the perpetrator is to instil in his victim not only fear of death but also gratitude for being allowed to live.[13] As with all pathological narcissists, it becomes important for his sanity that he, the leader, alone feels shameless. While apparently inviting others to attain his state of perfection (shamelessness) by following him, the charismatic cult leader is actually constantly involved in inducing shame in his followers, thereby maintaining dominance and control. The therapist Shaw calls this sado-masochistic *danse macabre* the 'dark side of enlightenment'.[14] Often the 'ego' is seen as something small and full of selfish pride that needs to be defeated as part of self-surrender to the charismatic leader, and thereby to God, so that it can be transformed into something 'higher'. Nothing should belong to the self, so, strangely, enslavement is reframed as the highest form of liberation and alienation from oneself as the highest form of connection. This explains why people, once they have managed to get themselves away from such a leader, need time to regain a sense of who they are. One church leader whose pathology gradually unravelled is discussed in this next section.

The Charismatic Cult Leadership of Chris Brain

A cult can often be defined largely on the basis of the personality of the leader. In this part of the chapter we explore the rise and fall of Chris Brain and the Nine O'Clock Service (NOS), an organisation fêted, acclaimed and hugely admired by the Church of England hierarchy for bringing in large numbers of young people to an exciting and radically different form of worship that could be called neo-charismatic evangelism. While Peter Ball followed the Anglo-Catholic tradition, Chris Brain was inspired by the charismatic movement that emerged from the Pentecostal Church and influenced by John Wimber a founding leader of the Vineyard Church. The glossary of the Church of England defines the emphasis of charismatics as 'on the working of the Holy Spirit in healing, prophecy and miracles in the church today, and on the direct revelation of God's will to the individual believer'.[15]

As Parsons writes, 'much good has been released into the church by the charismatic movement, but... charismatic churches have, in some places, become infected with authoritarian styles of leadership of a fundamentalist kind'.[16] Writing about such church communities, Parsons notes the way in which the 'discipling process' causes 'the personalities of members to be changed to fit in with the group norm' and how this was 'chillingly and abusively at work in the Nine O'Clock Service in Sheffield in the mid-1990s'. One of the interesting things about the rise of the unconventional NOS was the full support and endorsement of the hierarchy: 'NOS was a Church of England flagship congregation not simply because of its experimental worship, which resembled a state-of-the-art nightclub with film loops, projections, multi-track mixing desks and "attitude", but also because of its radical state-of-the-art "post-modern" theology.'[17]

Roland Howard in his examination of what happened in NOS describes how this new church was facing up to important issues of the day, largely ignored by the mainstream churches, such as the environment, poverty, racism and sexuality, and reaching out in an intelligent way to those aged under 30. At its height it attracted huge numbers – over 400 young people – and appeared a radical, challenging and vibrant form of Christianity. Many disillusioned evangelicals and charismatics felt they had found a new home. Most people look for leaders and all of us search for psychological or spiritual transformation, especially in young adulthood. One late teen is quoted as saying, 'It was incredible. I loved the music, I experienced God, it was a dream come true and the people were real, normal people, not the usual church types. They accepted and valued me for who I was.'[18] Undoubtedly, Brain's use of theatricality in ritual and in the music and light shows amplified his charisma and stimulated many into transformative states, what the sociologist Émile Durkheim referred to as 'collective effervescence'.[19] Within such a setting, spiritual ecstasy can become expected and Brain relied on the professionalism and power of the rituals to affect those attending.[20] Ultimately, Brain's sound and light services were impression management and, once his abusive narcissism and frailties began to undermine the illusion of specialness that had been cultivated, then disenchantment set in. Behaviour presented frontstage began to conflict with behaviour backstage and, once the cognitive dissonance became too great to be accommodated, then the illusion collapsed.[21]

Brain had converted to the evangelical wing as a teenager and initially attended a Baptist church, before moving to attend an Anglican church with livelier worship and charismatic leanings. He set up a rock band and through this he and other band members began to promote a vision of how church could be and to experiment with prophecy and speaking in tongues. They set up a community where income was shared and relationship boundaries began to blur, based largely on the vision and ideas of Brain who was beginning to be seen by many as a prophet. He had a powerful and charismatic personality and, after John Wimber's visit to Sheffield, Canon Robert Warren of St Thomas' Church persuaded Brain and the community he had established to set up a weekly service. This took place at nine in the evening and became a huge success. As Howard writes, the church authorities really started to take notice when, in 1989, David Lunn, the Bishop of Sheffield confirmed nearly one hundred people, 'they were thrilled by the growth in numbers among these young people that the church had thus far failed to reach'.[22] Many clergy attended the services, one archdeacon stating on a documentary made about the NOS, that he found it, 'creative, exciting, dynamic'.[23] Phil Catalfo, who attended the 'Planetary Mass' in San Francisco in 1994 described the whole service and the press conference held afterwards, and commented:

> Apparently the Anglican hierarchy embraces this trend not only as a cool way to attract the media-bred younger generation back into the church, but also as a natural expression of contemporary spirituality and an appropriate response to humanity's predicament. At this same press conference, Bishop Swing [the aptly named then Episcopal Bishop of California] – who was seen shaking his holiness during the service – also spoke. 'The Mass we saw tonight was like John the Baptist – a forerunner. I was very excited by tonight.'[24]

Brain was taken by Warren to meet George Carey just before he was made Archbishop of Canterbury in 1990 and Warren recalls how impressed Carey was by Brain and his alternative worship. However, with the success of his own prophetic and Christ-like role, Brain's need to dominate and control deepened. He initiated a system which was extremely good at controlling both the leaders that he had put in place and the membership. Over the years his increasingly angry outbursts and mind-controlling techniques meant that the followers began to adapt to the abuses of power, including what they wore (black clothes with strong make-up for the women), what they ordered when out with him (only what Brain drank and ate), what they did with their money (donate it) and what they did, including giving up their work and, for some, sexual involvement with Brain. Many of the followers: 'thinking that they had a special relationship with him, had shared their vulnerabilities with him on a deep and intimate level. Most thought he had divinely given insights and gifts' and that to please Brain was to please God.[25] This meant that those being abused became increasingly fragile.

Hypersensitivity surrounded any behaviour that might be seen as a challenge to Brain; there was genuine fear of his reaction and the humiliation of being on the end of his verbal attacks. In 1990 the church authorities encouraged Brain to go for ordination and, while training, Brain instituted something he called the Homebase Team. This was a group of women (and one man) to help around his house (by then he and his wife had a baby, although the followers were discouraged from having children). For the women, duties included putting Brain to bed with sexual contact; they were to be seen as post-modern nuns. One member of NOS, who was head of the pastoral department, thought that Brain had a psychological need to sexually dominate women because he had initiated a process of sexual grooming which the NOS member likened to an abuse factory. In 1992 Brain's ordination was rushed through by the Church and the normal procedure of being a curate under an experienced vicar was waived by the bishop. After a huge success at the Greenbelt Arts Festival, a rave worship in front of 15,000 people that also elicited criticism for the erotic overtones and post-modern theology, Brain demanded a new venue for NOS and the diocese put in a huge effort to find them accommodation in central Sheffield. It was here that Brain staged the first 'Planetary Mass', the forerunner to the one described above and where he became involved with the American creation spirituality theologian Matthew Fox and drawn into the offer of setting up similar worship in California.

However, 'it was inevitable that – with a leader abusing dozens of women [one estimate put this at between 40-60], undermining the marriages of his leaders, emotionally and psychologically abusing those that had contact with him – the bubble was going to burst'.[26] The first woman, who raised the alarm in 1992 with the bishop of Sheffield, had her concerns about idolatry and abuse of power dismissed and her complaints blamed on her 'mental illness'. However, in early 1994 Brain took a break from leading services and moved to California. Stephen Lowe, the archdeacon who had found the service so dynamic, was by this time relieved, 'there was increasing evidence . . . of what one might call Chris's hyper-messianic qualities, and I was becoming increasingly uneasy and said to the bishop that I was worried that he was looking and sounding too much like someone playing Jesus'. He had shoulder-length hair, a grand pectoral cross and was surrounded by disciples.[27] When some clergy complained about the post-modern theology, they were reassured that the diocese was overseeing NOS. When Brain's mother-in-law expressed her reservations about his abuse of power, Lowe, believing that Brain had reduced his involvement in the Church, saw it only as a relationship issue between a mother and her daughter. Early in 1995 one woman contacted Bishop Lunn and Stephen Lowe to say that she wanted NOS stopped, she recounted her experiences of sexual improprieties and said she thought it was a cult. Lowe reassured her by saying he attended regularly; her response was: 'They're used to dealing with people like you; go and look in the corners and find out what's really going on.' She believed that 'they weren't interested in hearing what she had to say, they were only interested in their showcase theological experiment'.[28] Brain was given a formal warning but later that year NOS was made an Extra-Parochial Place by an Act of Parliament, 'the Church of England's first sociological parish'.[29]

THE RESPONSE OF THE CHURCH HIERARCHY TO THE COLLAPSE OF NOS

When Brain provocatively described NOS as putting 'a bomb in the back pocket of the Anglican Church',[30] he had not been prophesying the media interest that surrounded its disintegration in 1995. That summer Archdeacon Lowe was contacted again by a number of women who told him about the manipulation and abuse and that the service was a sham, a grand elaborate façade. They were finally heard and believed. This led to the resignation of the NOS leadership team and the internal collapse of the organisation, once it was clear how many victims were involved. Brain was moved by the church hierarchy to a psychiatric hospital for a fortnight as the extent of his powers of manipulation and unreality became clearer and the Church tried to find counsellors and listeners for nearly 150 victims: 'NOS members' trauma was such that some people were hitting themselves against walls and mutilating themselves . . . the trauma was so great because of the sexual, emotional and spiritual nature of the manipulation.'[31] The decision by the diocese that they had insufficient funds to pay for all the victims' counselling caused fury among the members who felt that the Church was in some part responsible for their priest's destructive behaviour, and who wanted experts in cult behaviour to be involved: 'It seemed to many congregation members that the Anglican Church was unwilling to use the word "cult" because of the negative publicity that such an admission would create.'³² Lowe's response was to question whether he had been attending a cult that was open for public worship on a Sunday. The media attention was huge and the church hierarchy found itself at the forefront. George Carey was reported as saying that he felt really let down and 'saddened', statements that evoked fury amongst the victims who in turn stated that they were let down by the church hierarchy who had pastoral responsibility and who should have managed Brain. On the documentary made about NOS, one victim said about Carey, '*He* felt let down . . .' Another said:

> I feel incredibly let down by the hierarchy's response . . . at least come and stand with us . . . and come and say 'yes' this happened in the Church. It is possible for this to happen . . . you came to trust and this has happened to you because you wanted God and something good.³³

Clearly, as Lowe stated, everyone from the top down had been hoodwinked by Brain. Carey in his autobiography (in which, incidentally, he makes no mention of Peter Ball) shows no insight into the psychology of what happens in cults and abusive relationships, when he lays part of the blame on the victims, especially those caught up in Brain's sexual improprieties:

> They were, I said, intelligent and articulate people. How could they say that they were misled and duped by the Church? They were responsible adults. If Christian morality had any part to play in their faith, surely they too must share some of the blame? There seemed no willingness to hear this. Nevertheless, I was determined that lessons should be learnt from the affair and that any other experiments in the Church of England should be properly supervised.³⁴

His last comment suggests some acknowledgement that there was culpability in the lack of supervision of Brain. Bishop Lunn similarly fought back against the failure of the hierarchy to monitor what was going on by refusing to accept any blame; he viewed what happened as reflecting a time of 'extraordinarily loose sexual morals' and that 'sin is with us always'. He added, 'If the bishop

7. Charismatic Power and Control

was responsible for every sermon preached, every service taken, every action of every clergyman and lay leader in the diocese it wouldn't work. . . . I am puzzled what sort of accountability people are seeking for.'[35] Lunn denied the enormity of the collapse of NOS, although five years earlier in 1990 he had stated on BBC Radio 4 that NOS had 'a permanent significance',[36] such that, when the history books were written, 'a new development in the way we understand the Christian religion' could be traced to what was happening at St Thomas'. Following the allegations, Lunn stated: 'I still find it difficult to understand why the BBC and the media in general have managed to convince themselves that the problems of a single congregation in a single diocese have represented a crisis of management of mega proportions for the Church of England.'[37] Brain had successfully groomed the church hierarchy by increasingly pushing the boundaries in the liturgy, openly abusing them, and at the same time tantalising them by offering them reflected glory in his success with attracting young adults. However, their response lacked any understanding of what happens in such manipulative power games. It also left them unable to accept the part they had played – also as apparently responsible adults – and the general lack of accountability and supervision.

Linda Woodhead, commenting on the relationship between NOS and the hierarchy, notes that Brain and the leadership team held the Anglican Church in contempt.[38] Brain had spoken of himself as a 'Moses leading his people out of the Egypt of Anglicanism into the Promised Land of club culture reclaimed for God'. His teaching contradicted nearly every custom, practice and rule in the Anglican book. Woodhead sees 'this willingness of some of our senior churchmen to abandon all that has historically made Anglicanism what it is . . . stands out as one of the most shocking features of the whole NOS affair'. She sees what she terms the 'wise monkey syndrome . . . a refusal to see, hear, or speak of evil'.

The Christian faith is founded on a charismatic figure – Jesus Christ, who invites followers to change their lives and reflect his teachings. Jesus also warned against false prophets 'who come to you in sheep's clothing but inwardly are ravenous wolves' (Matthew 7.15). Both Peter Ball and Chris Brain appeared as welcome prophets, not only to individual seekers of spiritual inspiration and guidance, but also in the sense of enlivening and reviving the church. This meant that the hierarchy were willingly seduced by both men and embraced them, even when serious doubts were raised about their authenticity. The Church is hungry for success and power, to salvation and redemption, and relief from frustration and inhibition. This makes the institution itself vulnerable for what the charismatic leader appears to offer. On that basis, the hierarchy and many of the followers will staunchly defend the charismatic leader for as long as they can.

8.
The Influence of the Public School Ethos within the Institutional Church

> I also recall him talking about his own days as a pupil at Lancing College in Sussex and how prefects would beat younger boys as a release of sexual frustration. He said that was not the reason for the beating that I had endured.[1]
> *Quoted by David Greenwood*

Dame Moira Gibb, in her report, *An Abuse of Faith*, noted the links between Peter Ball and public schools, and his connections with such schools both as governor and in ministry.[2] Ball had also established personal relationships with the heads of the schools he visited – some of whom continued to champion his cause even after his resignation. Indeed, Ball continued to go into schools following his demotion. In 1996, George Carey agreed to Ball carrying out priestly duties in schools, although later Carey raised concerns 'apparently forgetting that he had already sanctioned this'.[3] Ball clearly felt at home in these schools, part of the system, and, as it turns out, incorporated a number of the experiences that he would have known about as a public schoolboy into the way that he ran his projects and his quasi-monastic community before his first arrest.

In this chapter it is suggested that some of the same traditional values found in British public schools have deeply influenced the institutional church and so continue to affect the way that the Church responds to child sexual abuse allegations against clergy. Historically Britain's public schools were closely tied to the church and many continue to have close links, some sharing priests and teachers. The focus is on boys' boarding schools, and in the first part of this chapter their general ethos is explored. Whilst there is an argument that things have changed now that many of the schools have become co-educational and there is increased understanding on safeguarding, the basic idea of removing children from their parents to be formed by others is still fundamental, and the emotional damage done by this is key to understanding the way that the Church has responded to abuse allegations. Such schooling aims to achieve entry into the upper parts of the professions, and social access to resources and opportunities, where the boy feels entitled and deserving of being part of the elite. However, such privilege and sense of entitlement comes at a cost, and in the second part of the chapter the painful experiences of the abuse perpetrated through the Iwerne camps – Christian evangelical summer camps run for public school boys – is discussed. The third part links the effect of the schooling on both the adult individual and on the institutional church, and teases out how the public school/boarding school ethos has infiltrated and embedded itself to the extent of generally framing the responses to allegations against the clergy.

What Is the Ethos?

The ethos includes various male values and attitudes developed in both preparatory schools and public schools; some preparatory schools are day, whilst others are boarding schools. The good schools guide explains that, 'the main aim of prep schools is to prepare pupils for entry to private secondary schools at either eleven or thirteen. Traditionally, pre-preps take children from age three or four and prepare them to move to a prep school at age seven or eight.'[4] There have been a number of books published and documentaries broadcast about the emotional disorientation and long-term damage for children leaving home to start at boarding prep schools.[5] One parent, also a director at the Independent Association of Prep Schools, has other views.

8. The Influence of the Public School Ethos within the Institutional Church

'Never let someone at a dinner party tell you you're heartless for sending a child to board,' she says. 'From the outside, it seems odd and parents can be easily criticised but in fact it's so good for the child that it is often the parents who put their children first, who are choosing boarding prep schools.' Another writes, 'A governor of Stowe told me that boys are better brought up by their peer group – a positive one, fostered in a good environment, and in that moment I got it.' As the website notes, 'Keeping children busy is what boarding preps excel at; busy children don't have time to be homesick.'[6] Homesickness is another term for the loss and grief experienced when the child is taken from his home.

Traditionally, boys' boarding schools stressed the values of sportsmanship, manliness and devotion to duty, and one hundred and fifty years ago sought to prepare boys for a life of imperial service.[7] The end result was to be 'a Christian gentleman . . . who played by the rules, and whose highest aim was to serve others'.[8] The training of boys on the playing fields of public schools was supposed to produce 'manly' men, and biographies of military heroes presented a picture of the idealised Christian gentleman, represented as being at the forefront of empire, spreading civilisation and Christianity to the 'darker' regions of the earth.[9] 'Christ would have played hard for his school. . . . He might have rowed for his Varsity, if there'd been a Varsity to row for', the novelist Arthur Calder-Marshall was told at St Paul's. Calder-Marshall states that he soon gave up religion for mutual masturbation.[10]

This outdated ethos lingers on, partly because men who went to public schools (as their fathers and grandfathers did before them) are still dominant in positions of power in the core of the establishment – including the Church. This means that there is a difficulty in changing the structure of the institutional church because the commitment of a powerful group to the institution derives not only from the institution itself, but also from their earlier experience of having been formed apart from parents and family to be part of the elite. In the law, the army, the Church, politics and in journalism are men with what has been called a sense of entitlement 'that in adulthood expresses itself as a feeling of belonging and comfort, and a willingness to ask for what the individual wants or needs'. There is a sense of self-assurance which arises from an appreciation of one's own qualities or abilities, and that these will be recognised. This kind of confidence 'whispers "you're special" – just like those who came before you'. It is feeling entitled to be present, entitled to be there, entitled to be heard, entitled to be recognised, entitled to be promoted[11] and, one might add in the context of this book, entitled to have sexual conquests where and when you want and to beat others the way you were beaten. This is also entitlement but destructive entitlement – the 'it didn't do me any harm' kind.

The influence of boarding schools on the Church is not only about values and traditions but also about direct experience, because the privilege offered through such an education is also inevitably painful. Two studies, in 2014 and 2016, confirm that 'a significant percentage of clergy. . . and the greater part of the senior leadership of the church were educated privately'. David Runcorn notes, 'formed within a very particular male-only educational culture that was characterised by such values as: toughness as character building, devotion to the team, distrust of women, suppression of emotion, assumptions of patriarchal and hierarchical social ordering, mocking of any feminine trait in men and minimal empathy for the weak and ordinary.'[12] There is every chance that many senior officials responding to hearing an abuse allegation have also been damaged by some level of trauma themselves, although clearly in a different context. They will have inevitably experienced abandonment, broken parental attachments and hidden despair but will also have learnt to deny and compartmentalise all feelings attached to this.

Studies have shown that to survive their 'homesick soul' children develop a 'boarded heart'[13] and an 'armoured self'[14] because weakness, dependence and vulnerability had to be repressed. Mark Stibbe, a former Anglican vicar, gives the seven most common statements of deprivation from ex-boarders: deprived of love, home, safety, childhood, siblings, innocence and freedom. The reality of bullying, physical formation through team sport, obsession with rules and authoritarianism, and knowledge of all forms of abuse: emotional, neglect, sexual and physical, jostle uneasily somewhere in the child's psyche: 'The conclusion is inevitable: this experience turns boarders into orphans and boarding houses into orphanages.'[15]

The emotional suppression demanded is sadly exemplified, albeit unintentionally, in one promotional example given, where a boy attended a day school which required leaving on a bus at 7.30 in the morning and getting home at 5pm, 'he was always exhausted and vile to her [his mother]'. The parents then sent him to board at the Dragon School in Oxford and 'got their son back, a charming, mature and polite young boy now on his way to Eton.' The Dragon School will be encountered in a more negative context below. Boarding schools successfully deny feelings and produce a polished persona – supposedly much less trouble until it all catches up with you.[16] For, unless you have accepted and integrated your own trauma, it is not possible to hear and appropriately respond to trauma in another. This may go some way in explaining the manner that certain church officials use to respond to victims, including rejecting the reality of what has happened. The associated lack of understanding and subsequent careless ill-treatment reflects how their earlier trauma was handled and minimised. The victim also presents as a danger, a reminder of the hidden victimhood within the church official. Stibbe calls the damage done an untreated wound that affects almost every sphere of British society including the institutional church: 'Many in these different arenas betray this unhealed desolation. They succeed in what they do at work but they fail at what matters most at home . . . emotionally handicapped, incapable of empathy.' He describes how many go from the boarding school into further institutions, such as the bar, the Church or the army, because the life there feels like home. Stibbe adds, 'I know. I was one of them.'[17] The public schoolboy entering the Church brings his personal unconscious pain alongside conscious privilege and also brings the experience of having grown up in a system where homosexuality and abuse is rife, where bullying covertly or overtly is almost seen as normative, where rules and keeping to the rules is the structural frame and where in the past physical punishment was seen as acceptable. The ethos includes a dislike of 'sneaking' or 'telling', alongside a dislike of the victim (despite their suffering), and some admiration for the power of the bully. All this rests uneasily alongside the suffering of Jesus Christ, which may explain the attraction of 'muscular Christianity'. In this next section I highlight the abuses perpetrated through the Iwerne camps characterised by 'muscular Christianity'.

Abuse and Bullying at the Iwerne Camps

When people write about boarding schools, they often use the word 'beatings', for being beaten was until, relatively recently, an acceptable part of the culture and given often under the guise of Christian teaching by teachers or senior pupils. This tradition of violent abuse is part of public school philosophy, but it is physical abuse. The Anglican priest and broadcaster Giles Fraser says:

> The popularity of beating children in the British educational system, and the idea that it had moral, character-forming properties, cannot be understood without the rise of so-called muscular Christianity during the second half of the nineteenth century. . . . The whole culture of public school beatings was dominated by [a] narrative of violent atonement – old men with beards thrashing young boys, apparently for their moral and spiritual education.[18]

Even when physical assault for disciplinary purposes was made illegal in the private sector (in 1998 in England and Wales, twelve years after it was outlawed in state schools), in 2001 'forty Christian schools challenged the law, arguing (unsuccessfully) in the High Court that there was a "God-given right" to chastise'.[19] Stephen Parsons draws our attention to this focus on violence:

> The tendency of generations of Protestant teachers to read into the New Testament a doctrine of atonement in terms of a wrathful Old Testament God requiring in some way the hideously cruel death of Jesus. However much the doctrine of substitutionary atonement is qualified and muted by modern writers, there are large numbers of Christians today who have a picture in their minds of God's fatherhood involving violence against his child. . . . It is small wonder that such teaching is sometimes carried over into violence against children in fundamentalist schools and families.[20]

It is this teaching that 'justified' the sadistic abuse meted out by John Smyth, who was educated at Strathcona School, a leading private school in Calgary, Canada, and at Trinity Hall, Cambridge and Trinity College, Bristol. Smyth became a barrister who chaired the Iwerne Trust during the 1970s and 1980s and, as a Christian evangelist, was a central figure in the organisation. The Iwerne Trust ran summer camps set up by E.J.H. Nash known as 'Bash' (1898-1982) as a Christian evangelical ministry to preach the gospel to the top public schools. The camp prayer was 'Lord, we claim the leading public schools for your kingdom'[21] and under Nash's leadership over 7,000 boys attended.[22] The ethos was that, if you convert the 'elite' and they were 'saved', then everyone else will follow. Nash used military terminology: he was 'commandant', his deputy, 'adjutant', and the leaders were 'officers', and this profound authoritarianism and associated control was continued after his death. Nash believed in the centrality of the crucifixion, saying: 'the only way to Mansion House is via King's Cross'.[23]

Allegations of physical abuse by Smyth that included severe naked beatings and inappropriate questioning about masturbation led to the commissioning of a report in 1982. However, the findings were not reported to the police and Smyth moved to Zimbabwe where he set up the Zambesi Ministries which ran similar summer camps for boys from elite schools and in which Smyth continued his abuse. Following pressure and publicity, Smyth was due to be extradited to the UK from South Africa to be questioned about the sado-masochistic beatings but died of a heart attack in 2018.[24]

Jonathan Fletcher, another prominent conservative evangelical, was also involved in the Iwerne organisation, alongside his brother, also a priest, David Fletcher, who actually ran the camps in the 1970s and 1980s and who commissioned the 1982 report on Smyth. Jonathan Fletcher had attended the Iwerne camps from the age of fourteen and went on to become a regular speaker and dormitory leader and remained very much linked to the regime there. He had been educated at Repton School in the 1950s and 1960s, a school from which a number of headmasters in the twentieth century moved on to senior positions in the Church of England. It is also a school where 'fagging' apparently continued into the late twentieth century and where, according to Jeremy Clarkson, bullying was rife in the 1970s. In 2018 there were a number of serious concerns about safeguarding raised, involving four members of staff and allegations of sexual abuse and inappropriate behaviour.[25] Fletcher moved in 'the upper echelons of society' and, following his ordination, remained involved in boarding schools, as director of Stowe School for over twenty years, and serving on the council for the evangelical college Wycliffe Hall. Worth noting also is Fletcher's membership of the private dining club, Nobody's Friends, discussed in Chapter 6 (which Peter Ball was rumoured to attend). Fletcher ministered at a number of churches and was seen as gifted and charismatic and hugely influential, a senior player in the conservative movement of the Church which has led opposition to women and LGB people. He was the vicar at Emmanuel Church in Wimbledon, southwest London, for 30 years from 1982 until 2012, which is when allegations of spiritual abuse were levelled against him and Fletcher agreed to withdraw from all aspects of ministry. The alleged abuse by Fletcher of young men in the Church has all the hallmarks of the Smyth naked beatings and bullying, and the sexual perversity of the Ball cold showers, naked massage and sexually inappropriate comments and questions on and punishment for masturbation.[26] It included evidence of boarding school culture as Fletcher minimised what happened in the statement he produced, explaining his actions as 'Going without chocolate, cold baths and school-type gym punishments'. One adult victim from Emmanuel Church who had, like a number of the others, first met Fletcher at the Iwerne summer camps stated that 'among the carrots offered by Mr Fletcher, was the sense that "you were joining the elite"' He added, 'There is a part of the church that's absorbed that public school fagging system – where the older boys treat the younger boys in a demeaning way.... It's all set up perfectly, so that you can never sustain any criticism.'[27] Press articles and further publicity from victims, plus reports of the flouting by Fletcher of his 2017 ban from further ministry, led to a statement by Emmanuel Church in late 2019 detailing the commission of an independent review. This will investigate to what extent the cultural context at the church provided an environment for such abuse to occur and not be disclosed and in which way safeguarding policy has evolved. Fletcher has denied abuse and claims that anything that happened was agreed and non-sexual, saying 'the punishments were (a) consensual and (b) mutual'. Here the effect of the public school regime is clear, the sexual activity is aggressive and narcissistic, characteristic of early adolescence with the interweaving of forbidden pleasure and punishment linked to confessions of masturbation. Fletcher claims that for him the activities were mutual, thus demonstrating both his lack of concern for the victim and his inability to appreciate the other man as separate and different, hence the significance of his use of the term 'we' in his apology and his focus on the reputation of the organisation: 'Although at the time we definitely did not think we were doing anything wrong, I've seen since that it could have caused much harm both to individuals and to the reputation of conservative evangelicalism for which I am profoundly sorry.'[28]

The physical abuse alleged against Smyth and Fletcher contains a sexual aspect, as the 1982 report on Smyth admits, so, clearly, the biblical teaching on atonement followed by both men was experienced as at some level, consciously or unconsciously, exciting. Sigmund Freud in his study of male beating phantasies links it originally to an incestuous attachment to the father, where the beating is a form of homoerotic love.[29] Smyth reworked what Freud called a 'sexual perversion' through his atonement theology into a form of warranted redemption or purification. He groomed and coerced boys and young men through this theology. As Charles Foster, who attended Iwerne camps for a number of years, writes, 'Without penal substitution, John Smyth would have had no thrashing shed in his back garden.' He continues:

> The theology was banal, stern, and cruel – a set of suffocatingly simple propositions held with steely eyed zeal. Its insistence on penal substitution and nothing but penal substitution embodied and tacitly encouraged the notion that ultimate good depended on violence. . . . [It] chimed perfectly with our politics, our sociology, and the grounds of our self-esteem. . . . God . . . was a headmaster, and we liked it that way, since headmasters were one of the only things we really understood. Mystery and nuance were diabolical. . . . Emotion was taboo. . . . For most of us it was a relief to hear this: our schooling and conditioning had left us emotionally stunted, and it was good to know that this stuntedness was what God wanted.[30]

Foster now sees Iwerne as a cult that encouraged a 'sort of nostalgic infantilism' and helped to manage the insecurity, the emotional immaturity and the damage from the public school experience: 'We needed personal and theological assurance more than most – perhaps particularly because we had to keep up the pretence of poise and infallibility. And, like most people, we loved easy answers'. In the UK a number of the Iwerne camp teenage victims attended Winchester College; Smyth also lived in Winchester and at least twenty-two boys were physically abused in Smyth's garden shed in Winchester 'to purge them from their sins . . . some so severe the victims were left bleeding'. One victim disclosed that Smyth made the boys admit to masturbation and told them they 'must bleed for Jesus' – before the beating they were made to say a prayer. The unnamed victim said that he received 8,000 strokes of the cane over a number of years.[32] Justin Welby Archbishop of Canterbury was a dormitory officer at the camps but denied knowledge of the abuses, saying that he first knew about the allegations in 2013. He did eventually issue an 'unreserved and unequivocal' apology on behalf of the Church, admitting that it had 'failed terribly' to tackle institutional abuse.[33] The physical abuse went on for many years and young men, such as the late Simon Doggart, who had previously himself been beaten by Smyth, were recruited to repeat the abuse on others. A victim told the BBC, 'Simon was completely brainwashed. I think even then I sensed that it wasn't my friend beating me: it was actually John Smyth beating me, using my friend to carry out his abuse.'[34] It is worth noting that Doggart later became headmaster of Caldicott, a prestigious preparatory boarding school, where, although there has been no suggestion that any pupils were harmed by him, teachers based at the school, who were members of a paedophile ring which included a former headmaster, Peter Wright, were convicted in 2014 of serious child sexual abuse.[35]

Bullying, which is unwanted aggressive behaviour against someone, is associated with both physical and sexual abuse, and has in the past been seen as another part of the required toughening up process of the public school system. Bullying can, of course, happen in any school setting, or indeed in any organisation, including the institutional church, despite measures to tackle this. Unfortunately, those who are vulnerable excite sadism in those whose vulnerability needs to be kept hidden and the greater the vulnerability of the victim, the greater the sadistic excitement for the one who bullies. This defensive thrill and the intoxicating feeling of power that goes with it can become addictive, which certainly seems to have been the case for Smyth, and possibly for Fletcher. In some schools licensed bullying and exploitation was built into the structure, for example, fagging, in which younger pupils were required to act as personal servants to 'entitled' seniors, featured 'at Eton until 1980, and at many of its cohorts until more recently'[36] and insubordination could result in a beating. The actor Simon Williams remembers his morning duties at Harrow, 'to spit and polish my prefect's shoes (even his rugby boots), to serve him tea and toast, make his bed, run his bath and fetch his paper (the *Daily Express*, for heaven's sake). It was also my duty to sit on the lavatory he intended to use after breakfast in order to warm the seat for him. "And don't you bloody well do anything in there, Williams, I don't want you stinking the place out."'[37]

Bullies usually feel inadequate inside and defend against being bullied but being part of a bullying culture as a child makes working co-operatively difficult later in life unless the inner bully has been owned and integrated. Reporting bullying is sometimes called 'sneaking'. George Orwell called this 'the unforgiveable sin'[38] as misfortune is seen as disgraceful and therefore has to be concealed. Might some church officials feel contempt at an unconscious level for those who complain about abuse? Might the discloser of clergy abuse be an easy recipient of bullying, judged as 'weak' in an institution where victimhood is best denied and emotions left unexpressed? The toughening up from being bullied but not disclosing is both physical and mental and the result is to make the victim become impervious by emotional withdrawal. The analyst Joy Schaverien in her study of boarding school syndrome describes this as an unconscious defensive structure where in order to survive:

> A hidden compartment in the self is acquired where such experiences are locked away.... Emotionally the true self shrinks into a tiny sphere where it is no longer known.... Deep within is the hidden vulnerable child who trusts no one. The outer presentation is a tough invincible masculine image.[39]

Sexual bullying is part of the continuum of abuse experienced at public schools; this may come from other boys, prefects or teachers. The journalist George Monbiot writes about his prep school in the 1970s: 'New boys were routinely groped and occasionally sodomized by the prefects. Sexual assault was and possibly still is a feature of prep school life as innate as fried bread and British bulldogs.'[40] There may also be a fair amount of mutual masturbation, crushes and comfort from sexual behaviour, alongside abuse. The writer Francis Wheen explains:

> At my prep school, Copthorne, there was a fair bit of leaping in and out of beds in dormitories, comparing notes, and general exploration. I was sexually molested by a gym master called Charles Napier, who was always putting his hand down boys' gym shorts. . . . The only thing I can remember from Harrow is a story about a veteran physics master who, according to legend, found a couple of boys doing something in his house, and said, 'I don't mind mutual masturbation, but I draw the line at buggery.' It was quoted from time to time as a bit of an accepted rule.[41]

The boy mentioned in promotional material earlier in the chapter, who was taken from his day school and so successfully boarded at the Dragon preparatory school, may have known Dr Paul Dean, head of English in the school, who was convicted in February 2020 for possessing indecent images of children. The same small boy may have heard whispers about Derek Slade, who began his career at the Dragon School, leaving for unacceptable use of the cane when teaching Latin, and who was convicted at Ipswich Crown Court in 2010 of physically and sexually abusing pupils at two other preparatory schools, and sentenced to 21 years' imprisonment.[42] As Robert Verkaik writes, 'the history of public schools has shown that for long periods our boarding schools were breeding grounds for abuse. Predatory paedophiles and sadists roamed dormitories with impunity'.[43]

Public schools have been slow to adopt safeguarding procedures and abuse inevitably continues in the present. For example, in 2018 research using data from 24 police forces in the UK showed that, since 2012, 425 people have been accused of carrying out sexual attacks at UK boarding schools, some are historical but at least 125 people have been accused by children of recent sex attacks at boarding schools.[44] Many children, and of course this includes girls abused at girls' boarding schools, have found it extraordinarily difficult to disclose for a variety of reasons, some of which were explored earlier in the book. The added pressure in the boarding school sector is that the child is away from home and, in some cases, abuse investigations have been stopped by the combined power of ambitious parents and school heads. The reputation of the school is crucial with fee-paying parents concerned about their child's access to later education and careers and so the abusive teacher may be moved and the cases hushed-up.[45]

How the Painful Privilege of a Sense of Entitlement Influences the Church's Response to Allegations

In this section the influence of the boarding school ethos on how the Church has responded to the cases of Smyth and Fletcher is analysed, looking at the psychological strategies used personally by church officials and collectively within the institution. As discussed earlier, those who have been exposed to trauma at public school remain traumatised in adulthood; though this may not be willingly acknowledged and may be repressed. It emerges unconsciously through behaviour and reaction to events. The dismissive-avoidant style of attachment and the strategic survival personality are two ways in which boarding school survivors have learnt to cope personally, and both have greatly and insidiously influenced the collective ethos of the institutional church. A dismissive-avoidant style in relationships is shown by those who have a positive view of self and a negative view of others; such people desire a high degree of independence as they have been brought up not to depend on anyone or to reveal their needs and feelings. They tend to be defensive, suppress and hide their feelings, seek less intimacy with others and, if rejected, they distance themselves from the source of rejection.[46] The strategic survival personality has some of the same traits and is also a defensively organised personality style, 'rooted in dissociation and typical of the ex-boarder . . . this has a protective and adaptive function dedicated to avoiding trouble and surviving at all costs'.[47] At a collective level this has characterised so much of the Church's response to allegations. Nick Duffell sees two features of strategic survival which include the immediate employment of aggression as the best form of defence or, alternatively, and largely favoured by the Church, 'a "duck-dive and freeze" conflict avoidance style'. This strategic survival personality is durable partly because it becomes normalized and also because it maintains a façade of confidence and success, 'masking (sometimes barely) rigid emotional illiteracy and intimacy avoidance'.

The dismissive-avoidant style is well demonstrated by John Thorn, the headmaster of Winchester School, who, presented with the 1982 report of Smyth's abuse, responded, 'Somehow it didn't occur to one at that point to bother the police. I think now in retrospect to this ghastly man, it probably would have been more sensible to do that, but people at the time. . . . The boys on the whole didn't want that to happen.'[48] The school motto, 'Manners makyth man', lays emphasis on positive superficial appearance rather than underlying reality. The statement that the boys 'on the whole' did not want the police involved can be seen as a form of dissociation projected out onto the boys and turned into a form of bullying masquerading as innocence. The headmaster did not want the report to go further so through covert bullying, whereby the 'uncomfortable aggression is disowned . . . and the uncomfortable identity is projected',[49] the boys got the message that the allegations were to be more or less dismissed. In reality the boys were left for years carrying all the projections from Smyth, but also a projection of public school ethos which can include distaste and vicarious excitement about sex, plus feelings of shame, despair and loneliness. Collectively, as Duffell notes, the elite 'are seamlessly versed in splitting and projecting and any challenge is automatically treated with bullying'.[50] The police were not informed because the sense of entitlement enabled the Iwerne Trust to decide to ignore the criminal behaviour; the reputation of the Iwerne Trust trumped the pain of the victim, the dubious theology more important than the individual soul, the leader preserved at the expense of others. Parsons in his thorough research on the Smyth and Fletcher cases uses the words 'cover-up of monumental proportions'.[51] This includes events after Winchester when, in 1997, Smyth was charged with culpable homicide over the death of Guide Nyachuru, a sixteen-year-old who had attended an Iwerne camp in Zimbabwe. Smyth was also charged with further counts related to the treatment of other boys but the prosecution collapsed when it emerged that there was a conflict of interest.[52] After much pressure and negative publicity, an independent review was finally set up in August 2019 to include the experiences of survivors and 'also consider the actions of Church of England participants'.[53] At roughly the same time pressure led to a separate 'lessons learnt' review set up by the Scripture Union who were connected with the Iwerne summer camps.[54] In April 2020 the Trustees of the Titus Trust (previously the Iwerne Trust) finally agreed a settlement with three of Smyth's victims, stating: 'the abuse by John Smyth and Jonathan Fletcher has caused us to reflect deeply on our current culture and the historic influences upon us. . . . An independent Cultural Review will begin shortly . . .'[55]

The flurry of concern following pressure contrasts with the fact that the Smyth scandal was allowed to be hidden for so long; nothing decisive happened, even although by 2012-13 it was known about at the highest levels. Both aspects of the strategic survival personality are displayed by the institution over Smyth and Fletcher: aggression and duck-dive and freeze. Parsons writes of the enormous energy involved in allowing and arranging for Smyth to leave the UK and so continue to abuse in Zimbabwe. Here is the aggressive response of supporters and financial backers determined not only to preserve reputations and defend institutions and ideas.[56] A duck-dive and freeze response is well illustrated by Archbishop Justin Welby, who in 2018 disingenuously affirmed that Smyth was 'not actually an Anglican' (despite having been a reader in the Church of England), thereby dismissing any association with Smyth or the Iwerne organisation. Eventually, under pressure, Welby as noted earlier issued a fulsome apology.[57]

A similar dismissal and freeze have taken place in the response of the Church to Jonathan Fletcher. What Parsons calls a 'Great Silence' followed publicity about the alleged Fletcher abuses:

> No one in the Church of England has said a thing, either through an official statement or through one of the safeguarding organisations that look after this side of the Church's life. What is going on when a major national newspaper describes a scandal in the Church of England but this story is met with blanket silence? Without such statements and a determination to take action, the public is going to believe that the Church is losing (has lost?) the will to remove the appalling blight of bullying, sexual harassment and power games from within its midst. In other words, the person in the street will conclude that the Church has become institutionally abusive.[58]

Here is a strategy to dismiss/avoid/freeze and hope for the best rather than admit and confront a reality that part of the Church's structure – a special part of the structure – appears free from episcopal control. Parsons suggests that the conservative evangelical wing under the umbrella grouping of ReNew has been operating separately from the control of central church structures, and this has included Fletcher at Emmanuel in Wimbledon.

The power and money involved has meant that victims too were silenced and secrecy predominated. Fletcher, seemingly embodying the Repton school motto of *'Porta Vacat Culpa'* ('The gate is free from blame') continued a public ministry despite the withdrawal of his permission to officiate. It is worth noting that the Church of England National Safeguarding Team declined to take action against Fletcher on 'the grounds that he didn't technically work for the C of E, even though he had been a parish priest for 35 years'.[59] Martin Sewell writes that Fletcher, 'had been prematurely rehabilitated within his niche constituency which deliberately or recklessly restored him to the status of a respected teacher which enabled him to continue abusing the trust which the imprimatur confers'. As with Ball, Fletcher's supporters:

> were willing to ignore all the safeguarding training and processes which the Church of England has painstakingly put in place over recent years, in order to facilitate his continued influence. They saw the plusses, ignored the minuses, and like neglectful servants let the fox into the henhouse.... There is a breathtaking sense of arrogance about this in an area of expertise which lay wholly beyond their sphere of competence.[60]

Sewell sees this self-confidence almost as 'a church within a church'; here again is the link with the public schools 'special boys from special schools'.[61] Perhaps like the 'Bloods' that C.S. Lewis writes about at Malvern College they were 'the adored athletes and prefects [who] were an embodiment of all worldly pomp, power, and glory . . . a member of the school aristocracy', where in some settings there is a sort of diarchy. The 'Bloods' supported by popular sentiment stand over against 'an official ruling class of prefects appointed by the Masters'.[62] So evidence has emerged of lies, manipulation and Fletcher's passive aggression to his victims and to his supporters. Like Ball and Smyth, Fletcher has been protected by privilege and the powerful elite following his religious brand.[63]

Such personality types and styles of coping with relationships are encouraged by the rule-bound regimes of public schools, and some of this undoubtedly has been incorporated into the structure of the institutional church where there is the 'preoccupation with rules and the imperative not to be wrong'.[64] Again, this characteristic affects the response to allegations where it may seem that the victim has somehow broken the 'rules' of the institution by disclosing and so betraying the abuser. Perhaps it feels as if the victims have let the reputation of the side, the team, the school, the Church down. For bullying is of itself an expression of an obsession with rules, and these are rules not necessarily written down like safeguarding guidelines but deeply embedded rules that belong in the tradition of maintaining the institution. One of these may be on not 'sneaking' or telling tales about what has happened – hence the 'stiff upper lip'. This belief in regimes based on power and control is fortified by the hierarchical way the Church is structured and the emphasis on organisational rules and arcane governance. This then creates a self-generating patriarchal world and at times a self-governing world, apart and distinct from those outside.

The façade of confidence and success, the sense of entitlement affects the way the Church has responded, if only at the level of duplicity. Changing any of this immediately evokes resistance, and it is only when public pressure becomes too great that the Church has reacted. Any regime, whether the boarding school or the institutional church, demands obedience and commitment to its ways, and this can include hushing things up and hoping the trouble will die down. The Church is often likened to a family but one where what goes on behind closed doors is kept within the house, as in John Thorn's comment earlier in the chapter. The theory of hegemonic masculinity where the dominant position of men is guaranteed helps explain some of what went on in the conservative evangelical wing, but also contributes to the common culture between the institutional church and boys' public schools and this theory will be explored further in the next chapter.

9.
Sex and Gender

In the previous chapter the boys' boarding school system was discussed in terms of its influence on the culture of the institutional church. Hegemonic masculinity is about the dominant position of men and their values,[1] for example, as found in the 'muscular Christianity' favoured by some conservative evangelicals. Hegemonic masculinity believes that men are in charge, in the world and in the family. It emphasises performance, rationality, repudiating the feminine and everything associated with it which is equated with weakness. This leads to a mistrust of public displays of emotion and is partly why the apologies to the victims by church officials are sometimes so wooden and unempathic. The public face of hegemonic masculinity is the image that sustains their power. While male headship has been challenged in various ways within the Anglican Church, 'it persists amongst Conservative Evangelicals and also amongst Anglo-Catholics. Just as disturbingly, it can also persist as unrecognised gender bias amongst those who might well believe themselves to be liberal or progressive.' The Rev. Canon Wyn Beynon writes that such power and control is always about 'abusive possession ... done in the name of the God of love. There will be women who will defend male headship. And that is perhaps the most evil result of all.'[2] This value system has led not only to sexism, but also to misogyny and homophobia in the Church.

In this chapter sex and gender are discussed in the context of power and control, both central to any understanding of the response to child sexual abuse allegations. The dilemma of the ordination of women and the issue of gay clergy (married or not) have provided and continue to provide preoccupying diversions from tackling the inherent discomfort and reluctance to acknowledge that sexuality, in all its diverse manifestations, is an essential aspect of what makes us human and alive.

CHRISTIANITY'S SEARCH FOR INNER PURITY AND THE INEVITABLE RESULTS

In the Church the subject of sex is fraught with contradictory moral worries and also invested with amazing and paradoxical powers. The Noah's Ark two-of-everything paradigm of sexuality – male and female – is thought to be foundational to the family and so implicitly to the future of the Church; after all, without children, engendered by a male and a female having sex, there will be no future church attendees nor for that matter clergy. Yet, at the same time, sex is thought to be such a powerful force that it threatens to break up the same family and imperil the Church. On the one hand, it is a 'private' matter and yet, on the other, the Church is impelled to keep returning to the subject in public proclamations telling people what they can and cannot 'do' – so much so that often the comment is made that sex is all the Church is interested in. Why *is* the church so interested in sex and telling people what not to do? It seems that, once you accept and promote this fantasy of the wholesome sex of a married heterosexual couple, then its shadow inevitably emerges as the nightmare of 'loose morals' outside the married heterosexual couple, with any adult having sex with any other.

The fear of the loss of the fantasy makes it absolutely imperative to control sex, where it can happen and between whom. The wild power suggested by the shadow means that sex has to be contained and tamed – domesticated – and kept firmly in the Christian heterosexual marital bed, under the covers. Such is the power of the nightmare of sex outside this set-up that it seems as if for the church *all* sex is a scandal and even the officially sanctioned occurrence is tinged with anxiety. There is hesitancy about sexual pleasure, reluctance for any serious discussion and, yet, as I found when I worked for the Church, this exists oddly, though perhaps inevitably, alongside an everyday office culture of sexualised banter, with risqué jokes and double entendre from the men and occasionally from a few of the women.

Early in the first century, St Paul, echoing contemporary neo-Platonic and Jewish ascetic writings, pronounced on the role of women and railed against both male homosexuality and cross-dressing (or what would now be called male-to-female transgender behaviour). His contribution to Christian morality cannot be underestimated with his emphasis on the intrinsic evil of matter and the flesh, innate sinfulness and concern with the individual soul. The resulting 'morality' has been the greatest single source in world history of prejudice against male homosexuals, male-to-female transpeople, and male transvestites. As Christianity became established so did the sin of concupiscence (strong sexual lust) and sexuality, as explored in Augustine's *Confessions*; this meant that chastity became the highest virtue and the idea of original sin, that we are all marked with evil, took hold. There is also, undoubtedly, a fear of incest and the breaking of family morals. Later ascetics rejected sex, any pleasure from food, their families and, especially striking, in many instances, refused even to look at their mothers. David Beres in his analysis of religious morality, quotes from a description of St Jerome, 'Sitting alone in a parching desert, he remembered the pleasures of Rome; filthy from not bathing, clothed in rags, emaciated and ill, surrounded by beasts and scorpions, he thought of shapely virgins and the fire of lust would almost consume him.'[3] It is but a short step from these ascetic practices to the alleged self-castration of the theologian Origen.

The religious life with its emphasis on chastity became idealised (as in veneration of the Virgin Mary) with celibate monks and nuns seen as closer to God than the masses with their lascivious ways and their morality determined by external pressures and commands transmitted by nominally celibate church dignitaries. However, one perceptive Desert Father, John Cassian, warned Christians in the fifth century against focusing on the evils of sexual desire. He perceived this as in reality a defence against aggression, and denying Christian awareness of inherent instinctuality.[4] Sigmund Freud would have appreciated his insight, for Freud famously wrote about the 'return of the repressed', a process whereby what has been pushed out of our consciousness remains indestructible and therefore tends to reappear, often by distorted and devious routes, especially when it involves forbidden feelings of anger or sexuality in a religious context. Freud comments on the watercolour painting by Félicien Rops called 'The Temptation of Saint Anthony' (1878):

> An ascetic monk has fled, no doubt from the temptations of the world, to the image of the crucified Saviour. And now the cross sinks down like a shadow, and in its place, radiant there arises instead the image of a voluptuous, naked woman, in the same crucified attitude. Other artists with less psychological insight have, in similar representations of temptation, shown Sin, insolent and triumphant, in some position alongside of the Saviour on the cross. Only Rops has placed Sin in the very place of the Saviour of the cross. He seems to know that, when what has been repressed returns, it emerges from the repressing force itself.[5]

In other words, placing God as a defence against what one is trying *not* to think about rarely works; instead, the repressed needs to be brought into conscious awareness and recognised for what it is. Freud draws our attention to the observation that 'complete backslidings into sin are more common among pious people', and the fear of sexual or aggressive feelings may cause distress and lead to further acts of penance which Freud equated to an obsessional neurosis.[6] Interestingly, the theologian Hans Küng made common cause with Freud over the Church's misuse of power in its attempts generally to keep control; he also criticised how the Church had responded to sexual abuse scandals:

How abundant are the examples of arrogance of power and misuses of power in the history of the churches: intolerance and cruelty toward deviationists, crusades, inquisition, extermination of heretics, obsession with witches, struggle against theological research, oppression of their own theologians – right up to the present time.

How over the centuries the churches have acted like a superego.[7]

Sanctioned Sexism in the Church of England

The anxiety caused by the impossible demand, given our human instincts, to lead a 'sinless' life and develop 'purity' ultimately leads to the conflation of the sacred and sexless, which is then pitted against the secular and sexual. This mistaken equation has dogged the Christian Church from the early days and quickly led to the need to project the blame for the perils and temptations of sex onto women, leaving men free to be sacred and thereby sexless. Sometimes the belief that God intends that men should dominate and that women should submit is quoted and backed up by the creation of Eve in Genesis chapter 2. The Pauline contribution and the instructions found in the epistle to Timothy provided a basis for women's subordination in the Church and acted to refute any ideas that this subordination had been overcome in Christ. 1 Timothy chapter 2 locates women as inherently secondary in creation and also as punished for initiating the fall into sin: 'The consequences of this status are made clear. Women are to exercise no authority in the church'.[8]

Women seen as sexual and secular temptation (as in the figure of Eve), and in contrast to the innocent (sexless) and sacred Virgin Mary, have for centuries provided a scapegoat for the tension about sex within the Church. The splitting of women into two types in this way was a traditional stereotypical view taught by patriarchal religious authorities and leading directly to a system of domination in religious institutions. However, there are also indirect connections that come from broader values incorporated into religious teachings. This links back to a hierarchy of masculine values present in religiosity with great weight placed on stability and certainty from tradition, so that anything that deviates from these norms is avoided or controlled. This emphasis on traditional values in the Church of England has led to what has been described as benevolent sexism; this differs from hostile sexism in its presentation but comes from the same roots. Sexism is understood here as systematic discrimination and the use of gender stereotypes.[9]

Benevolent sexism, that still permeates the institutional church at all levels, holds a supportive and patronising view towards women, reflected in the notions that Christian women may at times even be morally superior to men and yet very much require male protection and guidance, and the obedient wife and mother does not question her subordination. This means that even in the twenty-first century it is still assumed, almost always without question, that in the parish church setting the women remain responsible for childcare, hospitality, flowers and catering. The men are on the building and finance committees. Benevolent sexism may not appear unpleasant but, as with hostile sexism, its consequences are often negative and certainly implicitly controlling; it can lead to any and all forms of domestic abuse including coercive control. Ironically, while men can impose on women a greater responsibility for morals, they also see them as leading men astray, and benevolent sexism can move quickly to hostile sexism. It is hostile sexism that causes the small but powerful section of the Anglican Church still to contest the ordination of women; although the arguments are presented as theological. Rosemary Ruether writes that the reasoning is that 'the normative masculinity of both the humanity and the divinity of Christ imply a close relation of a masculine Christology with normative masculine priesthood or ministry in the church'[10] – in other words, if Christ was a man then only men can be priests. Ruether argues that if Christ was also a Jew, then why not argue that all priests must be Jews in order to represent Christ. It is instead possible, she suggests, to imagine how the same symbols and touchstones can be used in a prophetic and liberating way that creates communities of egalitarian mutuality. This would be about redemptive communities of equals but, she suggests, would also require the dismantling of clericalism where ministry and community are dynamically interconnected and not 'a clerical caste ruling over a silenced disempowered laity'.

The current maintenance of the protective structure and arrangements that allow those who do not accept women priests to continue to have a role remains damaging to women's status in the Church and deeply insulting. Imagine how repellent it would be if part of the Church would openly not allow black and ethnic minority people to be ordained and this apartheid was seen as 'mutually flourishing', the term used about the current arrangement with women. It is of course also important to note that institutional racism is present in the Church of England and has 'seeped into our structures and organisation'.[11]

In some instances, the hostile sexism that officially sanctions those who see women as alien to the priesthood and inferior veers into misogyny – hatred and an entrenched prejudice against women. As Barbara Harris, the first woman bishop in the Anglican Communion said, recalling the response to her appointment, 'Nobody can hate like Christians. The nasty letters I got were from church people, and you would not believe some of the things that they said in those letters – I laughed to keep from crying.'[12] However, when women protest against sexism, the backlash is significant. For example, when the appointment of Philip North to be bishop of Sheffield was resisted because of his refusal to acknowledge female priesthood, and he stood down, he was seen as the vulnerable and wounded victim of public bullying. Those against his appointment were judged as 'wicked' and their actions as 'diabolical'. The Archbishop of York urged the protesters to 'disagree Christianly', presumably a call to be silent and accept the institutionalised sexism. Incidentally, this is a similar response to what has happened to many victims of abuse and their supporters, who have been seen as troublemakers, while the perpetrator of the abuse is seen as the victim of their unjustified attacks.[13] Many women experienced sexism and misogyny as they began to take office in the Church, some still do. As Stephen Parsons writes, 'The mindset that creates abuse in a church setting will always have its roots in the wider institution and the attitudes and assumptions that have been nurtured there.' He continues, 'prejudice and assumptions in churches about women . . . will occasionally be acted out by an individual in a deed of cruelty or humiliation against a particular woman'.[14] This is sexual harassment and can take the form of sexual abuse, emotional abuse and, inevitably, given the context, also spiritual abuse where the adult is 'trapped' in a professional relationship and the perpetrator holds the power.

The following account from a woman called Anne details what happened to her when she was starting her ministry as a deacon in a big city centre church. Her training incumbent whom she calls 'Fred' was dynamic, with a charismatic personality, and showed an enthusiasm for outreach that initially Anne felt was positive. However, she quickly found him to be abrasive and unfair, sometimes bullying and displaying an explosive temper. What she initially took to be friendliness became sexualised. After he held her inappropriately, she tried to avoid being alone with him but it was impossible. She protested after he pinched her bottom but Fred was 'unabashed' calling Anne 'a bad sport' and getting confirmation of this from a fellow curate. Anne writes: 'I had learnt to be very afraid of Fred. I had seen him set out to destroy one person after another – and he usually succeeded . . . slander, bullying, aggression, false accusations – all were weapons in his armoury.'[15] The emotional abuse continued, and Anne went to talk to the bishop about the bullying and sexual harassment. The bishop refused to help, sided with the vicar and said that he would tell Fred that Anne had reported him. Finally, Anne found a way out through another diocese which well knew about Fred's reputation, though she said that the bishop continued to take various vindictive actions against her. Three months after she left, Fred was promoted. In the Church's eyes, it seemed that his sexually predatory and generally aggressive behaviour did not make him unfit for high office. The bishop also later moved to a bigger and more important diocese where his inaction over cases of abuse continued. One of the after-effects for Anne included self-blame: 'Did I unintentionally "lead Fred on"? Did I allow him to think I would welcome his advances?' She also describes a sense of guilt, so familiar to many women following a sexual attack. After counselling Anne knew that she was not responsible and it turned out that others had also experienced his sexual harassment. Yet, despite Anne reporting the abuse to the National Safeguarding Team, no action was taken. It seems, she reflects, that speaking out does the abuser no harm but there is a backlash against the complainant in the eyes of the Church: 'There are so many ways whistle-blowers can be punished: difficulty in changing jobs if you're labelled a "troublemaker"; lack of diocesan co-operation when applying for grants and funding; harsh ministerial reviews.'

Anne's experience of cumulative abuse – emotional, physical, sexual, spiritual, highlights how the power dynamic involves the submission of the abused to the dominance of the abuser. It also reflects hostile sexism, as does the response of the bishop. What

Anne experienced in her curacy was unboundaried, aggressive and predatory, by speaking out she risked rejection and, in terms of her career potential, 'obliteration'. Furthermore, the power and control displayed by Fred demonstrated misogyny, as she was placed by him in a position of relative passivity and weakness with her pain, distaste and discomfort disregarded. His open displays of rage and aggression and his critical stance towards those who opposed him, left Anne with little choice – though to her great credit she found a way out. However, the events of the first curacy affected all her ordained ministry: 'I have never felt again that I could trust my superiors in the Church, never again felt that it was my "mother Church". At the same time, I have partly blamed myself for what happened.'

One of the effects of misogyny and all sexism is a lingering sense of shame about what has happened and why; it is this that contributes to women not wanting to speak out. This leads to a certain amount of stoicism that can lead to masochism – the 'mustn't grumble' school of thought. In this way sexism is not just about discrimination but acts as a powerful mechanism for control; when victims of sexism are silenced, then the sexists and misogynists are free to continue abusing. Sexism and homophobia sadly are found side by side, as homophobia is a prejudice that does not exist outside contexts where sexism is endemic, as its forms – and they are plural – are all variants of sexism. In this next section we explore how divisive this issue has become in the Church of England.

The Significance of Sexualities Other than Heterosexual in the Way that the Church Responds to Abuse

> The C of E is unable to get over its fixation on homosexuality, which is driving the national church into a position more like a fundamentalist sect and does not speak to the vast majority of younger people today.[16]
>
> Linda Woodhead

Among progressive people around the world, homosexuality can be considered an ordinary, non-pathological type of sexuality – different but equal. However, the institutional church remains prescriptive about how people define themselves and view a practice as defining an identity, and some practices and identities are not acceptable. If 'sex is guilty until proven innocent,' as anthropologist Gayle Rubin[17] famously quipped, then homosexuality provides the perfect scapegoat. 'Homosexuals become the repository, the degraded and devalued holding place, for these buried remainders, those disavowed aspects of the self that must be, at all costs, charged to the account of the other.'[18] This means that all these uncomfortable feelings about sexual intimacy have become projected often, and certainly always in the past onto women, and almost always and certainly still now onto homosexuals. Towards the end of the review of the Peter Ball case, Moira Gibb includes a section on homosexuality,[19] noting that, when Ball was first a priest, and then a bishop, homosexuality was the subject of clear legal and religious proscription. There was at that time a more overt level of societal prejudice against homosexuality and, for clerics and some of the faithful, these religious, legal and social pressures served to reinforce a strong taboo. This made it hard for Ball's victims to speak out as they 'had good cause to fear legal action, social ostracisation and damage to their careers'. This taboo, whilst giving Ball confidence that the victims would remain silent, may have contributed, Gibb adds, to what appears to be his own denial and self-deceit. There was also in some parts of the Church, 'an inexperience and naïveté in relation to homosexuality', a surprising thought given the numbers in the church hierarchy who would probably have known about homosexuality from their public school years. Gibb urged the promotion of 'an open and accepting culture', whilst noting the subject still remained a source of division and conflict. Perhaps this naïveté and the ongoing conflict about the subject are linked and are rather more to do with a conscious denial of awareness alongside the unconscious repression of the homosexual part that is indeed present in every person no matter their gender, 'every human being is bisexual . . . either in a manifest or latent fashion'.[20] The inability to accept this lies at the heart of the conflict in the Church.

Parsons in his book, *Ungodly Fear*, examines the Church's response to homosexuality and, in particular, the 'incredibly powerful antipathy towards homosexuals from part of the evangelical world'.[21] He suggests a paranoid fear of homosexuality with the belief that the behaviour is subversive: 'Were homosexuality to be considered an allowable option within the Christian community, that would be a challenge to the idea that only Christian heterosexual marriage can be read out of the Bible.' The homophobic stance is defensive and interestingly often invoked whilst a Christian group is fending off either imaginary or real persecution or humiliation:

> Prejudice against sexual minorities, including homosexuals, seems strongest in groups who have achieved cohesion defensively through an ideology of active, self-punishing asceticism or body rejection. In persecuted, defended groups, sexual minorities are accused of being the reason for the group's weakness, or of being a threat to the reproductive strength that might overcome weakness. . . . The hated sexual minorities are usually said to inhibit or undermine . . . by not contributing to the regular reproduction that would reinforce the group's imperial strength.[22]

George Carey, Archbishop of Canterbury from 1991-2002, voted against equality legislation in 1994 and 1998 in the House of Lords and, after leaving office, continued to oppose same-sex marriage and church blessings of same-sex partnerships, speaking out many times against any changes in both the Church and in society. Interestingly, whilst a whole chapter of his memoir is on 'The Challenge of Homosexuality' and eighteen threads on the subject are listed in the index, there is no mention of clergy abuse.[23] He called the decision to legalise same-sex marriage in 2012 as 'cultural vandalism'[24] and in 2013 spoke of being 'very suspicious' that behind plans for gay marriage lurked an aggressive secularist and relativist approach towards an institution that has glued society.[25] A few months later Carey claimed same-sex marriage could set a 'dangerous precedent' which could lead to sibling marriage or polygamy.[26] Whilst rightly attracting criticism, Carey's homophobic and frightened discourse also reveals his ignorance. Recent studies of sexuality show that prejudice against women, sexual minorities, or both, has always gone along with and promoted misinformation about sexuality. For example, paedophilia was widely and wrongly assumed for some time to be a sub-species of homosexuality. There are organisations within the Church actively trying to remedy this ignorance and prejudice.[28]

The profound disagreements in worldwide Anglicanism, encapsulated in the Lambeth Conference of 1998 under Carey, are still being debated, with all the associated damage. For example, a report published by the Oasis Foundation in 2018 showed how negativity towards those who are LGB (used as shorthand for LGBTQI+ lesbian, gay, bisexual, transgender, queer, intersex and plus – any other identities that might fall under this umbrella) is fuelled by churches. The research demonstrates that the majority of negative messages about same-sex relationships in the mainstream media are driven by churches or churchgoers, and that most political opposition to the liberalisation of laws around same-sex relationships is from those who can be publicly identified as Christian. The report concludes that attitudes and pastoral practices of the Church and local churches are significantly contributing to a narrative that is causing serious emotional and physical harm to LGB people.[29]

In January 2017, in *Marriage and Same Sex Relationships after the Shared Conversations: A Report from the House of Bishops*, the Church of England urged the establishment of a fresh tone and culture but, in the same paper, agonised about how welcoming and supporting LGB people and their families might fit with moral judgements regarding the choices people make about relationships, marriage and family life: 'Can the Church of England establish a consistent tone and culture when it encompasses those who hold to some sharply differing moral judgments about those choices in this case?'[30] The same paper reaffirms the well-established exemplary role of the clergy:

> It is clear, then, that there are good grounds in law for holding the clergy to an exemplary standard of behaviour consistent with the Church of England's doctrine where the laity are not bound in the same way . . . clergy who are same-sex oriented or are in a relationship with a person of the same sex may be questioned about the nature of their relationships, with the explicit expectation that they be celibate.[31]

In 2017, the Church of England began a new process to replace 1991's *Issues in Human Sexuality*, with working parties focusing on various aspects to find a way forward between the two opposing positions on full acceptance of those with sexualities differing from heterosexuality. However, initial evidence from pastoral guidance issued by bishops in January 2020 suggests that little progress has been made. *It was* stated that sex belongs only within heterosexual marriage, that sex in gay or straight civil partnerships 'falls short of God's purpose for human beings' and that 'For Christians, marriage – that is, the lifelong union between a man and a woman, contracted with the making of vows – remains the proper context for sexual activity.'[32] Following protests, including from a number of bishops, an apology was given by the two archbishops for the timing of the guidance but they did not retract its substance. One protester wrote, 'The bishops, some of whom are now women, of course, seem to regard sexual activity as an entirely avoidable activity, separate from a normal, intimate, mutually supportive, committed and loving relationship between two civil partners, whether they are men, women or men and women.'[33]

Jayne Ozanne, in a talk about love, sex and power, links this to the sexual abuse of both adults and children 'often perpetrated by the very people who pronounce from their pulpits ... that sex is for marriage between a man and a woman', adding, 'I believe it's time to end this hypocritical charade'. Drawing on her past experience of rape by a priest and how she was dissuaded by a bishop from reporting the allegation to the police, Ozanne also spoke of a further sexual assault by a married conservative evangelical. She points out that, although the latter never apologised, 'he does keep pronouncing about sex being only between a man and a woman in marriage. I'm not sure which is worse – the abuse I suffered that night or the hypocrisy of hearing him constantly pronounce his views on this subject, knowing what I do.' Controlling people through fear seems at odds with the promotion of the unconditional love of God.[34] The subject of inclusion seems far from being resolved, leaving those who have watched the 'Living in Love and Faith project' develop over the years currently concluding that there is no evidence of learning from experience. Judith Maltby and Helen King write, 'we're no longer convinced that the House and College of Bishops are capable of breaking the repeated, destructive pattern of behaviour'. Referring here to an earlier rejection of the House of Bishops report, *Marriage and Same Sex Relationships after the Shared Conversations*, they comment: 'History never precisely "repeats itself" but we regretfully conclude that our bishops have shown a collective inability to learn from it.'[35]

Being tolerant has often been put forward as the best way to manage irreconcilable difficulties, indeed it has become a central coping mechanism for the institutional church, yet this is so clearly a false solution that can quickly unravel: for example, assuring LGB churchgoers of the Church's love and support, whilst simultaneously harbouring, and maybe even letting slip out loud, the wish that the person was not gay. This is a wishing away of difference and, given the Church likes to portray itself as a family, it reflects the 'we still love you in spite of everything' approach, a family portrait of in/tolerance. Whilst clearly tolerance is an improvement over homophobic violence and hate, it still affirms the basic social hierarchy by establishing an 'us' and 'them' relationship from the centre to the margins, an idea that was discussed earlier in the book. This kind of tolerance offers those who define themselves as LGB the right to worship without fear of persecution but withholds from them certain rights and privileges – to get married in church or easily to become ordained.[36] As Pellegrini and Jakobsen state, 'Tolerance is a wedge against recognizing and grappling with loss. . . . The moralizing strains of tolerance are conceivable as self-reproach turned outward onto those others whose ongoing inequality (and the irksome noisiness with which "they" proclaim it) threatens to bring lost ideals back into view.'[37]

What happened to Jeffrey John, a gay senior Anglican churchman, passed over for promotion to a bishopric seven times since the Church of England rescinded his appointment as bishop of Reading in 2003 amid homophobic protests, reveals the weakness and superficiality of the statements of tolerance. In February 2017 he was put forward for the post of bishop of Sodor and Man but failed to make it onto the shortlist, despite positive feedback. This rejection came shortly before he was passed over for appointment as bishop of Llandaff, after objections to his sexuality were allegedly raised.[38] Apparently tolerant, an open vote confirmed that the panel considering him for Sodor and the Isle of Man had no objection to John's sexuality and his long-term civil partnership with Anglican priest Grant Holmes. However, at the next stage once the ballots became secret, John failed even to be shortlisted. Whilst his record and attributes (including his stated celibacy) fitted the role of bishop, his repeated rejection seems only explicable by homophobia. This suggests that tolerance can go only so far and no further. In the selection for Llandaff,

John was told by a member of the electoral college that the only arguments made against his appointment 'were directly related to my homosexuality and/or civil partnership – namely, that my appointment would bring unwelcome and unsettling publicity to the diocese, and that it might create difficulties for the future archbishop [of Wales] in relation to the Anglican communion'. Inevitably, the Church rejected allegations of homophobia and said the process had been carried out 'properly and fairly'. Dr Alan Wilson, Bishop of Buckinghamshire, said: 'There is a pattern here, and I'm amazed that after all these years there is still so much mendacious obfuscation about appointing Jeffrey John as a bishop. It calls into question the sincerity of all the church's hand-wringing apologies to gay and lesbian people.'[39] Many agreed that sexuality lay at the heart of the opposition to John as a bishop, given his championing of a theology that does not condemn gay and lesbian sex.[40]

Yet, the Church of England does have a gay bishop who is in a long-term relationship, whose sexuality and living arrangements were apparently 'no secret within the Church' but which were not made public during the time at which the appointment was being made because the relationship was 'private'. The Bishop of Grantham, Dr Nicholas Chamberlain was appointed November 2015 but declared his sexual status in September 2016 when he was threatened with being 'outed' by a national newspaper.[41] This raises the interesting possibility that the concern is more about the publicity and appearance rather than the reality. LGB campaigning groups and GAFCON (the Bible-based, conservative Global Anglican Future Conference, very much opposed to LGB clergy) were both critical that they had not known beforehand about Chamberlain's sexuality. The LGB groups' statement said it was, 'regrettable' that his relationship had not been acknowledged at the time of his appointment and that Chamberlain should have been able to be open about his sexuality. After Chamberlain's sexuality was the subject of media reports, he received about 500 letters and e-mails; 96 per cent of the letters contained unequivocal support for him and only a smaller percentage of these letters (30 per cent) were from people he knew. The researchers analysing the letters described them as a 'tsunami of prayer and love'. One response was, 'The Church claims to preach a gospel of love whilst failing to understand what love looks like in people's lives. The boundaries that the

Church tries to keep don't make sense anymore.' Another, 'Thank you for giving so many thousands of gay people encouragement and hope after so many decades of being trampled into the mud by the Church they love.' Worth noting is that roughly half of those who wrote were not affiliated to any particular religion or community but expressed their desire for the Church to behave differently – to be supportive, to be accepting and to be kind.[42]

Real tolerance, or appreciation and acceptance of 'different but equal', would involve the end of splitting genders (or, in theoretical terms, not embracing binarism – the Noah's Ark view). In a psychological and spiritual sense this is about integrating what is felt to be male/masculine and what is felt to be female/feminine within the self.[43] Unfortunately, the reverence for purity and the holy discussed earlier is instead a focus on suppressing both parts of the self, an extreme form of splitting so that both parts become disembodied. However, if there can be some integration of variant sexuality, then rather than define what is diverse, or seen as deviant in terms of practice, the focus can be in terms of the quality of the relationship existing between persons engaging in sexual behaviour. Young-Bruehl sees it more helpful to refocus sex pathology by looking at sexual behaviour that is non-relational or relationship denying, where the pathological person does not treat another as an equal as a human with human rights. There is instead some form of ownership with no consent or respect for the other's wishes so such abuse cannot be in any way companionable.[44]

Finally, it is worth noting that the Church's attachment to what has been called 'the reification' of masculinity and femininity shuts down healthy reflection on the range of sexualities. It makes it difficult for clergy to discuss what will be judged 'inappropriate' sexual thoughts or fantasies and it has been shown that repression of thinking about difference and otherness can lead to acting out – as in the abuse of children, young people or other adults. The institutional church is stuck in an inability to reflect on the acceptance of difference and otherness.[45] This affects the way that the institutional church responds to allegations of abuse by clergy perpetrators. Sexual acts and sexed embodiment have become overburdened areas of spiritual, religious and psychological conflict within the Church. This then affects how the Church has responded to allegations and what it has projected onto victims and survivors. It is as if the 'sexual' part of sexual abuse contributes to the inability of the Church to respond with appropriate pastoral concern. If mature thinking about sex and sexuality has been barred, the subject then becomes imbued with huge fear, vicarious excitement and distaste. This contributes to spiritual sickness within the Church, an idea that is further explored in the last chapter.

10.
Spiritual Abuse, the Spiritual Sickness within the Church and Signs of Hope

> But the thing that eats one up is the anguish over the Church . . . there is this conviction that the Church is full of a spiritual sickness, even though there is always that inexpressible life.[1]
>
> *Thomas Merton*

'The response to the damage done the survivors of clerical abuse has been parsimonious and late', Alana Lawrence, of Minister and Clergy Sexual Abuse Survivors, wrote to Archbishop Justin Welby in 2014, identifying that those who have disclosed abuse have been dismissed, vilified or told to get over it. Five years later, Jo Kind, also of MACSAS, told the IICSA hearing in 2019 that complainants, victims and survivors continue to be met with polite obstinacy and an unwillingness to acknowledge the scale of the problem or the structural inadequacies of the safeguarding system.[2]

The way that the church hierarchy has failed adequately to respond to allegations of clergy abuse is a form of sickness – a spiritual sickness. The sickness is caused by institutional narcissism, an idea that has run through this book. All organisations and institutions are to a certain extent healthily narcissistic – they have to be to survive and to thrive. However, the Church has become stuck at the level of survival to the detriment of thriving. In an individual a narcissistic personality disorder is seen as a sign of mental ill health and the same can be said at the collective level in an organisation. The institutional church has become dominated by its own internal self-preoccupations, to the extent that it is increasingly out of touch with society, and reliant on self-generating authoritarian structures. Complacency, arrogance and a lack of empathic concern are other characteristics to be noted. As discussed in the previous chapter, the Church has been introspective and absorbed by issues, initially, about the ordination of women and women bishops and, then, by divisions over homosexual clergy. At root is the question of who can join the elite hierarchy. The divisions over these subjects amongst the conservative evangelicals, the Anglo-Catholics and the liberals have been well documented by Andrew Brown and Linda Woodhead[3] and the issues have absorbed energy and have restricted perspectives. All these concerns are not generally understood by the wider society, or indeed by many in the Church, but certainly they have contributed to obscuring the Church's response to disclosures of abusive 'in-house' sex involving clergy. The complacent culture and tradition of elite masculine power, control and emotional repression, discussed in Chapter 8, has worked strongly against efforts to engage empathically and fairly with survivors.

Furthermore, institutional narcissism is present in the powerful assumption that the Church offers something 'special' (a word sadly tainted from its overuse by some abusers), something sacred, something loving and, as discussed earlier in this book, something superior to the secular. It offers this, presided over by 'special' people chosen by God, who have been 'called' to become clergy. The Church offers a place for anyone – especially for the troubled – to come and be 'saved'. As Cliff James says, and his words are used as the epigraph to this book: 'If you look at it from the outside, it is beautifully decorated. It has lovely stories, it promises so much, it promises everlasting life and redemption; but, if you strip away the veneer, it is a cold machine, it is gunmetal coloured.' James clearly sees from his experience as a survivor of episcopal abuse that this is because for the Church the maintenance of the corporation is its raison d'être. The Church prides itself on being about love, compassion and kindness but no one gets love from an institution; it is a contradiction in terms. Clearly there are many individual clergy and laity capable of love, kindness and compassion – it is obviously not full of psychopaths or narcissists – but the institution as a collective does not have the capacity for this. Inevitably, when under pressure from an allegation against a member of the clergy, especially if this involves a senior or charismatic cleric, the institution moves onto the defensive. The institution is unable to cope with the realisation that the abuser is clergy and that the Church does *not* have the collective capacity or ability to love; such an insight could destroy it. The awareness that the Church has spiritually abused victims is a challenge to the institution's very identity – hence the move to defensive deceptions, avoidance and eventually inauthentic and half-baked apologies. Because of the power and control derived from institutional narcissism, the Church is compelled to respond in the way it has; it seems there has not been a choice. The manner in which all the victims and survivors discussed in this book have been treated is as a compulsive defence against the realisation that the institution is betraying its spurious identity as a loving institution.

This is because a central aspect of narcissism concerns power and here the analytical psychologist Carl Jung can offer insight: 'Where love reigns, there is no will to power; and where the will to power is paramount, love is lacking.'[4] The institutional church (unlike its founder Jesus Christ) is preoccupied with power and control, and these have been confused with value. A contemporary analyst has reframed Jung's statement using the associated opposites as having value and having no value, thus: 'Where there is a sense of personal value there is no will to power; and where the will to power is paramount then there is no sense of personal value.'[5] This is why the Church has been unable to honour the personal distress of the victims and survivors. It is not possible to value others without a sense of personal value, and here is where the narcissistic institution struggles. Ideally, there needs to be a balance of power and love but that would require change. This inability to respond to the personal value of the victim is demonstrated distressingly in the account of what happened to Neil Todd, one of Peter Ball's young victims.

The Church's Spiritual Abuse of Neil Todd

Throughout this book the direct words of survivors have been used, where possible, to describe what happened to them. The abuses were sexual, physical, emotional and, given the religious context for all of them, always spiritual. The survivors have then experienced further abuse in the way that the Church handled their disclosures, that is, more spiritual abuse. Spiritual abuse is a term that has proved hard to define, perhaps because sometimes it is quite subtle and often it is hidden, but it is easy to see how many of us looking for love, acceptance, joy and healing can become drawn into a relationship characterised by control, criticism and coercion, albeit in the name of obedience to God. Lisa Oakley and Justin Humphreys define spiritual abuse as 'a form of emotional and psychological abuse. It is characterized by a systematic pattern of coercive and controlling behaviour in a religious context.'[6] From analysis of the mind of the abuser in Chapter 3, and the attraction of charismatic leaders in Chapter 7, it is easy to see how coercive control can happen and how God is often used to justify what is happening. In a talk given to the Royal College of Psychiatrists in 2017, Jayne Ozanne spoke about a 'group model of spiritual abuse', in which a church community – rather than an individual – perpetrates spiritual abuse, and so causes significant long-term harm to their victims.[7] The church hierarchy has responded in a defensive manner that can be seen as spiritually abusive through their coercive control following the disclosure of allegations. The question is how much of this was consciously intended and how much just carelessly 'allowed' to happen. The Home Office definition of coercive control is: 'a purposeful pattern of behaviour which takes place over time in order . . . to exert power, control or coercion over another'.[8] Oakley and Humphreys see this as hallmarks of spiritual abuse and 'just as relevant to the church or Christian context'.[9] Another relevant aspect of the spiritual abuse perpetrated against victims following disclosure is that of 'gaslighting', a term taken from the 1940 film, *Gaslight* (dir. Thorold Dickinson). This is understood as manipulating and pressuring someone, or a group, to doubt themselves, leading them to question their memory, their view of what has happened and sometimes their sanity. Both coercive control and gaslighting are found in the post-abuse trauma inflicted by the authorities on Neil Todd. The disclosures Todd made in 1992 are now completely vindicated and his words live on. In 2012, shortly before he killed himself, Todd was interviewed by the BBC from his home in Australia. Commenting on the recent Church investigation and hearing that the information had been passed to the Sussex police, Todd said that the abuse had 'stayed with me throughout my life's journey and even this far down the track it doesn't feel like there's any real closure . . . obviously there was a component of sexual abuse. But basically it was mind games and controlling behaviour.' Furthermore, he said: 'When it came to the abuse, the abuse was sexual, mental and physical. He [Ball] was just not a very nice human being.' He added: 'It took a long time for people to be convinced the events that actually took place actually took place.' In fact, it took twenty years for the Church to believe Todd and seriously take action.[10]

From early adolescence, Todd had wanted to find out more about entering a religious community and, in his statement to Gloucester police in December 1992, Todd describes how he was given details of Peter Ball's scheme for young people to have a year receiving instruction in monastic life and monastic obedience.[11] Joining the community as a 'postulant' in July 1992, Todd describes the abuse of naked praying, the cold showers with Ball watching and the threat of naked beatings for disobedience. Deeply embarrassed and discomforted Todd believed that Ball, who was by then a bishop, must be right. Frightened by the threat of the naked beatings, Todd left with the kindly housekeeper and her chauffeur husband, Mr and Mrs Moss, who were going on holiday to France and who were deeply concerned for Todd. Incidentally, Mr and Mrs Moss spoke to two bishops about their concerns but no action was taken by either of these senior clerics. In October 1992, when Todd returned to Bishopscourt where Ball lived, further abuse took place. However, when Todd disclosed to another religious shortly after this, he was told that what had occurred was not part of monastic life. Distraught and feeling he had been deceived by the bishop – in other words, spiritually as well as sexually abused, Todd attempted suicide that November. Todd disclosed to a local vicar and then to the bishop of Southwark, and also met with Bishop Eric Kemp [Ball's former diocesan bishop]. Others had also expressed concern so there were a number of people aware of what had happened but, at this point, the church hierarchy sought to minimise the damage through denial and saying that Todd was lying.[12] This is noted in the IICSA report:

By the time of Peter Ball's arrest, at least three senior bishops and a number of other clergy knew of the allegations by Mr Todd. None of them told the police or thought to do so. Overall, this has the appearance of an attempt to ensure that the matter did not become known to the authorities. The reputation of the Church and Peter Ball was given a higher priority than the obvious distress of a vulnerable young man.[13]

Todd made a further suicide attempt on 11 December 1992; his parents, who visited him in hospital, described him as 'a physical and emotional wreck'.[14] The IICSA report highlights that Todd had received no support or reassurance from senior church figures, who instead were busy rallying around Ball. 'No action was taken to put a stop to Peter Ball's behaviour or to protect others from it. The Church failed to support and protect a vulnerable young man who had done nothing wrong . . . the response of the Church was weak and focussed on protecting its own reputation.'[15] The police took Todd's statement from his parents' home in Nottingham and his account was then found to be consistent with other young men who also disclosed abusive experiences. It was at this point that both Peter and his twin brother Michael Ball began their campaign of intimidation and pressure on witnesses, asking for support from people of influence. Interestingly, among the elite group who supported Ball against the Neil Todd's allegations, were Tim Renton MP (now Lord Renton) and his wife, who wrote, on parliamentary headed paper, to the DPP, Dame Barbara Mills, in February 1993. This was before the case had even been submitted by the police. Renton said he had never written to a DPP about an individual case before but he did so for Peter Ball because he believed him to be 'a man of outstanding Christian sincerity and goodness'. He wrote with the explicit intention that he might have an effect on the outcome of the case:

> In all the years he was with us in Sussex, surrounded by his Order or young men, we never heard a breath of any suggestion of impropriety. I do hope you will not mind my writing to you personally and that you will take these thoughts . . . into consideration when reaching your decision.[16]

(Interestingly these are the parents of Alex Renton, author of *Stiff Upper Lip*, referred to earlier in this book, who described his own traumatic experiences of having been sexually abused on three occasions at boarding school.) At this time, and as has since become known, George Carey suppressed letters from other victims and their parents and did not pass on this information to the police. As a result of the allegations, Ball was only given a police caution in 1993 and he resigned as bishop of Gloucester. He retired and received a disability pension. No action was taken under the Church's disciplinary procedures. He was at first restricted from ministry but repeatedly challenged this and, in 1995, was given permission to officiate as a retired priest. Ball was supported throughout by Carey (see Chapter 3), even following his retirement as archbishop. Carey not only failed to pass on significant information to the police but vociferously added weight to the developing false narrative of the wronged good Christian by a troubled young man. For example, in September 1993, Carey wrote, 'for in the end I believed him to be basically innocent' and, in 2000, 'Peter Ball lost everything. I stand by a man who, overall, has been a wonderful Priest and Bishop.'[17] Carey would not take seriously what had happened to Neil Todd and so failed him. Carey could not accept that abusive behaviour had taken place. He attached 'more weight to Peter Ball's word than that of Mr Todd', probably because Ball was a bishop. He prayed for the matter to end and prayed for Ball, no mention was made of Todd and no prayers offered for his wellbeing. In a 1992 Lambeth Palace press release unqualified support was expressed for Ball, 'who has a proven record of outstanding pastoral work, particularly amongst young people'. The public and Mr Todd were 'left in no doubt as to where the Church's sympathies lay'.[18]

Ball could also draw on his friendship with Prince Charles when complaining about a 'malicious campaign' against him and the 'fraudulent accusers'. Prince Charles in 1995 said: 'I wish I could do more. I feel so desperately strong about the monstrous wrongs that have been done to you.' He wrote of a 'horrid man' and in 1997 described one apparent accuser (presumed to be Neil Todd) as a 'ghastly man . . . up to his dastardly tricks again'.[19] With such friends in high places it is easy to see how the false narrative became embedded, so that attempts to restrict Ball were met by a similar campaign. Even in 2010 when the police were increasingly interested in pursuing an investigation, the firmly held story in the village of Aller, where the Ball twins lived, was that Todd was a mentally ill young man who had unfairly damaged the innocent Ball's reputation. In 2012 the criminal investigations began, led by Sussex police. Soon after learning of this and, having spoken to police officers and journalists, Neil Todd, aged 38, took his life. One can only surmise that he was simply unable to face a repetition of the isolating and destructive treatment he had received from the Church over the previous twenty years. The stress and fear of the post-abuse trauma repeating itself was too great. Following his death and the eventual imprisonment of Ball, Marc Hawley, who was Todd's partner, commented on the leniency of the sentence for the gravity of Ball's offences. He added that Todd, who had moved away to build a new life after the authorities failed to prosecute Ball in 1993, was a religious man who 'did nothing except want to pledge his life to God but fell foul of the filthy devil incarnate'.[20] In the film *Gaslight*, the husband's interpretation of reality, of what actually happened, all but overwhelms his wife's actual experience. In the Ball/Todd case, Ball and his supporters did, for a long time, overwhelm Todd's actual experience by their concerted denial of it and calling Todd a liar. Having experienced this denial, to the extent of removing himself to the other side of the globe, Todd could not live once more with this pressure. Ultimately, Ball and his supporters can be seen as responsible for Todd's death. Whilst individual clergy offered Todd some support, the institution closed ranks and turned away. He was openly maligned.

I experienced the same denial of reality that Todd experienced, albeit on a far smaller scale, in my attempts, first, to have a professional risk assessment made on Ball and, second, to remove his PTO. On one occasion I was 'invited' to walk round the bishop's palace grounds by a senior diocesan cleric and asked (or was it told?) to stop harassing Ball. He spoke of Ball's great spirituality and goodness, and my findings about his past were dismissed as of less importance. This stance was confirmed by a second member of the bishop's staff who criticised my approach, accusing me of being over-zealous. The third approach came from an official in Lambeth Palace, who rang to tell me that I could be seen as persecuting an elderly man inappropriately. This ran alongside Ball's own campaign and attempts at coercive control by letter (sometimes three or four a week) and from his influential friends by telephone, including a warning to me that Prince Charles could get involved. It is hard to hold to one's convictions under this sort of powerful pressure.

A number of people in the diocesan hierarchy whom I came across in my work as safeguarding advisor would ask, 'How can you stand it?' At the time I thought the 'it' they referred to was the suffering of children and the complexities of working with those who might pose a risk of harm, or the difficulties of the lack of a good management and professional support structure. Since leaving this work I have reinterpreted this comment in the light of the spiritual sickness of the institution. In other words, there was something that I was able to stand in my role that other parts in the institutional church could not, something that seemed to be unthinkable or unbearable to the hierarchy. Initially I thought that this 'it' that could not be stood was something to do with the unwanted emergence of sexuality in a perverted manifestation. However, on further reflection, the 'it' was what was being seen as an attack on the assumption that the Church is a special place of sanctity and love, somewhere holy and different from the sinful world – an illusory 'it' that had become too difficult to think about. When someone responsible for safeguarding is employed, the institution is able to profit by the association of having them in this role, so 'it' is being taken care of and nobody else need think about 'it'. However, the appearance that the problem is being tackled is another dynamic of deception. This is the arrogance of the institutional narcissism, that not only is it then possible to put the unthinkable aspects of the institution into the person of the safeguarding advisor (so that 'it' can be rendered generally more tolerable), but also an accompanying patronising idealisation of the object ('we don't know how you do it').[21]

SMALL CHANGES

> We hate an evil and we hate a change. Hating the evil most, we make the change but we make it as small as possible.[22]
>
> *George Carey, quoting Trollope*

The current (2020) layers of safeguarding structures are complex and, whilst changes have been made over the years, concerns are increasingly being voiced about 'impaired transparency and intermittent accountability', particularly in the National

Safeguarding Team.[23] There remain the local teams in each of the 42 dioceses plus the National Safeguarding Team that reports to the Secretary General through a National Safeguarding Director. Policy is devised and guidelines issued by the House of Bishops, with a Lead Bishop for Safeguarding working with two assistant bishops (a relatively new innovation) and with further responsibility undertaken by the National Safeguarding Steering Group chaired by the Lead Bishop with its members appointed by the two Archbishops. There is also the National Safeguarding Panel, operating under an independent (external) chair. But the current system within the current culture does not work.

A variety of preferable options have been suggested, some of these are big changes and others smaller. The biggest change would be for legislative mandatory reporting with failure to report made a criminal offence. David Greenwood, together with the campaigning and support group, Minister and Clergy Sexual Abuse Survivors, suggests this.[24] He emphasises there should be 'no exemption, excuse, protection or privilege granted to clergy for failing to report information disclosed in, or in connection with, a religious confession'. Another big change would be to remove the whole responsibility for safeguarding from the Church through the creation of a new independent statutory body. This could enforce basic standards of safeguarding and deal with complaints. It could cover all institutions which care for children and would require part funding from the Church as one of those institutions. The Church would be required to give generous funding for survivor support and compensation. Greenwood also raises the need to consider the introduction of an offence of failing to protect a child from the risk of sexual abuse. The criminal offence of 'abuse of position of trust' could also be reviewed with the possibility of extending the categories beyond the age of eighteen. Josephine Stein, too, puts forward radical options for cultural changes including a widespread process of learning about ecclesiastical abuse, 'from the causes of pastoral failures by individual priests to contributory social factors such as a sense of entitlement amongst the elite in English society'. She also suggests adopting policies and practices from the health sector, including embedding the idea of professional ethics into the ecclesiastical culture, where there could be annual assessments of fitness. Learning from other organisations, including the police and the press, could lead to 'an Independent

Ecclesiastical Complaints Commission that could issue binding rulings'.[25] This would see a change in focus onto transparent accountability where both the individual and the organisation are taken into account. These big structural and systemic changes would require accepting letting go of the power and control issues that have been explored in earlier chapters, alongside an opening up of the 'traditions' that have kept the institutional church such a closed, or, at the very least, such a congested, system. Sadly, the relatively new current arrangement with the National Safeguarding Team and the setting up of a 'core group' to investigate concerns seems fraught in the way it has recently operated. Far from transparent accountability there appears the disappointing continuation of the old pattern of obfuscation and conflicts of interest, so much so that its dysfunctionality has been referred to by Bishop Pete Broadbent as Kafka-esque.[26]

If safeguarding remains within the remit of the institutional church, then it seems generally agreed that a whole church approach to safeguarding is needed. This could include an arrangement equivalent to the Truth and Reconciliation Commission in South Africa, tasked with bringing out into the open all the past wrongdoings by the institutional church towards victims and survivors. This would make an absolute priority of the return of the true narrative of events to its proper position in the mainstream accounts of what actually happened. This would be a reversal of the established power and control and indeed 'the truth will set you free' (John 8:32). The 2019 Shemmings Report on the prevalence of abuse in the diocese of Chichester commended a suggestion made by one survivor they interviewed, which is to hold an official Day of Reconciliation across that diocese: 'It was also suggested that the focus of such a day – a Sunday, it was recommended – could become a feature of the diocese calendar on an annual basis . . . "lest we forget".'[27] The report also gave three proposals, 'developed as an organic, co-produced, open and transparent process, with diverse individuals and organisations to achieve genuine "ownership", because it is now well-known and accepted that the protection and safeguarding of individuals from sexual abuse and exploitation requires the whole community to take an active part.' These included a series of filmed conferences and seminars on subjects such as '"Supporting Survivors", "Screening New Applicants", "Maintaining Openness", "Celibacy and Close, Intimate

Relationships", "(so called) Desistant Paedophiles" etc.' Key speakers could be invited and the events filmed with survivors very much present as participants or speakers. The Shemmings Report also advocated further research into understanding sexual offending and an action research programme to evaluate progress on key areas. These areas include: recruitment and training of clergy; generally restricting access by clergy to children on their own or unsupervised; prosecuting offenders; further thinking about the concept of forgiveness; and continuing support for survivors. It also includes the idea of changing the culture of the organisation.

There is no shortage of ideas around for significant changes but, as noted before, the Church appears stuck in a self-destructive and self-defeating pattern. This pattern, or modus operandi, is following bad publicity eventually to admit to past mistakes, issue apologies, then point to procedural and administrative changes and claim all is improved. The IICSA hearings noted that the Church has already accepted in the course of the investigations that it has failed victims and survivors and has stated that it is acutely aware of its historic failings in this area. The question remains whether change can take place and, if so, how.[28] Interestingly, a survey carried out by the Social Care Institute for Excellence[29] invited contributions from survivors and those who had expressed concerns and asked about their experience of the response of the Church. The majority of people who took part had not been satisfied with the response that they got. However, they did offer good ideas of some basic smaller changes that they would like the Church to make. Whilst seeming small changes, they would in fact have a relatively big impact. The first suggestion was that, where possible, the experiences of abuse needed to be widely heard and the experiences of the survivor honoured and their reality validated. This would also increase vigilance within the church context. The second was the wish for the Church to recognise the contributions of survivors in public narratives about safeguarding and value their 'real wealth of knowledge'. Those who have spoken out and had a key role in the recent history of bringing perpetrators to justice have been given no public recognition. This would mean seeing survivors as part of the new life of the Church. The third suggested change was that senior officials should become role models by admitting when they have got it wrong. The fourth was for long-term support. The fifth idea was for a person-centred approach in which survivors would be directly acknowledged and action driven by their needs and not by the reputation of the institution. It would be essential that this did not become a niche area but rather where safeguarding informed the whole business of the Church and where survivors were seen as on an equal footing to those making decisions.

A small change that initially promised much when it was first put forward in 2014 was that of Safe Spaces.[30] Over the last six years the project seemed to have stalled but in June 2020 it was announced that it would be run by Victim Support to provide time and space for survivors to be listened to and supported, individually and in groups. This decision was taken in partnership with survivor representatives: 'Their knowledge, skill and personal experience in shaping the model for Safe Spaces, alongside their commitment and support during the procurement process, was integral to finding the right organisation to deliver the project.'[31] The Bishop of London, Sarah Mullally, current chairwoman of the Safe Spaces management board said: 'for some this project has not come quickly enough and as we have previously said this is a matter of regret which the Church of England acknowledges and apologises for. But it is good news that we now have a charity with proven experience of putting survivors first.'[32] There needs to be generous provision for appropriate support and therapy and for spiritual recovery.[33]

Whilst the suggestion for survivor-led responses is important, it inevitably holds a potential danger which is that the responsibility for change is left with survivors. In a sense this is what has already happened by default. The worry is that this would become another avoidance strategy by the hierarchy and perhaps even replicate the original abusive trauma where the victim ends up carrying the responsibility and often the guilt of the abuser. It is also worth noting that survivors were offered 'a new dawn' in 2002 but the sun has not yet risen on this promise.[34] This could presage that the talked-about 'survivor-led' changes merely become window-dressing and so 'safeguarding-washing', leaving it fundamentally business as usual. After all, power is not easily relinquished. Calcified structures, such as those described in this book, cannot change by themselves. Any small changes so far have been driven by survivors and their supporters, and the strength to do this has come from the power that the survivors do have. This is the inner authentic power that comes from the pride of knowing that you did survive and are seeking justice. There is a personal strength and resilience that comes from confronting trauma, despite all the heartache and pain, and this comes from the inexpressible and vital life force. Inexpressible because some feelings are hard to put into words and even harder to translate into projects or policy documents or discuss at committees:

> There will be moments when it will be impossible to put into words what you're feeling, what you're going through, when you instinctively know that no one will *properly* understand, and yet you need to muster up the confidence to stay the course, and keep believing that around the corner lies the new landscape. . . . Nothing – no job rejection, no break-up, no other tragedy – would ever be as bad. I could put that on the list under resilience demonstrated, survival displayed, experience acquired.[35]

The final words belong with Phil Johnson, survivor and heroic campaigner:

> The Church is trying much harder than it used to. I think it's trying to learn from its mistakes but it's still not getting it right. I sit on the National Safeguarding Panel for the Church of England. I've tried extremely hard, but sometimes I still think they'd rather I wasn't there . . . they'd rather I went away.[3]

Afterword

On 6 October 2020 the latest IICSA report was published. It included many of the situations, and some of the extracts, from the hearings discussed in this book. The conclusions were as expected: that for decades the Anglican Church has failed to protect children and young people under its care, failed to respond appropriately to abuse allegations and failed to provide adequate safeguarding policies and practices. As illustrated in this book, excessive attention was paid to the well-being and reputation of perpetrators, rather than to the needs of the traumatised victims. The issues of clericalism, deference to the institutional church and its reputation, and taboos around discussing the issues realistically and with appropriately qualified people, all contributed to the neglect, humiliation and further abuse of victims.

The report's publication was followed by the inevitable apologies and expressions of regret. Archbishop Welby commented that the report acted as a reminder of the many times that survivors have been failed and that, whilst apologies were important, there needed to be better listening, learning and action. This was echoed by the Lead Safeguarding Bishop, Dr Jonathan Gibb, and the then Church's Director of Safeguarding, Melissa Caslake, who agreed that the Church needed to learn lessons to get safeguarding right and focus on the victims and survivors.

The report made a number of recommendations but, in the opinion of many survivors, these were disappointing and largely underwhelming; the Church will still retain substantial control and thus there is a likelihood that past errors will be repeated in the future. There was, for example, no recommendation on mandatory reporting. One survivor noted that, whilst the tenor of the report was highly critical, it was as if the recommendations were drafted by a different group influenced by central church committees.

In the wider church the final IICSA review of the Roman Catholic Church published 10 November 2020 noted, as expected, the church's neglect of the protection of children and young people in favour of its reputation. In the Church of England there are more hearings still to be held and more reports to be written with a final IICSA report expected in due course. There are further reviews due out in 2021. It is inevitable that there will be more instances of clergy abuse and the capacity of the institutional church will be further tested to respond appropriately, sensitively and consistently to cases brought before them. Until there are serious cultural changes within the institutional church, the distressing 'game' of pawns and bishops will continue to get played out.

Endnotes

1. Introduction – Stripping away the Veneer

1. A vicar on the abuse by Jonathan Fletcher, quoted in *Private Eye*, 29 December 2019.
2. Josephine Stein, 'Safeguarding Policy at a Crossroads', in Janet Fife and Gilo (eds), *Letters to a Broken Church* (London: Ekklesia, 2019), pp. 160-61.
3. Josephine Anne Stein, 'Clerical Abuse and Christian Discipleship', *Modern Believing*, Vol. 61, no. 2 (2020), p. 154.
4. David Gamble and Kathy Galloway, *Time for Action: Sexual Abuse, the Churches and a New Dawn for Survivors* (London: Churches Together in Britain and Ireland [CTBI], 2002), https://ctbi.org.uk/books/time-for-action-paperback/.
5. https://www.theguardian.com/world/2020/feb/12/church-of-england-may-have-to-payout-millions-to-child-sexual-abuse.
6. Rosie Harper, 'What's under the Bonnet', in Fife and Gilo (eds), *Letters to a Broken Church*, p. 77.
7. Simon Barrow, 'Preface', in Fife and Gilo (eds), *Letters to a Broken Church*, p. x.
8. Donald Campbell, 'Foreword', in Cosimo Schinaia, *On Paedophilia* (London and New York: Routledge, 2010), p. xiv.
9. https://www.theguardian.com/world/2019/jun/19/church-of-england-reveals-50-rise-in-abuse-claims-and-concerns.
10. https://www.macsas.org.uk/.
11. Andrew Brown and Linda Woodhead, *That Was the Church That Was: How the Church of England Lost the English People* (London: Bloomsbury, 2016), pp. 72 and 96.
12. https://www.opendemocracy.net/en/5050/victim-vs-survivor-feminism-and-language/.
13. https://www.harpersbazaar.com/culture/features/a20138398/stop-using-survivor-to-describe-sexual-assault-victims/.
14. Harry Ferguson, 'The Paedophile Priest: A Deconstruction', *Studies: An Irish Quarterly Review*, Vol. 84, no. 335 (1995), pp. 247-56.

15. Carl Jung, *C.G. Jung: Letters, Volume 2: 1951-1961*, ed. Gerhard Adler (London: Routledge & Kegan Paul, 1976), p. 265.
16. Alistair McFadyen, *Bound to Sin: Abuse, Holocaust and the Christian Doctrine of Sin* (Cambridge: Cambridge University Press, 2000).
17. Gamble and Galloway, *Time for Action*, p. 125.
18. Fiona Gardner, 'Telling Places and Healing Spaces: Theological Reflections on Projects that Give a Voice to Those Who Have Been Silenced in the Church', Faith, Spirituality and Social Change Conference paper, University of Winchester, April 2007.
19. Margaret Kennedy, *The Courage to Tell*, eds David Gamble and Anne van Staveren (London: CTBI, 1999), p. 50.
20. Alex Renton, *Stiff Upper Lip: Secrets, Crimes and the Schooling of a Ruling Class* (London: Weidenfeld & Nicolson, 2017), pp. 332-33.
21. Harper, 'What's under the Bonnet', pp. 74 and 77.
22. Cf. Rosie Harper and Alan Wilson, *To Heal and Not to Hurt: A Fresh Approach to Safeguarding in Church* (London: Darton, Longman & Todd, 2019).

2. Survivor Accounts

1. Donald Kalsched, *The Inner World of Trauma: Archetypal Defenses of the Personal Spirit* (London and New York: Routledge, 1996), p. 1. Also, cf. Caroline Garland (ed.), *Understanding Trauma: A Psychoanalytical Approach* (London: Tavistock Clinic Series, 1998).
2. Kalsched, *The Inner World of Trauma*, pp. 12-13, and cf. Lisa McCann and Laurie Anne Pearlman, *Psychological Trauma and the Adult Survivor: Theory, Therapy and Transformation* (London and New York: Routledge, 2015), pp. 6-7.
3. Angharad Woolcott, *Church Times*, 17 January 2020, https://www.churchtimes.co.uk/articles/2020/17-january/comment/opinion/as-a-survivor-i-believe-that-by-talking-out-i-may-be-able-to-help-others.
4. Kalsched, *The Inner World of Trauma*, p. 1.
5. Janet Lord, 'The Power of Purple', in Fife and Gilo (eds), *Letters to a Broken Church*, pp. 97-100.
6. Ibid., p. 99.
7. Judith Herman, *Trauma and Recovery: The Aftermath of Violence* (New York: Basic Books, 1992), p. 8.
8. Ernst Becker, 1973, quoted by Daniel Shaw, 'Traumatic Abuse in Cults: A Psychoanalytic Perspective', *Cultic Studies Review*, Vol. 2, no. 2 (2003), pp. 101-31, p. 104, http://www.danielshawlcsw.com/danielshaw/wp-content/uploads/2018/04/traumabusecults.pdf.
9. Donald Campbell, 'Foreword', p. xv.
10. Ibid., p. xv.
11. Ibid., p. xvi.
12. Henrik Ibsen, *John Gabriel Borkman*, in *The Master Builder and Other Plays*, ed. Betty Radice and Robert Baldrick (London: Penguin, 1958), pp. 285-376, p. 331.

13. Leonard Shengold, *Soul Murder Revisited: Thoughts about Therapy, Hate, Love, and Memory* (New Haven, CT and London: Yale University Press, 1999), p. 1.
14. Sigmund Freud's famous statement is found in several places. The earliest reference is in 'The Neuroses of Defence', in J. Strachey (ed.), *The Standard Edition of the Complete Psychological Works of Sigmund Freud, Volume I (1886-1899): Pre-Psycho-Analytic Publications and Unpublished Drafts* (London: Hogarth Press, 1966), p. 227.
15. https://www.cheshire-live.co.uk/news/chester-cheshire-news/sexual-abuse-victim-former-bishop-13775212; https://www.cheshire-live.co.uk/news/chester-cheshire-news/child-sex-attack-shame-former-13772353.
16. https://www.cheshire-live.co.uk/news/chester-cheshire-news/former-bishop-chester-sexually-abused-16312837; https://www.churchofengland.org/news-and-media/news-and-statements/publication-review-bishop-whitsey
17. Campbell, 'Foreword', p. xviii.
18. L. Newman, 'Sexual Abuse within the Family', *19 Magazine*, September 1982, pp. 35-39.
19. Sandor Ferenczi, quoted by Campbell, 'Foreword', p. xix.
20. Loretta R. Loeb, 'The Consequences of Child Sexual Abuse', in Charles W. Socarides and Loretta R. Loeb (eds), *The Mind of the Paedophile: Psychoanalytic Perspectives* (London and New York: Karnac, 2004), pp. 177-86, p. 181.
21. Herman, *Trauma and Recovery*, p. 75.
22. Fiona Gardner, 'Mastery and Guilt', *Free Associations*, Vol. 29, no. 4 (1993), pp. 63-78.
23. Dylan Thomas, 'Reminiscences of Childhood', in *Quite Early One Morning* (London: Dent, 1987), p. 8.
24. There is currently no mandatory reporting of abuse for psychotherapists and counsellors in private practice; they can decide in consultation with their supervisor. If the perpetrator is still alive, then the work might include encouraging the survivor to consider reporting the abuse to the police.
25. Fiona Gardner, 'Transgenerational Processes and the Trauma of Sexual Abuse', *European Journal of Psychotherapy, Counselling and Health*, Vol. 2, issue 3 (1999), pp. 297-308.
26. Kalsched, *The Inner World of Trauma*, p. 5.
27. Fiona Gardner, *Self-Harm: A Psychotherapeutic Approach* (London and New York: Brunner-Routledge, 2001), and 'Working Psychotherapeutically with Adult Survivors of Child Sexual Abuse', in J. Heller et al. (eds), *Mental Health Matters* (Basingstoke and London: Macmillan Press, 1996).
28. Harper and Wilson, *To Heal and Not to Hurt*, p. 168.

3. THE MIND OF THE ABUSER

1. The report by Lord Carlile of Berriew, https://www.churchofengland.org/sites/default/files/2017-12/Bishop%20George%20Bell%20-%20The%20Independent%20Review.pdf (2017), p. 14.

2. Fiona Gardner, 'Review of the Film, *Lolita*, Dir. Stanley Kubrick (Metro-Goldwyn-Mayer, 1962)', *British Journal of Psychotherapy*, Vol.16, no. 4 (June 2000), p. 517.
3. Robert van Handel document available at: https://abcnews.go.com/US/confessions-pedophile-priest-released/story?id=16474982; https://www.dailymail.co.uk/news/article-2153224/Robert-Van-Handel-A-disturbing-look-mind-pedophile-priest.html.
4. Carol Travis and Elliot Aronson, *Mistakes Were Made (but Not by Me): Why We Justify Foolish Beliefs, Bad Decisions, and Hurtful Acts* (Boston, MA, and New York: Mariner Books, Houghton Mifflin Harcourt, 2007).
5. https://www.scribd.com/document/379336016/Paul-Andre-Harvey-documents; https://www.theinquiry.ca/wordpress/accused/charged/accused-g-to-l/harvey-father-paul-andre-harvey/unofficial-english-translation-of-father-paul-andre-harvey-statements-and-affidavit/.
6. https://thehill.com/blogs/blog-briefing-room/news/410401-pope-says-devil-trying-to-divide-attack-the-catholic-church.
7. https://www.theguardian.com/world/2019/feb/17/catholic-church-still-making-excuses-paedophilia-pope.
8. Meaghan O'Keefe, *American Catholic Bishops and the Politics of Scandal: Rhetoric of Authority* (London and New York: Routledge, 2019).
9. Cosimo Schinaia, *On Paedophilia* (London and New York: Routledge, 2018), p. xxxv.
10. American Psychiatric Association, *Diagnostic and Statistical Manual of Mental Disorders, 5th edition* (DSM-5) (Arlington, VA: American Psychiatric Pub. Inc., 2013), pp. 697-700.
11. https://www.stopitnow.org.uk/concerned-about-your-own-thoughts-or-behaviour/help-with-inappropriate-thoughts-or-behaviour/get-the-facts/is-it-illegal-to-be-a-paedophile/.
12. Cf. David Finkelhor, *Child Sexual Abuse: New Theory and Research* (New York: Free Press, 1984).
13. T. Ward and S.M. Hudson, 'Finkelhor's Precondition Model of Child Sexual Abuse: A Critique', *Psychology, Crime and Law* (online) Vol. 7, issue 4 (2001), pp. 291-307; D. Finkelhor, R.K. Ormrod, H.A. Turner and S.L. Hamby, 'Child and Youth Victimization Known to Police, School, and Other Medical Authorities', *OJJDP Juvenile Justice Bulletin – NCJ235394* (pp. 1-8) (Washington, DC: US Government Printing Office, 2012).
14. Schinaia, *On Paedophilia*, p. 233.
15. C.S. Lewis, *Surprised by Joy: The Shape of My Early Life* (London: Fount Paperbacks, 1955).
16. Renton, *Stiff Upper Lip*, p. 318.
17. Personal communication.
18. Witness statement of Bishop Peter Ball, Independent Inquiry into Child Sexual Abuse, 2018 (ANGOOO301), pp. 1-88, p. 18, https://www.iicsa.org.uk/document/ang000301; https://www.iicsa.org.uk/key-documents/4888/view/ang000209.pdf.
19. Ibid., p. 18.

20. Ibid., p. 29.
21. Ibid., p. 22.
22. Ibid., p. 31.
23. Dave Tregaskis, https://www.iicsa.org.uk/key-documents/8862/view/ACE001424_015-020.pdf.
24. Campbell, 'Foreword', p. xix.
25. Daniel E. Greenberg, 'A Review of *Traumatic Narcissism: Relational Systems of Subjugation* by Daniel Shaw (New York: Routledge, 2014)'. *Contemporary Psychoanalysis*, Vol. 52, no. 1 (2016), pp. 130-43, p. 131.
26. Harold Blum, quoted by Loretta L. Loeb, 'The Consequences of Child Sexual Abuse', p. 181.
27. Ibid., p. 182.
28. https://www.independent.co.uk/news/long_reads/chichester-paedophile-child-abuse-reverends-church-of-england-diocese-sex-offenders-a8270601.html.
29. Cf. David Greenwood, *Responding Badly: Church and Institutional Cover-up of Sex Abuse Allegations* (Independently published, 2018), pp. 65-68; https://cofechichestersafeguarding.contentfiles.net/media/documents/document/2017/05/RM_report__EBS_Comments_1202282.pdf.
30. https://safeguarding.chichester.anglican.org/documents/meekings-report-butler-sloss-comments/; https://cofechichestersafeguarding.contentfiles.net/media/documents/document/2017/05/EBSReport_Addendum1202282.pdf.
31. https://www.iicsa.org.uk/key-documents/4418/view/WWS000133.pdf.
32. https://safeguarding.chichester.anglican.org/shemmings-report/.
33. https://www.iicsa.org.uk/key-documents/8800/view/ACE025954_079.pdf.
34. 'Church of England ordained known paedophile Roy Cotton', 26 May 2011, https://www.bbc.co.uk/news/uk-england-sussex-13560976; 'Priest Roy Cotton sex abuse victim "ready to move on"', 9 September 2013, https://www.bbc.co.uk/news/uk-england-sussex-24017063.
35. Schinaia, *On Paedophilia*, p. 232.
36. https://www.bexhillobserver.net/news/crime/former-bexhill-vicar-sentenced-child-sex-offences-2058010; https://www.bbc.co.uk/news/uk-england-sussex-43141768.
37. https://www.iicsa.org.uk/publications/investigation/anglican-chichester-peter-ball/case-study-1-diocese-chichester/b3-cases-roy-cotton-and-colin-pritchard, para. 202.
38. 'Bishop of Chichester admits child abuse cover-up', 23 April 2013, https://www.bbc.co.uk/news/uk-england-sussex-22248572.
39. Renton, *Stiff Upper Lip*, p. 335.
40. https://www.iicsa.org.uk/publications/investigation/anglican-chichester-peter-ball/case-study-1-diocese-chichester/b3-cases-roy-cotton-and-colin-pritchard; https://www.iicsa.org.uk/publications/investigation/anglican-chichester-peter-ball/case-study-1-diocese-chichester/b8-allegations-against-gordon-rideout-robert-coles-and-jonathan-graves.

41. https://www.iicsa.org.uk/key-documents/4418/view/WWS000133.pdf.
42. Leon Festinger, *A Theory of Cognitive Dissonance* (Redwood City, CA: Stanford University Press, 1957).
43. Travis and Aronson, *Mistakes Were Made (but Not by Me)*, p. 22.
44. https://www.churchtimes.co.uk/articles/2019/3-may/news/uk/bishop-apologises-for-mistakes-after-lincoln-abuse-featured-on-panorama.
45. 'Paedophiles need help, not condemnation – I should know', 11 September 2020, https://www.bbc.co.uk/bbcthree/article/3216b48d-3195-4f67-8149-54586689ae3c;
https://stopso.org.uk/my-experience-as-a-paedophile-cured-by-nhs-psychoanalysis.

4. How the Church Has Responded

1. Archbishop Rowan Williams, https://www.communitycare.co.uk/2007/05/04/church-of-england-apologises-for-child-abuse-committed-by-vicar-david-smith/.
2. Neil Todd's sister, quoted by Angharad Woolcott, *Church Times*, 17 January 2020, https://www.churchtimes.co.uk/articles/2020/17-january/comment/opinion/as-a-survivor-i-believe-that-by-talking-out-i-may-be-able-to-help-others.
3. https://www.telegraph.co.uk/news/uknews/1550588/Church-failed-to-act-against-sex-abuse-vicar.html.
4. 'Boy "abused by vicar in vicarage"', 25 April 2007, http://news.bbc.co.uk/1/hi/england/somerset/6592333.stm;
'Vicar jailed for child sex abuse', 3 May 2007; http://news.bbc.co.uk/1/hi/england/bristol/6620445.stm.
5. https://www.communitycare.co.uk/2007/05/04/church-of-england-apologises-for-child-abuse-committed-by-vicar-david-smith/;
http://www.ekklesia.co.uk/node/5226.
6. https://www.communitycare.co.uk/2006/04/19/churches-complacent-about-the-need-for-child-protection-policies/.
7. 'Church choirmaster jailed for child sex abuse', 27 April 2007, https://www.theguardian.com/uk/2007/apr/27/topstories3.ukcrime.
8. 'Anger over Church abuse cover-up', 24 April 2007, http://news.bbc.co.uk/1/hi/6594439.stm.
9. http://www.bishop-accountability.org/news2007/09_ 10/2007_10_26_BBCNews_ChurchAbuse.htm.
10. https://www.churchofengland.org/more/media-centre/news/report-handling-past-cases-review.
11. https://www.churchofengland.org/sites/default/files/2019-08/PCR2%20Background%20and%20Overview.pdf;
https://www.thinkinganglicans.org.uk/church-of-england-announces-past-cases-review-2/.
12. Cf. I.E.P. Menzies, The Functioning of Social Systems as a Defence against Anxiety, Tavistock Pamphlet No. 3 (London: Tavistock Institute

Endnotes

of Human Relations, 1960); A. Obholzer and V. Zagier Roberts (eds), *The Unconscious at Work: Individual and Organizational Stress in the Human Services* (London: Routledge, 1994).
13. https://www.portsmouth.co.uk/news/crime/victim-pervert-chichester-priest-warns-there-are-more-victims-out-there -1365033.
14. https://www.churchtimes.co.uk/articles/2015/11-december/comment/opinion/church-litigation-means-my-ordeal-continues.
15. 'Meirion Griffiths: Chichester abuse vicar's sentence appeal dismissed', 19 May 2020, https://www.bbc.co.uk/news/uk-england-sussex-52724532.
16. Stein, 'Safeguarding Policy at a Crossroads', pp. 160, 161 and 163.
17. https://www.iicsa.org.uk/key-documents/12767/view/public-hearing-transcript-10-july-2019.pdf, p. 16.
18. https://www.theguardian.com/uk-news/2019/nov/23/church-of-england-reviews-its-handling-of-sexual-abuse-case.
19. https://www.iicsa.org.uk/key-documents/12767/view/public-hearing-transcript-10-july-2019.pdf, p. 30.
20. Ibid., pp. 31 and 32.
21. Ibid., pp. 47 and 48.
22. Ibid., p. 56.
23. Ibid., pp. 60 and 61.
24. https://www.theguardian.com/uk-news/2019/nov/23/church-of-england-reviews-its-handling-of-sexual-abuse-case.

5. Surface Awareness – Policies, Guidelines and Training

1. Ian Elliott, 'Recognising Dangerous Safeguarding Practices', in Fife and Gilo (eds), *Letters to a Broken Church*, p. 21.
2. https://www.churchofengland.org/safeguarding/promoting-safer-church/how-we-work-and-governance; https://www.churchofengland.org/safeguarding/safeguarding-principles.
3. https://www.iicsa.org.uk/key-documents/12363/view/public-hearing-transcript-2-july-2019.pdf, p. 12.
4. Elliott, 'Recognising Dangerous Safeguarding Practices', p. 21.
5. https://www.iicsa.org.uk/key-documents/12363/view/public-hearing-transcript-2-july-2019.pdf, p. 24; https://www.churchofengland.org/sites/default/files/2017-11/Elliot%20Review%20Findings.pdf.
6. https://www.iicsa.org.uk/key-documents/12363/view/public-hearing-transcript-2-july-2019.pdf, pp. 42-43.
7. https://www.wirralglobe.co.uk/news/10970850.wirral-child-porn-vicar-jailed-for-12-months-as-judge-tells-him-your-dark-secret-is-out/.
8. https://www.iicsa.org.uk/key-documents/12423/view/public-hearing-transcript-3-july-2019.pdf, pp. 31-41.
9. Ibid., p. 78; https://www.iicsa.org.uk/video/iicsa-anglican-investigation-day-3-03072019-am2, pp. 83-127;

Edi Carmi and Sheila Fish, Final Overview Report of the Independent Diocesan Safeguarding Audits and Additional Work on Improving Responses to Survivors of Abuse (2019), https://www.scie.org.uk/consultancy/safeguarding-reviews-audits.
10. https://www.iicsa.org.uk/key-documents/12363/view/public-hearing-transcript-2-july-2019.pdf, p. 144.
11. Elliott, 'Recognising Dangerous Safeguarding Practices', p. 21.
12. https://www.theguardian.com/world/2016/mar/15/i-told-so-many-bishops-survivor-tells-of-system-that-protected-priest.
13. Obituary of Garth More, plus postscript, *Ecclesiastical Law Journal*, https://www.cambridge.org/core/services/aop-cambridge-core/content/view/S0956618X00000892.
14. https://www.theguardian.com/world/2016/mar/15/i-told-so-many-bishops-survivor-tells-of-system-that-protected-priest.
15. https://www.theguardian.com/world/2015/dec/04/church-of-england-pays-35000-abuse-expert-canon-law-garth-moore;
https://www.churchofengland.org/more/safeguarding/safeguarding-news-statements/Elliottt-review-findings;
https://www.churchofengland.org/sites/default/files/2017-11/Elliot%20Review%20Findings.pdf.
16. https://www.churchofengland.org/sites/default/files/2017-11/Elliot%20Review%20Findings.pdf.
17. https://www.iicsa.org.uk/key-documents/12363/view/public-hearing-transcript-2-july-2019.pdf, p. 22.
18. Ibid., pp. 130-1.
19. https://richardwsymonds.wordpress.com/tag/the-lambeth-list/;
https://www.iicsa.org.uk/key-documents/12363/view/public-hearing-transcript-2-july-2019.pdf, pp. 129-30.
20. Ibid., p. 132.
21. See Policy for Bishops and their Staff Approved by the House of Bishops May 2018 (marked draft), https://www.churchofengland.org/sites/default/files/2019-09/Personal%20Files%20Relating%20to%20Clergy%202018%20Edition.pdf.
22. https://www.lawandreligionuk.com/2014/07/03/clergy-blacklists-blue-files-and-the-archbishops-list/;
https://www.theguardian.com/world/2019/may/07/rebel-priest-gay-church-campaign-same-sex-marriage.
23. https://www.iicsa.org.uk/key-documents/12363/view/public-hearing-transcript-2-july-2019.pdf, p. 139.
24. https://www.ecclesiastical.com/.
25. Gilo, 'The Virtuous Circle', in Fife and Gilo (eds), *Letters to a Broken Church*, pp. 48-54.
26. http://www.allchurches.co.uk/news/new-chairman-for-allchurches-trust/.
27. Gilo, 'The Virtuous Circle', pp. 49-50.
28. http://survivingchurch.org/2020/03/, 7 March 2020.
29. https://www.churchtimes.co.uk/articles/2020/14-august/news/uk/money-for-abuse-survivors-is-dwarfed-by-legal-and-admin-bill.

Endnotes 175

30. https://www.churchofengland.org/safeguarding/promoting-safer-church/how-we-work-and-governance.
31. Hashi Mohamed, *People Like Us: What it Takes to Make it in Modern Britain* (London: Profile Books, 2020), p. 133. He quotes from James Ball and Andrew Greenway, 'The Rise of the Bluffocracy', *The Spectator*, 18 August 2018, https://www.spectator.co.uk/article/the-rise-of-the-bluffocracy.
32. https://chairnsp.org/2020/02/19/annual-report-2019-national-safeguarding-panel/.

6. DYNAMICS OF POWER AND CONTROL IN THE INSTITUTIONAL CHURCH

1. https://www.iicsa.org.uk/key-documents/12363/view/public-hearing-transcript-2-july-2019.pdf, p. 155.
2. Jane Chevous, comment, 9 March 2020, on Stephen Parsons' blog, 'Safeguarding, Compassion and the Law', posted 7 March 2020, http://survivingchurch.org/2020/03/07/safeguarding-compassion-and-the-law/.
3. Anthony Giddens, *Runaway World: How Globalisation Is Reshaping Our Lives* (London: Profile Books, 2002).
4. Gary Younge, 'Notes from the Margins', *Free Associations*, Issue 30 (Spring 2020), p. 1.
5. Sally Cahill QC, with Joe Cocker and Nichola Harding, *Cahill Report: Inquiry into the Church of England's Response to Child Abuse Allegations Made against Robert Waddington* (2014), available from Church House Bookshop; see Amanda Gearing, 'Litany of Failure', posted 5 November 2014, https://www.onlineopinion.com.au/view.asp?article=16831&page=0.
6. Younge, 'Notes from the Margins', p.1.
7. https://www.iicsa.org.uk/key-documents/12363/view/public-hearing-transcript-2-july-2019.pdf, p. 155.
8. Ibid., pp. 157-60.
9. Gearing, 'Litany of Failure', https://www.onlineopinion.com.au/view.asp?article=16831&page=0.
10. Mohamed, *People Like Us*, pp. 168, 224 and 242. Unconscious bias has now been legally established by the case in law of Nagarajan.
11. Ibid., pp. 243, 244 and 245.
12. Eric Luis Uhlmann and Geoffrey L. Cohen, '"I Think It, Therefore It's True": Effects of Self-perceived Objectivity on Hiring Discrimination,' *Organizational Behavior and Human Decision Processes*, Vol. 104, issue 2 (2007), pp. 207-23.
13. https://ianpace.wordpress.com/2013/05/; https://ianpace.wordpress.com/2013/05/12/robert-waddington-former-dean-of-manchester-cathedral-and-chethams-school-of-music/.
14. https://www.independent.co.uk/news/uk/crime/church-of-england-sex-abuse-investigation-into-manchester-cathedral-dean-robert-waddington-expected-8617712.html;

https://blogs.city.ac.uk/music/2015/03/03/ian-pace-articles-on-elite-music-teaching-and-abuse-in-the-telegraph-and-the-conversation/;
https://www.theguardian.com/uk/2013/feb/12/chethams-music-school-allegations-increase;
https://slippedisc.com/2019/10/distressing-evidence-at-sex-abuse-inquiry-into-english-music-schools/.
15. https://www.iicsa.org.uk/key-documents/12363/view/public-hearing-transcript-2-july-2019.pdf, p. 158.
16. https://archbishopcranmer.com/safeguarding-church-england-house-rebuilt/.
17. https://www.churchofengland.org/more/media-centre/news/overwhelming-support-synod-safeguarding-motion.
18. Ibid., speeches in the debate.
19. David Campbell and Marianne Groenback, *Taking Positions in the Organization*, (London: Karnac, 2006).
20. http://survivingchurch.org/2020/07/10/general-synod-and-the-questions-around-safeguarding/.
21. R. Stacey, 'Complexity at the "Edge" of the Basic Assumption Group', in L.F. Gould, L.F. Stapley and M. Stein (eds), *The Systems Psychodynamics of Organizations: Integrating the Group Relations Approach, Psychoanalytic and Open Systems Perspectives* (New York and London: Karnac, 2001), pp. 91-114, p. 106.
22. Campbell and Groenback, *Taking Positions in the Organization*, p. 16.
23. https://www.iicsa.org.uk/key-documents/6346/view/public-hearing-transcript-27-july-2018.pdf, pp. 13-14;
https://www.secularism.org.uk/opinion/2018/08/religious-power-and-privilege-failed-the-victims-in-the-peter-ball-affair; https://archbishopcranmer.com/nobody-knows-nobodys-friends/.
24. http://survivingchurch.org/2018/09/30/toxic-masculinity-a-problem-for-the-church.
25. http://survivingchurch.org/2019/08/20/gilo-writes-safeguarding-the-secrets-part-1-nobodys-friends/.
26. Brown and Woodhead, *That Was the Church That Was*, p. 105.
27. http://survivingchurch.org/2019/08/20/gilo-writes-safeguarding-the-secrets-part-1-nobodys-friends/;
28. George Orwell, 'England your England', 1941, https://orwell.ru/library/essays/lion/english/e_eye.
29. Mohamed, *People Like Us*, pp. 58, 66, 13 and 49.
30. Lord Carlile of Berriew CBE QC, *Bishop George Bell: The Independent Review*, 16 December 2017, p. 19, https://www.churchofengland.org/sites/default/files/2017-12/Bishop%20George%20Bell%20-%20The%20Independent%20Review.pdf.
31. Ibid.; and https://archbishopcranmer.com/bishop-george-bell-reputation-restored-cloud/.
32. https://www.irishtimes.com/opinion/britain-is-run-by-a-self-serving-clique-that-s-why-it-s-in-crisis-1.3947592.
33. https://www.theguardian.com/commentisfree/2020/jun/07/how-can-

the-church-of-england-speak-about-race-when-its-leaders-are-so-white-george-floyd-covid-19.
34. Lynsey Hanley, *Respectable: The Experience of Class* (London: Penguin Books, 2017), p. xi.

7. CHARISMATIC POWER AND CONTROL

1. Bishop Alan Wilson, https://www.iicsa.org.uk/key-documents/12363/view/public-hearing-transcript-2-july-2019.pdf, pp. 158-59.
2. Max Weber, *Economy and Society*, eds. G. Roth and C. Wittich (New York: Bedminster Press, 1968), p. 215.
3. Robert A. Dahl, quoted in Steven Lukes, *Power: A Radical View*, 2nd edition (London: Palgrave, 2005), p. 30.
4. Weber, *Economy and Society*, pp. 242 and 245.
5. Neil Todd's words, quoted in 'Exposed: The Church's Darkest Secret', Ep. 2 of 2, https://www.youtube.com/watch?v=adoDCbr5_SA.
6. John Keats, 'Ode to a Nightingale', https://www.poetryfoundation.org/poems/44479/ode-to-a-nightingale.
7. David Greenwood, *Basically Innocent? The Facts behind the Scandal of Bishop Peter Ball's Abuse of Children and Young Men and How the Establishment Helped Him Get away with It* (Independently published, 2019), pp. 21-38, quotes from pp. 21, 22, 25, 26, pp. 26-27 and pp. 32 and 38.
8. Dame Moira Gibb DBE, *An Abuse of Faith: The Independent Peter Ball Review*, June 2017, pp. 41-45, https://www.churchofengland.org/sites/default/files/2017-11/report-of-the-peter-ball-review-210617.pdf.
9. Alexander Deutsch, 'Psychological Perspectives on Cult Leadership', in Marc Galanter (ed.), *Cults and New Religious Movements* (Washington, DC: American Psychiatric Association, 1989), pp. 147-63.
10. Daniel Shaw, *Traumatic Narcissism: Relational Systems of Subjugation* (New York: Routledge, 2014), pp. 12-13.
11. Aung San Suu Kyi, acceptance message for the Sakharov Prize for Freedom of Thought, 1991.
12. Shaw, 'Traumatic Abuse in Cults: A Psychoanalytic Perspective', p. 106, http://www.danielshawlcsw.com/daniel shaw/wp-content/uploads/2018/04/traumabusecults.pdf.
13. Herman, *Trauma and Recovery*, p. 77.
14. Shaw, 'Traumatic Abuse in Cults: A Psychoanalytic Perspective', p. 112.
15. *The Church of England Companion: A Glossary*, https://www.churchofenglandglossary.co.uk/dictionary/definition/charismatic.
16. Stephen Parsons, *Ungodly Fear: Fundamentalist Christianity and the Abuse of Power* (Oxford: Lion Publishing, 2000), pp. 208 and 217.
17. Roland Howard, *The Rise and Fall of the Nine O'clock Service: A Cult within the Church?* (London: Mowbray, 1996), p. 5.
18. Ibid., p. 35.
19. Émile Durkheim, *The Elementary Forms of the Religious Life* (New York: Free Press, 1965).

20. K. Wu, 'Performing the Charismatic Ritual', in C. Lindholm (ed.), *The Anthropology of Religious Charisma: Ecstasies and Institutions* (New York: Palgrave Macmillan, 2013), pp. 33-57.
21. Erving Goffman, *The Presentation of Self in Everyday Life* (New York: Doubleday, 1959).
22. Howard, *The Rise and Fall of the Nine O'clock Service*, p. 28.
23. BBC Everyman Special, 'Breach of Faith', 26 November 1995, https://www.youtube.com/watch?v=QxwdyF3qZj8.
24. Phil Catalfo, 'Glory Be to Gaia', *New Age Journal*, no. 1 (1995), http://smokyhole.org/fem/fem0428.htm.
25. Howard, *The Rise and Fall of the Nine O'clock Service*, p. 31, p. 72.
26. Ibid., p. 107.
27. Ibid., p. 108.
28. Ibid., pp. 122-23.
29. Ibid., p. 124.
30. 'Breach of Faith', https://www.youtube.com/watch?v=Qxwd yF3qZj8.
31. Howard, *The Rise and Fall of the Nine O'clock Service*, p. 131.
32. Ibid., p. 135.
33. 'Breach of Faith', https://www.youtube.com/watch?v=Qxwd yF3qZj8.
34. George Carey, *Know the Truth: A Memoir* (London: Harper Collins, 2004), p. 188.
35. 'Breach of Faith', https://www.youtube.com/watch?v=Qxwdy F3qZj8.
36. BBC Radio 4, 'The Nine O'clock Service', 1990, https://www.youtube.com/watch?v=IYOunsaMZSU.
37. https://www.independent.co.uk/news/rave-vicar-resigns-1583712.html; https://www.independent.co.uk/news/sex-cult-leaves-150-in-need-of-counselling-1597498.html.
38. Linda Woodhead, 'Hear No Evil, See No Evil, Speak No Evil', 18 November 1996, http://trushare.com/18NOV96/NO96EVIL.htm.

8. The Influence of the Public School Ethos within the Institutional Church

1. David Greenwood, *Basically Innocent?*, p. 33.
2. Gibb, *An Abuse of Faith*, pp. 63ff., https://www.church ofengland.org/sites/default/files/2017-11/report-of-the-peter-ball-review-210617.pdf.
3. Gibb, *An Abuse of Faith*, p. 63, 6.2.5.
4. https://www.goodschoolsguide.co.uk/choosing-a-school/independent-schools/.
5. Two documentaries used are: The Channel 4 British Documentary Film Foundation, 'Chosen',
https://www.youtube.com/watch?v=WoOzqebOU1k, and 40 Minutes, 'The Making of Them', https://www.youtube.com/watch?v=2uRr77vju8U; Nick Duffell, *The Making of Them: The British Attitude to Children and the Boarding School System* (London: Lone Arrow Press, 2000); other books are included in the Bibliography.

6. https://www.independentschoolparent.com/school/prep/boarding-prep/boarding-prep-schools/.
7. G.R. Searle, *A New England? Peace and War 1886-1918* (Oxford: OUP, 2004), p. 65.
8. L. James, *The Rise and Fall of the British Empire* (London: Abacus, 1994), p. 207.
9. https://stephenbasdeo.wordpress.com/2013/09/01/the-public-school-ethos-and-late-nineteenth-century-juvenile-literature.
10. Renton, *Stiff Upper Lip*, p. 144.
11. Mohamed, *People Like Us*, pp. 49 and 130.
12. http://www.acceptingevangelicals.org/wp-content/uploads/2014/07/AE-synod-address-David-Runcorn.pdf; 2014, Church Times report that half of the serving bishops (whose schooling could be determined) were educated in the independent sector https://www.thinkinganglicans.org.uk/6718-2/; 2016, A study of the then current 40 enthroned or acting diocesan bishops showed that 85% studied at Oxbridge, 12.5% attended another Russell group University, 32.5% attended an independent school, and 32.5% attended a selective grammar school; https://www.secularism.org.uk/opinion/2016/04/church-of-england-bishops-are-more-elitist-than-david-camerons-cabinet.
13. Mark Stibbe, *Home at Last: Freedom from Boarding School Pain* (Milton Keynes: Malcolm Down Publishing, 2016), pp. 13 and 18.
14. Joy Schaverien, *Boarding School Syndrome: The Psychological Trauma of the 'Privileged' Child* (London: Routledge, 2015), p. 179.
15. Stibbe, *Home at Last*, p. 60.
16. Independent School Parent, 'Boarding Prep Schools: Are They Right for Your Child?', https://www.independentschoolparent.com/school/prep/boarding-prep/boarding-prep-schools/.
17. Stibbe, *Home at Last*, pp. 18-19.
18. Giles Fraser, quoted by Robert Verkaik in *Posh Boys: How the English Public Schools Ruin Britain* (London: OneWorld Publications, 2018), p. 211.
19. Renton, *Stiff Upper Lip*, p. 210.
20. Parsons, *Ungodly Fear*, p. 52.
21. Verkaik, *Posh Boys*, p. 212.
22. Donald A. MacLeod, *C. Stacey Woods and the Evangelical Rediscovery of the University* (Downers Grove, IL: IVP Academic, 2007), p. 246.
23. John Eddison (ed.), *A Study in Spiritual Power: An Appreciation of E.J.H Nash (Bash)* (Crowborough: Highland Books, 1992), p. 87.
24. Despite the scandal the conservative evangelical camps operate today but now under the auspices of the Titus Trust https://www.titustrust.org/. There is growing opposition to this continuing, cf. http://anglican.ink/2020/05/01/why-the-titus-trust-must-close/.
25. https://www.independent.co.uk/news/people/jeremy-clarkson-opens-up-about-bullying-at-public-school-i-was-made-to-lick-the-lavatories-clean-and-10336723.html;
https://www.derbytelegraph.co.uk/news/derby-news/repton-school-allegations-charity-commission-1394532.

26. https://www.patheos.com/blogs/thefreethinker/2019/06/bare-butt-beatings-and-naked-massages-at-prayer-group-meetings/.
27. https://premierchristian.news/en/news/article/bbc-s-martin-bashir-explains-how-vicar-jonathan-fletcher-dominated-his-church; https://www.telegraph.co.uk/news/2019/12/26/victims-jonathan-fletcher-speak-felt-like-neglected-abused-dog/.
28. http://anglican.ink/2019/06/29/joining-up-the-dots-the-jonathan-fletcher-story/; http://anglican.ink/2019/09/23/time-to-come-clean-response-to-jonathan-fletchers-letter/.
29. Sigmund Freud, 'A Child Is Being Beaten', in J. Strachey (ed.), *The Standard Edition of the Complete Psychological Works of Sigmund Freud, Volume XVII (1917-1919): An Infantile Neurosis and Other Works* (London: The Hogarth Press, 1955), pp. 179-204, p. 179.
30. http://anglican.ink/2019/11/28/smyth-fletcher-iwerne-and-the-theology-of-the-divided-self/.
31. Ibid.
32. Verkaik, *Posh Boys*, p. 214.
33. https://www.independent.co.uk/news/uk/home-news/archbishop-of-canterbury-justin-welby-child-abuse-links-apology-church-of-england.
34. https://www.bbc.co.uk/news/av/uk-39560235/further-abuse-allegations-uncovered-against-leading-qc; https://www.churchtimes.co.uk/articles/2017/13-april/news/uk/new-allegations-tell-of-savagery-of-smyth-beatings; https://www.telegraph.co.uk/news/2017/02/06/family-lawyer-accused-beating-boys-demanded-stopped-working/.
35. https://www.telegraph.co.uk/news/2017/04/11/john-smyth-recruited-victim-now-head-top-prep-school-help/; Channel 4 News, 4 February 2014, report that Peter Wright had been found guilty of twelve counts of sexual assault, https://www.youtube.com/watch?v=tOQ5glZfi6w; https://cathyfox.wordpress.com/2016/09/22/caldicott-school-child-sexual-abusers-and-timeline/;
entry on Wikiwand relating to Caldicott School, https://www.wikiwand.com/en/Caldicott_School#/Child_sex_abuse;
Channel 4 documentary, 'Chosen', https://www.youtube.com/watch?v=WoOzqebOU1k;
Channel 4 News, 'Former Caldicott headteacher jailed for years of abuse', 6 February 2014, https://www.youtube.com/watch?v=oOZdMKI2MYE.
36. Renton, *Stiff Upper Lip*, p. 70.
37. https://www.telegraph.co.uk/men/thinking-man/archers-simon-williams-public-school-fagging/.
38. Renton, *Stiff Upper Lip*, p. 80.
39. Schaverien, *Boarding School Syndrome*, pp. 187-88.
40. Renton, *Stiff Upper Lip*, p. 245.
41. 'When I was at school . . .', *The Guardian*, 12 October 2005, https://www.theguardian.com/education/2005/oct/12/publicschools.schools.
42. https://www.oxfordmail.co.uk/news/18267102.dragon-school-oxford-teacher-caught-images-children/;

https://www.verisonalaw.com/blog/derek-slade-conviction-results-in-numerous-compensation-claims/.
43. Verkaik, *Posh Boys*, p. 207.
44. https://www.itv.com/news/2018-02-18/shocking-scale-of-sexual-abuse-at-uk-boarding-schools-revealed-by-itv-documentary/.
45. Verkaik, *Posh Boys*, pp. 207 and 220, and Renton, *Stiff Upper Lip*, pp. 309-19.
46. Tirril Harris, 'Implications of Attachment Theory for Working in Psychoanalytic Psychotherapy', *International Forum of Psychoanalysis*, Vol. 13, issue 3 (2004), pp. 147-56.
47. Duffell, *The Making of Them*, p. xiii.
48. Verkaik, *Posh Boys*, p. 214.
49. Nick Duffell, *Wounded Leaders: British Elitism and the Entitlement Illusion – A Psychohistory* (London: Lone Arrow Press, 2015), p. 84.
50. Ibid., p. 88.
51. https://www.channel4.com/news/christian-lawyer-who-beat-boys-was-charged-over-zimbabwe-death;
http://survivingchurch.org/2019/10/20/open-letter-to-keith-makin-re-john-smyth-review/;
Channel 4 News, 'Church of England bishop admits he was victim of John Smyth abuse', 7 February 2017, https://www.youtube.com/watch?v=JXNS57yQWGI;
https://www.thinkinganglicans.org.uk/statement-from-victims-of-the-late-john-smyth-qc-and-the-titus-trust/.
52. https://www.channel4.com/news/christian-lawyer-who-beat-boys-was-charged-over-zimbabwe-death.
53. https://www.churchofengland.org/safeguarding/promoting-safer-church/safeguarding-news-statements/independent-review-smyth-case.
54. https://content.scriptureunion.org.uk/safeguarding.
55. https://www.titustrust.org/safeguarding-and-safety/john-smyth-statement-on-settlement/.
56. http://survivingchurch.org/2019/10/20/open-letter-to-keith-makin-re-john-smyth-review/.
57. https://www.theguardian.com/world/2019/aug/13/justin-welby-church-scrutiny-sadistic-christian-camp;
https://www.churchtimes.co.uk/articles/2019/18-april/news/uk/smyth-abuse-survivors-dispute-welby-claim.
58. http://survivingchurch.org/2020/01/03/reacting-to-the-jonathan-fletcher-story-the-great-silence.
59. *Private Eye*, no. 1513, 10 January 2020, and no. 1522, 22 May 2020.
60. https://archbishopcranmer.com/jonathan-fletcher-church-of-england-crisis-integrity/.
61. Ibid.
62. Lewis, *Surprised by Joy*, p. 65.
63. https://www.telegraph.co.uk/news/2019/12/26/jonathan-fletcher-son-cabinet-minister-village-vicar-gifted/;

http://survivingchurch.org/2019/06/27/joining-up-the-dots-the-jonathan-fletcher-story/powerful friends;
https://survivingchurch.org/2019/07/01/further-reflections-on-the-jonathan-fletcher-story/;
http://anglican.ink/2019/06/29/joining-up-the-dots-the-jonathan-fletcher-story/.
64. Duffell, *Wounded Leaders*, p. 77.

9. Sex and Gender

1. R.W. Connell and James W. Messerschmidt, 'Hegemonic Masculinity: Rethinking the Concept', *Gender Society*, Vol. 19, no. 6 (2005), pp. 829-59.
2. http://inclusive-church.org/blog/male-headship-and-patriarchal-theologies;
http://survivingchurch.org/2020/06/02/the-church-of-england-gentlemens-club/.
3. David Beres, 'Psychoanalytic Notes on the History of Morality', *Journal of the American Psychoanalytic Association*, Vol. 13 (1965), p. 21.
4. Cf. Thomas Merton, *Cassian and the Fathers: Initiation into the Monastic Tradition*, ed. Patrick O'Connell (Kalamazoo, MI: Cistercian Publications, 2005).
5. Sigmund Freud, 'Delusion and Dream in Jensen's "Gradiva"', in J. Strachey (ed.) *The Standard Edition of the Complete Psychological Works of Sigmund Freud, Volume IX (1906-1908): Jensen's 'Gradiva' and Other Works*, (London: Hogarth Press, 1907), p. 35.
6. Sigmund Freud, 'Obsessive Actions and Religious Activities', in ibid., p. 125.
7. M. Charney, 'Review of *Freud and the Problem of God* by Hans Küng (New Haven, CT: Yale University Press, 1979)', *Psychoanalytic Review*, Vol. 67, no. 3 (1980), pp. 415-16, p. 416.
8. Rosemary Radford Ruether, 'Sexism and Misogyny in the Christian Tradition: Liberating Alternatives', *Buddhist-Christian Studies*, Vol. 34 (2014), pp. 83-94, p. 85.
9. Małgorzata Mikołajczak and Janina Pietrzak, 'Ambivalent Sexism and Religion: Connected through Values, *Sex Roles: A Journal of Research*, Vol. 70, nos 9-10 (2014), pp. 387-99.
10. Ruether, 'Sexism and Misogyny in the Christian Tradition', pp. 89 and 94.
11. https://www.theguardian.com/world/2020/jun/10/c-of-e-systemic-racism-guli-francis-dehqani-bame-bishop-says.
12. https://www.telegraph.co.uk/obituaries/2020/04/09/rt-rev-barbara-harris-first-woman-bishop-anglican-communion/.
13. 'Church of England at war after Bishop Philip North's u-turn', 10 March 2017, https://www.bbc.co.uk/news/uk-39227033;
https://theconversation.com/as-metoo-harassment-claims-hit-the-church-of-england-its-an-institution-still-steeped-in-sexism-86884.
14. Parsons, *Ungodly Fear*, p. 24.

15. Anne, 'The Deacon's tale', in Fife and Gilo (eds), *Letters to a Broken Church*, p. 2.
16. https://www.theguardian.com/world/2020/jan/23/sex-married-heterosexual-couples-church-of-england-christians.
17. Gayle Rubin, 'Thinking Sex: Notes for a Radical Theory of the Politics of Sexuality', in H. Abelove, M.A. Barale and D.M. Halperin (eds), *The Lesbian and Gay Studies Reader* (New York: Routledge), pp. 3-44, p. 11.
18. Ann Pellegrini and Janet R. Jakobsen, 'Melancholy Hope and Other Psychic Remainders: Afterthoughts on "Love the Sin"', *Studies in Gender and Sexuality*, Vol. 6, no. 4 (2005), pp. 423-40.
19. Gibb, *An Abuse of Faith*, pp. 60ff., https://www.churchof england.org/sites/default/files/2017-11/report-of-the-peter-ball-review-210617.pdf.
20. Sigmund Freud, 'Analysis Terminable and Interminable', in J. Strachey (ed.), *The Standard Edition of the Complete Psychological Works of Sigmund Freud, Volume XXIII (1937-1939):Moses and Monotheism, An Outline of Psychoanalysis and Other Works* (London: Hogarth Press, 1964), p. 244.
21. Parsons, *Ungodly Fear*, p. 132.
22. E. Young-Bruehl, 'Sexual Diversity in Cosmopolitan Perspective', *Studies in Gender and Sexuality*, Vol. 11, no. 1 (2010), pp. 1-9, p. 5.
23. Carey, *Know the Truth*.
24. https://www.telegraph.co.uk/news/religion/9093297/Lord-Carey-gay-marriage-would-be-cultural-vandalism.html.
25. 'Lord Carey attacks PM over Christian support', 30 March 2013, https://www.bbc.co.uk/news/uk-21979034.
26. 'Gay marriage plan paves way for polygamy, says Lord Carey', 4 June 2013, https://www.bbc.co.uk/news/uk-politics -22727808.
27. Young-Bruehl, 'Sexual Diversity in Cosmopolitan Perspective'.
28. https://onebodyonefaith.org.uk/about-us/what-we-believe/; https://www.inclusive-church.org/;
    see also https://stopabusecampaign.org/2017/03/10/are-most-sex-abusers-heterosexual/ and other research studies.
29. https://www.onebodyonefaith.org.uk/site/assets/files/2320/in_the_name_of_love_-_oasis_trust.pdf.
30. https://www.churchofengland.org/sites/default/files/2017-11/GS%202055%20Marriage%20and%20Same%20Sex%20Relationships%20after%20the%20Shared%20Conversations%20A%20Report%20from%20the%20House%20of%20Bishops.pdf, p. 7.
31. Ibid., p. 11.
32. https://www.theguardian.com/world/2020/jan/23/sex-married-heterosexual-couples-church-of-england-christians.
33. https://www.theguardian.com/world/2020/jan/27/church-of-england-stance-on-sex-and-marriage-is-staggeringly-stupid.
34. https://www.theguardian.com/world/2020/feb/04/c-of-e-sex-guidance-row-synod-member-calls-out-deep-hypocrisy.
35. https://viamedia.news/2020/02/06/living-in-love-faith-what-the-bishops-need-to-learn/.

36. Janet R. Jakobsen and Ann Pellegrini, *Love the Sin: Sexual Regulation and the Limits of Religious Tolerance* (Boston, MA: Beacon Press, 2004)
37. Pellegrini and Jakobsen, 'Melancholy Hope and Other Psychic Remainders', p. 437.
38. https://www.theguardian.com/world/2017/apr/06/openly-gay-clergyman-passed-over-seven-times-for-promotion-to-bishop-jeffrey-john-reading; https://www.theguardian.com/world/2017/mar/19/jeffrey-john-anglican-church-in-wales-homophobia-llandaff.
39. https://www.theguardian.com/world/2017/apr/06/openly-gay-clergyman-passed-over-seven-times-for-promotion-to-bishop-jeffrey-john-reading.
40. https://www.thinkinganglicans.org.uk/7527-2/#comments.
41. https://www.churchtimes.co.uk/articles/2020/17-january/comment/opinion/a-tsunami-of-love-for-a-gay-bishop; https://www.churchtimes.co.uk/articles/2016/9-september/news/uk/gay-suffragan-says-he-hopes-to-be-standard-bearer.
42. blogs.lse.ac.uk/religionglobalsociety/2019/12/silence-and-words-unexpected-responses-to-a-gay-bishop.
43. Cf. C.G. Jung, 'The Development of Personality', in Sir Herbert Read, Gerhard Adler and Michael Fordham (eds), *The Collected Works of C.G. Jung, Vol. 17* (London and Henley: Routledge & Kegan Paul, 1954), p. 198.
44. Young-Bruehl, 'Sexual Diversity in Cosmopolitan Perspective', pp. 1-9.
45. Judith Butler, *The Psychic Life of Power: Theories in Subjection* (Stanford, CA: Stanford University Press, 1997).

10. Spiritual Abuse, the Spiritual Sickness within the Church and Signs of Hope

1. Thomas Merton, *The Hidden Ground of Love: Letters on Religious Experience and Social Concerns*, ed. William H. Shannon (London: Collins Flame, 1985), p. 19.
2. Opening note for Fiona Scolding QC, p. 21, https://www.iicsa.org.uk/key-documents/12229/view/2019-06-20-fsqc-draft-opening-wider-church-hearing.pdf.
3. Brown and Woodhead, *That Was the Church That Was*.
4. Carl Jung, *The Collected Works of C.G. Jung, Vol. 7: Two Essays in Analytical Psychology*, ed. Read, Adler and Fordham (London and Henley: Routledge & Kegan Paul, 1953), p. 78.
5. Hugh Gee (personal communication).
6. Lisa Oakley and Justin Humphreys, *Escaping the Maze of Spiritual Abuse: Creating Healthy Christian Cultures* (London: SPCK, 2019), p. xiv.
7. Jayne Ozanne, 'Spiritual Abuse – The Next Great Scandal for the Church', *Spirituality and Psychiatry Special Interest Group Newsletter*, no. 43 (June 2017), pp. 42-50, p. 46, https://www.rcpsych.ac.uk/docs/default-source/members/sigs/spirituality-spsig/newsletter-no-43-june-2017.pdf? sfvrsn=62c314cf_4.

8. Home Office Statutory Guidance Framework 2015, quoted by Oakley and Humphreys, *Escaping the Maze of Spiritual Abuse*, p. 42.
9. Ibid.
10. 'Church of England inquiry into Sussex abuse Bishop', 28 May 2012, https://www.bbc.co.uk/news/uk-england-sussex-18240733.
11. Gloucestershire Constabulary Witness Statement, 12 December 1992, https://www.iicsa.org.uk/key-documents/8892/view/OHY 000086_024-047.pdf.
12. 'Exposed: The Church's Darkest Secret', https://www.you tube.com/watch?v=adoDCbr5_SA.
13. IICSA, Anglican Church Case Studies, Case Study: 2: The Response to Allegations Against Peter Ball, Chapter 5: The Events Leading to Peter Ball's Arrest, paras 71f., para.87, https://www.iicsa.org.uk/publications/investigation/anglican-chichester-peter-ball/case-study-2-response-allegations-against-peter-ball/c5-events-leading-peter-balls-arrest.
14. Ibid., para. 91.
15. Ibid., paras 94-95.
16. IICSA, C.6: The Gloucestershire Constabulary Investigation, ibid., para. 147.
17. Greenwood, *Basically Innocent?*, pp. 70 and 73.
18. IICSA, C.7: The Response of the Church of England During the 1992 Police Investigation, https://www.iicsa.org.uk/publi cations/investigation/anglican-chichester-peter-ball/case-study-2-response-allegations-against-peter-ball/c7-response-church-england-during-1992-police-investigation, paras 158-63.
19. 'Peter Ball abuse inquiry: Prince Charles "misled" by bishop', 27 July 2018, https://www.bbc.co.uk/news/uk-england-44979209.
20. https://www.theguardian.com/uk-news/2015/oct/09/bishop-peter-ball-case-goddard-child-sex-abuse-inquiry.
21. Fiona Gardner, 'Defensive Processes and Deception: An Analysis of the Response of the Institutional Church to Disclosures of Child Sexual Abuse', *British Journal of Psychotherapy*, Vol. 28, no. 1 (2012), pp. 98-109.
22. Anthony Trollope, quoted by George Carey in his autobiography, *Know the Truth*, p. 175.
23. http://survivingchurch.org/2020/08/12/letter-to-charity-commissioners-over-concerns-about-church-of-england-safeguarding/.
24. David Greenwood, 'Potential Safeguarding Solutions', in Fife and Gilo (eds), *Letters to a Broken Church*, pp. 70-73.
25. Stein, 'Safeguarding Policy at a Crossroads, pp. 160-66, and Stein, 'Clerical Abuse and Christian Discipleship', pp. 153-68.
26. Quoted by Gilo, 14 July 2020, in comment on http://survivingchurch.org/2020/07/13/they-a-talking-head/;
see also http://survivingchurch.org/2020/07/20/revisiting-the-carlile-review-a-critique-of-church-core-groups/.
27. https://safeguarding.chichester.anglican.org/shemmings-report/, pp. 85ff.
28. https://www.iicsa.org.uk/key-documents/12229/view/2019-06-20-fsqc-draft-opening-wider-church-hearing.pdf, para. 39.

29. https://www.iicsa.org.uk/video/iicsa-anglican-investigation-day-3-03072019-am2, pp. 83-127;
    Carmi and Fish, Final Overview Report of the Independent Diocesan Safeguarding Audits, https://www.scie.org.uk/consultancy/safeguarding-reviews-audits.
30. https://www.thinkinganglicans.org.uk/update-on-safe-spaces-following-media-report/.
31. https://www.churchofengland.org/safeguarding/promoting-safer-church/news-and-statements/statement-safe-space-proposal.
32. https://www.salisbury.anglican.org/news/safe-spaces.
33. Cf. Fiona Gardner, 'Spiritual Recovery from Childhood Trauma', *Spirituality*, Vol. 8, no. 43 (2002), pp. 236-68.
34. Cf. Gamble and Galloway, *Time for Action*.
35. Mohamed, *People Like Us*, pp. 148 and 156.
36. 'Exposed: The Church's Darkest Secret', https://www.youtube.com/watch?v=adoDCbr5_SA.

Bibliography

American Psychiatric Association, *Diagnostic and Statistical Manual of Mental Disorders, 5th edition* (DSM-5) (Arlington, VA: American Psychiatric Pub. Inc., 2013)

Anne, 'The Deacon's tale', in Janet Fife and Gilo (eds), *Letters to a Broken Church* (London: Ekklesia, 2019)

Barrow, Simon, 'Preface', in Janet Fife and Gilo (eds), *Letters to a Broken Church* (London: Ekklesia, 2019)

Beres, David, 'Psychoanalytic Notes on the History of Morality', *Journal of the American Psychoanalytic Association*, Vol. 13 (1965), pp. 3-37

Brown, Andrew, and Linda Woodhead, *That Was the Church That Was: How the Church of England Lost the English People* (London: Bloomsbury, 2016)

Butler, Judith, *The Psychic Life of Power: Theories in Subjection* (Stanford, CA: Stanford University Press, 1997)

Campbell, David, and Marianne Groenback, *Taking Positions in the Organization* (London: Karnac, 2006)

Campbell, Donald, 'Foreword', in Cosimo Schinaia, *On Paedophilia* (London and New York: Routledge, 2010), pp. xiii-xix

Carey, George, *Know the Truth: A Memoir* (London: Harper Collins, 2004)

Charney, M., 'Review of *Freud and The Problem of God* by Hans Küng (New Haven, CT: Yale University Press, 1979)', *Psychoanalytic Review*, Vol. 67, no. 3 (1980), pp. 415-16

Connell, R.W., and James W. Messerschmidt, 'Hegemonic Masculinity: Rethinking the Concept', *Gender Society*, Vol. 19, no. 6 (2005), pp. 829-59

Deutsch, Alexander, 'Psychological Perspectives on Cult Leadership', in Marc Galanter (ed.), *Cults and New Religious Movements* (Washington, DC: American Psychiatric Association, 1989), pp. 147-63

Duffell, Nick, *The Making of Them: The British Attitude to Children and the Boarding School System* (London: Lone Arrow Press, 2000)

Duffell, Nick, *Wounded Leaders: British Leaders and the Entitlement Illusion – A Psychohistory* (London: Lone Arrow Press, 2015)

Durkheim, Émile, *The Elementary Forms of the Religious Life* (New York: Free Press, 1965)

Eddison, John (ed.), *A Study in Spiritual Power: An Appreciation of E.J.H Nash (Bash)* (Crowborough: Highland Books, 1992)

Elliott, Ian, 'Recognising Dangerous Safeguarding Practices', in Janet Fife and Gilo (eds), *Letters to a Broken Church* (London: Ekklesia, 2019)

Ferguson, Harry, 'The Paedophile Priest: A Deconstruction', *Studies: An Irish Quarterly Review*, Vol. 84, no. 335 (1995), pp. 247-56

Festinger, Leon, *A Theory of Cognitive Dissonance* (Redwood City, CA: Stanford University Press, 1957)

Finkelhor, David, *Child Sexual Abuse: New Theory and Research* (New York: Free Press, 1984)

Finkelhor, D., R.K. Ormrod, H.A. Turner and S.L. Hamby, 'Child and Youth Victimization Known to Police, School, and Other Medical Authorities', *OJJDP Juvenile Justice Bulletin – NCJ235394* (pp. 1-8) (Washington, DC: US Government Printing Office, 2012)

Freud, Sigmund, 'A Child Is Being Beaten', in J. Strachey (ed.), *The Standard Edition of the Complete Psychological Works of Sigmund Freud, Volume XVII (1917-19): An Infantile Neurosis and Other Works* (London: Hogarth Press, 1955)

Freud, Sigmund, 'Obsessive Actions and Religious Activities', in J. Strachey (ed.), *The Standard Edition of the Complete Psychological Works of Sigmund Freud, Volume IX (1906-1908): Jensen's 'Gradiva' and Other Works* (London: Hogarth Press, 1961)

Freud, Sigmund, 'Delusion and Dream in Jensen's "Gradiva"', in J. Strachey (ed.), *The Standard Edition of the Complete Psychological Works of Sigmund Freud, Volume IX (1906-1908): Jensen's 'Gradiva' and Other Works* (London: Hogarth Press, 1961)

Freud, Sigmund, 'Analysis Terminable and Interminable', in J. Strachey (ed.) *The Standard Edition of the Complete Psychological Works of Sigmund Freud, Volume XXIII (1937-1939): Moses and Monotheism, An Outline of Psychoanalysis and Other Works* (London: Hogarth Press, 1964)

Freud, Sigmund, 'The Neuroses of Defence', in J. Strachey (ed.), *The Standard Edition of the Complete Psychological Works of Sigmund Freud, Volume I (1886-1899): Pre-Psycho-Analytic Publications and Unpublished Drafts* (London: Hogarth Press, 1966)

Gamble, David, and Kathy Galloway, *Time for Action: Sexual Abuse, the Churches and a New Dawn for Survivors* (London: Churches Together in Britain and Ireland [CTBI], 2002)

Gardner, Fiona, 'Psychotherapy with Adult Survivors of Child Sexual Abuse', British Journal of Psychotherapy, Vol. 6, no. 3 (Spring 1990), pp. 285-294.

Gardner, Fiona, 'Mastery and Guilt', *Free Associations*, Vol. 29, no. 4 (1993), pp. 63-78

Gardner, Fiona, 'Working Psychotherapeutically with Adult Survivors of Child Sexual Abuse', in J. Heller et al. (eds), *Mental Health Matters* (Basingstoke and London: Macmillan Press, 1996)

Gardner, Fiona, 'Transgenerational Processes and the Trauma of Sexual Abuse', *European Journal of Psychotherapy, Counselling and Health*, Vol. 2, issue 3 (1999), pp. 297-308

Gardner, Fiona, 'Review of the Film, *Lolita*, Dir. Stanley Kubrick (Metro-Goldwyn-Mayer, 1962)', *British Journal of Psychotherapy*, Vol.16, no. 4, pp. 515-518 (June 2000)

Gardner, Fiona, *Self-Harm: A Psychotherapeutic Approach* (London and New York: Brunner-Routledge, 2001)

Gardner, Fiona, 'Spiritual Recovery from Childhood Trauma', *Spirituality* (2002), Vol. 8 no. 43, pp. 236-38

Gardner Fiona, 'Telling Places and Healing Spaces: Theological Reflections on Projects that Give a Voice to Those Who Have Been Silenced in the Church', Faith, Spirituality and Social Change Conference paper, University of Winchester, April 2007

Gardner, Fiona, 'Defensive Processes and Deception: An Analysis of the Response of the Institutional Church to Disclosures of Child Sexual Abuse', *British Journal of Psychotherapy*, Vol. 28, no, 1 (2012), pp. 98-109

Garland, Caroline, (ed.), *Understanding Trauma: A Psychoanalytical Approach* (London: Tavistock Clinic Series, 1998)

Giddens, Anthony, *Runaway World: How Globalisation Is Reshaping Our Lives* (London: Profile Books, 2002)

Gilo, 'The Virtuous Circle', in Janet Fife and Gilo (eds), *Letters to a Broken Church* (London: Ekklesia, 2019)

Goffman, Erving, *The Presentation of Self in Everyday Life* (New York: Doubleday, 1959)

Greenberg, Daniel E., 'A Review of *Traumatic Narcissism: Relational Systems of Subjugation* by Daniel Shaw (New York: Routledge, 2014)', *Contemporary Psychoanalysis*, Vol. 52, no. 1 (2016), pp. 130-43

Greenwood, David, *Responding Badly: Church and Institutional Cover-up of Sex Abuse Allegations* (Independently published, 2018)

Greenwood, David, *Basically Innocent? The Facts behind the Scandal of Bishop Peter Ball's Abuse of Children and Young Men and How the Establishment Helped Him Get Away With It* (Independently published, 2019)

Greenwood, David, 'Potential Safeguarding Solutions', in Janet Fife and Gilo (eds), *Letters to a Broken Church* (London: Ekklesia, 2019)

Hanley, Lynsey, *Respectable: Crossing the Class Divide* (London: Penguin Books, 2017)

Harper, Rosie, 'What's under the Bonnet', in Janet Fife and Gilo (eds), *Letters to a Broken Church* (London: Ekklesia, 2019)

Harper, Rosie, and Alan Wilson, *To Heal and Not to Hurt: A Fresh Approach to Safeguarding in Church* (London: Darton, Longman & Todd, 2019)

Harris, Tirril, 'Implications of Attachment Theory for Working in Psychoanalytic Psychotherapy', *International Forum of Psychoanalysis*, Vol. 13, issue 3 (2004), pp. 147-56

Herman, Judith, *Trauma and Recovery: The Aftermath of Violence* (New York: Basic Books, 1992)

Howard, Roland, *The Rise and Fall of the Nine O'clock Service: A Cult within the Church?* (London: Mowbray, 1996)

Ibsen, Henrik, *John Gabriel Borkman*, in *The Master Builder and Other Plays*, ed. Betty Radice and Robert Baldrick (London: Penguin, 1958)

Jakobsen, Janet R., and Ann Pellegrini, *Love the Sin: Sexual Regulation and the Limits of Religious Tolerance* (Boston, MA: Beacon Press, 2004)

James, L., 1994, *The Rise and Fall of the British Empire* (London: Abacus, 1994)

Jung, C.G., *The Collected Works of C.G. Jung, Vol. 7: Two Essays in Analytical Psychology*, ed. Sir Herbert Read, Gerhard Adler and Michael Fordham (London and Henley: Routledge & Kegan Paul, 1953)

Jung, C.G., 'The Development of Personality', in Sir Herbert Read, Gerhard Adler and Michael Fordham (eds), *The Collected Works of C.G. Jung, Vol. 17* (London and Henley: Routledge & Kegan Paul, 1954)

Jung, C.G., *C.G. Jung: Letters, Volume 2: 1951-1961*, ed. Gerhard Adler (London: Routledge & Kegan Paul, 1976)

Kalsched, Donald, *The Inner World of Trauma: Archetypal Defenses of the Personal Spirit* (London and New York: Routledge, 1996)

Kennedy, Margaret, *The Courage to Tell*, eds David Gamble and Anne van Staveren (London: CTBI, 1999)

Lewis, C.S., *Surprised by Joy: The Shape of My Early Life* (London: Fount Paperback, 1955)

Loeb, Loretta R., 'The Consequences of Child Sexual Abuse', in Charles W. Socarides and Loretta R. Loeb (eds), *The Mind of the Paedophile: Psychoanalytic Perspectives* (London and New York: Karnac, 2004), pp. 177-86

Lord, Janet, 'The Power of Purple', in Janet Fife and Gilo (eds), *Letters to a Broken Church* (London: Ekklesia, 2019)

Lukes, Steven, *Power: A Radical View*, 2nd edition (London: Palgrave, 2005)

MacLeod, Donald A., *C. Stacey Woods and the Evangelical Rediscovery of the University* (Downers Grove, IL: IVP Academic, 2007)

McCann, Lisa, and Laurie Anne Pearlman, *Psychological Trauma and the Adult Survivor: Theory, Therapy and Transformation* (London and New York: Routledge, 2015)

McFadyen, Alistair, *Bound to Sin: Abuse, Holocaust and the Christian Doctrine of Sin* (Cambridge: Cambridge University Press, 2000)

Menzies, I.E.P. 'The Functioning of Social Systems as a Defence against Anxiety', Tavistock Pamphlet No. 3 (London: Tavistock Institute of Human Relations, 1960)

Merton, Thomas, *The Hidden Ground of Love: Letters on Religious Experience and Social Concerns*, ed. William H. Shannon (London: Collins Flame, 1985)

Merton, Thomas, *Cassian and the Fathers: Initiation into the Monastic Tradition*, ed. Patrick O'Connell (Kalamazoo, MI: Cistercian Publications, 2005)

Mikołajczak, Małgorzata, and Janina Pietrzak, 'Ambivalent Sexism and Religion: Connected through Values, *Sex Roles: A Journal of Research*, Vol. 70, nos 9-10 (2014), pp. 387-99

Mohamed, Hashi, *People Like Us: What it Takes to Make it in Modern Britain* (London: Profile Books, 2020)

Newman, L., 'Sexual Abuse within the Family', *19 Magazine*, September 1982, pp. 35-39

Oakley, Lisa, and Justin Humphreys, *Escaping the Maze of Spiritual Abuse: Creating Healthy Christian Cultures* (London: SPCK, 2019)

Obholzer, A., and Zagier V. Roberts (eds), *The Unconscious at Work: Individual and Organizational Stress in the Human Services* (London: Routledge, 1994)

O'Keefe, Meaghan, *American Catholic Bishops and the Politics of Scandal: Rhetoric of Authority* (London and New York: Routledge, 2019)

Parsons, Stephen, *Ungodly Fear: Fundamentalist Christianity and the Abuse of Power* (Oxford: Lion Publishing, 2000)

Pellegrini, Ann, and Janet R. Jakobsen, 'Melancholy Hope and Other Psychic Remainders: Afterthoughts on "Love the Sin"', *Studies in Gender and Sexuality*, Vol. 6, no. 4 (2005), pp. 423-40

Renton, Alex, *Stiff Upper Lip: Secrets, Crimes and the Schooling of a Ruling Class* (London: Weidenfeld & Nicolson, 2017)

Rubin, Gayle, 'Thinking Sex: Notes for a Radical Theory of the Politics of Sexuality', in H. Abelove, M.A. Barale and D.M. Halperin (eds), *The Lesbian and Gay Studies Reader* (New York: Routledge, 1993), pp. 3-44

Ruether, Rosemary Radford, 'Sexism and Misogyny in the Christian Tradition: Liberating Alternatives', *Buddhist-Christian Studies*, Vol. 34 (2014), pp. 83-94

Schaverien, Joy, *Boarding School Syndrome: The Psychological Trauma of the 'Privileged' Child* (London: Routledge, 2015)

Schinaia, Cosimo, *On Paedophilia* (London and New York: Routledge, 2010)

Searle, G.R., *A New England? Peace and War 1886-1918* (Oxford: OUP, 2004)

Shaw, Daniel, 'Traumatic Abuse in Cults: A Psychoanalytic Perspective', *Cultic Studies Review*, Vol. 2, no. 2 (2003), pp. 101-31

Shaw, Daniel, *Traumatic Narcissism: Relational Systems of Subjugation* (New York: Routledge, 2014)

Shengold, Leonard, *Soul Murder Revisited: Thoughts about Therapy, Hate, Love, and Memory* (New Haven, CT, and London: Yale University Press, 1999)

Stacey, R., 'Complexity at the "Edge" of the Basic Assumption Group', in L.F. Gould, L.F. Stapley and M. Stein (eds), *The Systems Psychodynamics of Organizations: Integrating the Group Relations Approach and Open Systems Perspectives* (New York and London: Karnac, 2001)

Stein, Josephine, 'Safeguarding Policy at a Crossroads', in Janet Fife and Gilo (eds), *Letters to a Broken Church* (London: Ekklesia, 2019)

Stein, Josephine Anne, 'Clerical Abuse and Christian Discipleship', *Modern Believing*, Vol. 61, no. 2 (2020)

Stibbe, Mark, *Home at Last: Freedom from Boarding School Pain* (Milton Keynes: Malcolm Down Publishing, 2016)

Thomas, Dylan, 'Reminiscences of Childhood', in *Quite Early One Morning* (London: Dent, 1987)

Travis, Carol, and Elliot Aronson, *Mistakes Were Made (but Not by Me): Why We Justify Foolish Beliefs, Bad Decisions, and Hurtful Acts* (Boston, MA, and New York: Mariner Books, Houghton Mifflin Harcourt, 2007)

Uhlmann, Eric Luis, and Geoffrey L. Cohen, '"I Think It, Therefore It's True": Effects of Self-perceived Objectivity on Hiring Discrimination,' *Organizational Behavior and Human Decision Processes*, Vol. 104, issue 2 (2007), pp. 207-23

Verkaik, Robert, *Posh Boys: How the English Public Schools Ruin Britain* (London: OneWorld Publications, 2018)

Ward, T., and S.M. Hudson, 'Finkelhor's Precondition Model of Child Sexual Abuse: A Critique', *Psychology, Crime and Law* (online) Vol. 7, issue 4 (2001), pp. 291-307

Weber, Max, *Economy and Society*, eds G. Roth and C. Wittich (New York: Bedminster Press, 1968)

Wu, K., 'Performing the Charismatic Ritual', in C. Lindholm (ed.), *The Anthropology of Religious Charisma: Ecstasies and Institutions* (New York: Palgrave Macmillan, 2013)

Younge, Gary, 'Notes from the Margins', *Free Associations*, Issue 30 (Spring 2020)

Young-Bruehl, E., 'Sexual Diversity in Cosmopolitan Perspective', *Studies in Gender and Sexuality*, Vol. 11, no. 1 (2010), pp. 1-9

Index

Allchurches Trust Ltd (ATL), 80, 94
Aller, Somerset, 158
An Abuse of Faith, 104, 117
'Anne', 140–2
Archbishop of Canterbury's,
   ecumenical mission, 94; registrar,
   62–3; solicitors, 57, 58;
   see also Canterbury Archbishops'
   Council, 80, 82, 93; List 78, 79
Athenaeum Club, 94
Aung San Suu Kyi, 108
Ball, Michael, 36, 156; Peter, 2,
   10, 75, 78, 79, 109, 114, 115,
   123, 132; analysis of, 33, 36–40,
   105–7; at Chichester, 40, 44, 91;
   'community' of, 101, 102–5, 124;
   and intimidation, 143, 156–8; and
   Neil Todd, 153, 155, 156–7; and
   public schools, 117
Barnardo's Children's Home, 43, 55
Barrow, Simon, 4
Bath Abbey, 102
Bath and Wells, Bishop's chaplain,
   49, 50, 53, 67; Bishops of, 53, 54;
   diocese of, 1, 10, 31, 38, 49, 67;
   see also Thompson, Jim
BBC, 115, 126, 155
Beer, Stuart, 87
Bell, George, 96, 97, 98
Benn, Wallace, 42, 43, 44
Beres, David, 136
Betrayal of Trust, A, 22
Beynon, Wyn, 135

Bishopscourt, Gloucester, 155
Boarding schools, 12, 26, 36, 51, 89,
   157; influence of, 68, 88, 117–33,
   134
Bound to Sin, 8
Brain, Chris, 101, 109–16
Bristol, diocese of, 1;
   see also Trinity College, Bristol
Broadbent, Pete, 161
Brown, Andrew, 6, 152
Buckinghamshire, Bishop of, *see*
   Wilson, Alan
Burnley, Bishop of, *see* North, Philip
Burrows, Peter, 61, 62
Butler-Sloss, Baroness, 40; Report,
   41
Cahill, Sally, 84, 85
Calder-Marshall, Arthur, 119
Caldicott prep school, 126
Campbell, David, 92
Campbell, Donald, 18, 39
Canterbury, Archbishops of, *see*
   Carey, George; Coggan, Donald;
   Ramsey, Michael; Runcie, Robert;
   Welby, Justin; Williams, Rowan
Carey, George, 37, 106, 111, 114, 117,
   144, 145, 157, 159
Carlile, Lord, 30, 91, 95, 96
Carlile Review, 91
Carmi Review, 91
'Carol', 96–8
Caslake, Melissa, 165
Cassian, John, 137

Catalfo, Phil, 111
Chamberlain, Nicholas, 44, 148
Chester, Bishops of, see Forster, Peter; Whitsey, Victor; Bishop's Palace, 16
Chetham's School of Music, 89, 90
Chevous, Jane, 83
Chichester, Bishops of, see Benn, Wallace; Hind, John; Kemp, Eric; Warner, Martin; diocese of, 10, 33, 40–4, 56, 91, 161; rural dean of, 43
'Children First', 84
Church Commissioners, 82
Church of England statement of safeguarding, 65–6
Church House, 62, 91, 93
Church Times, 48, 56, 59
Church's Child Protection Advisory Service (CCPAS), 54
see also Thirtyone: Eight
Church's Director of Safeguarding, 160, 165
Clarkson, Jeremy, 123
Clergy Discipline Commission, 73
Clergy Discipline Measures (CDM), 2, 3, 61, 62, 69, 79
Clergy Discipline Tribunal, 73
Clevedon, Somerset, 49, 50, 52, 53; St John the Evangelist Church, 50, 51, 52
Coggan, Donald, 94
Compensation Act 2006, 2
Confessions, St Augustine, 136
Copthorne prep school, 128
Cotton, Roy, 40, 41, 42, 44
Criminal Records Bureau (CRB), 43
Croft, Steven, 61
Data Protection Act, 62
Day of Reconciliation, 161
Dean, Paul, 128
Devamanikkam, Trevor, 60–3
Dickenson, Gordon, 69
Dickinson, Thorold, 154
diocesan safeguarding adviser (DSA), 6, 43
Doggart, Simon, 126
Doncaster, Bishop of, see Burrows, Peter

Douai Abbey, Berkshire, 51
Dragon School, Oxford, 121, 128
Duffell, Nick, 129, 130
Durham diocese, Chancellor of, see Moore, Garth,
Durkheim, Émile, 110
Ebbsfleet, Bishop of, 51
Ecclesiastical Insurance Group (EIG), 79, 80, 94
Ecclesiastical Law Journal, 75
Economy and Society, 100
Ekklesia, 4
Elliott, Ian, 65, 66, 67, 68–9, 74, 76–8, 79, 91
Elliott report, 76–8, 91
Emmanuel Church, Wimbledon, 124, 131
Eton School, 121, 126
evangelical summer camps see Iwerne camps
Extra-Parochial Place, 113
Festinger, Leon, 44
Finkelhor, David, 34–5
Fisher, Michael, 75
Fletcher, David, 123; Jonathan, 91, 123–5, 126, 129, 130, 131–2
Forster, Peter, 68, 69–73
Foster, Charles, 125
Fox, Matthew, 112
Fraser, Giles, 122
'Fred', 141, 142
Freud, Sigmund, 15, 20, 125, 137
General Synod, 3, 80, 90, 91, 92, 93, 94
Gibb, Jonathan, 3, 165
Gibb, Moira, 117, 143
Gibb Report, 91, 105, 143
Gilbert, Patrick, 94
Gilbert, Peter, 89
Gilo, 79, 80, 94
Global Anglican Future Conference (GAFCON), 148
Gloucester, 155; Bishop of, see Ball, Peter; Chancellor of, see Moore, Garth
Grantham, Bishop of, see Chamberlain, Nicholas
Greaves, Barry, 89

Greenbelt Arts Festival, 112
Greenwood, David, 117, 160
Griffiths, Meirion, 55–6, 57, 59
Groenback, Marianne, 92
Guardian, The, 63
Halliday, Peter, 54, 55
Hanley, Lynsey, 99
Hare, David, 36
Harper, Rosie, 4, 12, 28
Harris, Barbara, 140
Harrow School, 127, 128
Harvey, Paul-André, 32
Hawley, Marc, 158
Hill, Christopher, 94
Hind, John, 40
Holmes, Grant, 147
Hope, David, 84, 85
House of Bishops, 6, 63, 78, 79, 82, 88, 90, 91, 93, 160; *Marriage and Same Sex Relationships* report, 145, 146; Safeguarding Monitoring and Reference Group, 81
House of Clergy, 90
House of Laity, 90
House of Lords, 86, 94, 144
Howard, Roland, 110, 111
Hughes, Ian, 69–72
Humphreys, Justin, 154
Ibsen, Henrik, 19
Independent Association of Prep Schools, 118
Independent Ecclesiastical Complaints Commission, 160–1
Independent Inquiry into Child Sexual Abuse (IICSA), 73, 80, 151, 162; and Ball, 36, 37, 39, 102, 155-6; and Chichester, 40, 42, 44; on deference, 86, 90, 94; and Elliott, 66, 68–9, 77–8; and Forster, 69–72; and Ineson, 61, 62; recommendations, 3, 91, 92, 93, 162; reports, 91, 165, 166
Ineson, Matthew, 60–3
insurers, ecclesiastical, 2, 11, 56–9, 60, 76;
  see also Ecclesiastical Insurance Group

Issues in Human Sexuality, 145
Iwerne camps, 12, 118, 121–6, 130; Trust, 122, 130–31
'Jack', 45–7
Jakobsen, Janet, 147
James, Cliff, 152
'Joe', 74–7, 79
John, Jeffrey, 147–8
Johnson, Phil, 164
Jones, Philip, 44
Jung, Carl, 8, 27, 153
Kemp, Eric, 41, 96, 155
King, Helen, 146
Kroll, Una, 37, 38
Küng, Hans, 137–8
Lambeth, the Bishop at, 82; Conference 1998, 145; List, 78; Palace, 37, 91, 93, 96, 157, 158
Lancing College, 36, 117
Lawrence, Alana, 151
Lawrence, D.H., 91
Lead Bishop for Safeguarding, 81, 160, 165
Lewes, Bishop of, *see* Ball, Peter
Lewes and Hastings, Archdeacon of, 40;
  see also Jones, Philip
Lewis, C.S., 36, 132
LGB (LGBTQI+), 124, 145, 147, 148
Lincoln, diocese of, 44
'Living in Love and Faith project', 146
Llandaff, Bishop of, 147
Lloyd, Lord, 93, 106
Lolita, 31
London, Bishop of, *see* Mullally, Sarah
Lord, Janet, 16–17, 18, 97
Lords Spiritual, 86
Lowe, Stephen, 112, 113, 114
Lucy Faithfull Foundation, 10, 43
Lunn, David, 111, 113, 114–15
Macfarlane, Julia, 56–60
McFadyen, Alistair, 8
McFarlane, Sir Andrew, 71, 73
McNeill, Nikita, 69–73
Maltby, Judith, 146

Malvern College, 36, 132
Manchester Cathedral, 84, 87, 88, 89
Marriage and Same Sex Relationships after the Shared Conversations, 145, 146
Mawer, Sir Philip, 80, 94
Meekings Report, 40, 41
Merton, Thomas, 151
Mills, Dame Barbara, 156
Minister and Clergy Sexual Abuse Survivors (MACSAS), 6, 151, 160
Mohamed, Hashi, 88, 95
Monbiot, George, 127
Moore, Garth, 74, 75
Moss, Mr and Mrs, 155
Mullally, Sarah, 92, 163
Nabokov, Vladimir, 31
Napier, Charles, 128
Nash, E.J.H., 122, 123
National Safeguarding Director, 160; Panel, 82, 160, 164; Steering Group (NSSG), 81, 92, 160; Team, 63, 82, 132, 141, 159–60, 161
News, The, (Portsmouth), 59
Nikaean Club, 94
Nine O'Clock Service (NOS), 109–13, 114, 115
Nobody's Friends, 93, 94, 123
North, Philip, 92, 140
North Queensland, Bishop of, 85
Nyachuru, Guide, 130
Oakley, Lisa, 154
Oasis Foundation, 145
Old Deanery, Wells, 2
On Paedophilia, 18
Origen, 136
Orwell, George, 95, 127
Ozanne, Jayne, 146, 154
Pace, Ian, 90
parochial church councils (PCC), 50, 86
Parsons, Stephen, 81, 94, 109, 122, 130, 131, 140, 143
Past Cases Reviews (PCR), 49, 50, 55, 91
Pearson, David, 54
Pellegrini, Ann, 147

Pentecostal Church, 109
Permission to Officiate (PTO), 42, 79, 84, 85, 132, 157, 158
'Planetary Mass', 111, 112
'Policy for Bishops and Their Staff', 78
Pope Benedict XVI, 33
Pope Francis, 32
Pope John Paul, II, 32
Portman Clinic, 45
Portsmouth, Bishop of, 41
prep schools *see* boarding schools
President of Clergy Discipline Tribunals, 69, 70, 71, 72, 73
Prince Charles, 106, 157, 159
Pritchard, Colin, 40, 41, 42
'Protecting All God's Children', 84
public schools *see* boarding schools
Ramsey, Michael, 41
Reading, Bishop of, 147
'Rebuild my House', 92
ReNew, 131
Renton, Alex, 10, 43, 157
Renton, Tim, 156
Repton School, 123, 132
Rideout, Gordon, 43, 44
Rise of the Bluffocracy, The, 82
Rops, Félicien, 137
Rouncefield, Angela, 38
Rubin, Gayle, 143
Runcie, Robert, 87
Runcorn, David, 120
Ruether, Rosemary, 139
Safe Spaces, 80, 163
'Sam', 20, 24, 25–6, 27, 28
St Augustine, 33, 136
St Barnabas boarding school, North Queensland, 89
St Francis, 102
St Germans, Cornwall, Bishop of, *see* Fisher, Michael
St Jerome, 136
St Mary's, Abchurch, 74
St Paul, 100, 136, 138
St Paul's School, 119
St Thomas' Church, Sheffield, 110, 115

Schaverien, Joy, 127
Schinaia, Cosimo, 18, 33, 42
Scout Association, 41, 42
Scripture Union, 130
Sentamu, John, 61
Sewell, Martin, 90, 91, 92, 132
Shaw, Daniel, 39, 106, 108
Sheffield, 109, 110, 112, 140; Bishop of, 111, 112;
 see also Lunn, David
Shemmings Report, 40, 161–2
Smith, David, 49–55
Smyth, John, 91, 122–3, 124, 125, 126; and boarding school ethos, 129, 130, 131, 132
Singleton, Roger, 55
Slade, Derek, 128
Snow, Martyn, 61
Social Care Institute of Excellence (SCIE), 73, 162–3
Society for Promoting Christian Knowledge, 94
Society of St Francis, 75
Sodor and Man diocese, 147
Southwark, Bishop of, 155; Chancellor of, see Moore, Garth
statute of limitations, 58
Stein, Josephine, 2, 3, 59, 60, 81, 160
Stibbe, Mark, 120, 121
Stiff Upper Lip, 157
Stowe School, 119, 123
Strathcona School, Canada, 122
Stuart, Gordon, 88
Swing, Episcopal Bishop, 111
Taunton, Bishop of, 50
Thirtyone: Eight, 54
Thomas, Dylan, 24
Thompson, Jim, 2, 51
Thorn, John, 129, 133
Time for Action, 3
Titus Trust, 130
To Heal and not to Hurt, 28–9
Todd, Neil, 38, 48, 102, 153–8
Trinity College, Bristol, 122

Trinity Hall, Cambridge, 122
Trollope, Anthony, 159
Truth and Reconciliation Commission, 161
Ty Mawr, Monmouth, 37
Ungodly Fear, 143
Vallins, John, 89, 90
Van Handel, Robert, 31
Verkaik, Robert, 128
Victim Support, 163
Vineyard Church, 109
Waddington, Robert, 84, 85, 87, 88, 89, 90
Ward, Eli, 88
Warner, Martin, 43
Warren, Robert, 110
Weber, Max, 100, 101
Webster, Glyn, 61
Welby, Justin, 61, 62, 91, 97, 126, 131, 151, 165
Wells Cathedral, 2
Wheen, Francis, 127
Whitsey, Victor, 16, 17, 20–2, 69, 97
Whittaker, Ifor, see Pritchard, Colin
Williams, Rowan, 48
Williams, Simon, 126–7
Wilson, Alan, 28–9, 73, 78, 79, 83, 86, 90, 100, 148
Wimber, John, 109, 110
Winchester, 125, 130; College, 125, 129
Wogan, Terry, 105
Woodhead, Linda, 6, 115, 142, 152
Woolcott, Angharad, 15, 16
Wotton-under-Edge, Gloucestershire, 51
Wright, Peter, 126
Wycliffe Hall, 123
York, Archbishops of, 61, 63, 140; see also, Hope, David; Sentamu, John
Young-Bruehl, E., 149
Zambesi Ministries, 123
Zimbabwe, 123, 130, 131